TRANSATLANTIC STUDIES

Will Kaufman
Heidi Slettedahl Macpherson

University Press of America
Lanham • New York • Oxford

Copyright © 2000 by
University Press of America,® Inc.
4720 Boston Way
Lanham, Maryland 20706

12 Hid's Copse Rd.
Cumnor Hill, Oxford OX2 9JJ

Library of Congress Cataloging-in-Publication Data

Transatlantic studies / (edited by) Will Kaufman and Heidi
Slettedahl Macpherson
p.   cm.
Essays based on on-going discussions at the Maastricht Center
for Transatlantic studies.
Includes index.
1.   Europe—Relations—America. 2. America—Relations—Europe.
3.   Globalization. 4. Citizenship—Cross-culture studies. 5. Aliens—
Cross-cultural studies. 6. Human rights—Cross-cultural studies.
7.   Popular culture—Cross-cultural studies. I. Kaufman,
Will. II. Macpherson, Heidi Slettedahl.
D1065.A4T73   2000   303.48'2407—dc21   00-060713 CIP

ISBN 0-7618-1789-1 (cloth: alk. ppr.)
ISBN 0-7618-1790-5 (pbk: alk. ppr.)

For Terry Rodenberg

Contents

Foreword

Paul Giles

As the contributors to this volume amply demonstrate, the study of culture from a transatlantic perspective is not a new phenomenon. Since the 16th century, the alternative horizons opened up by possibilities of transatlantic exchange have inspired emigration, mutual comparisons and reciprocal influences of every kind. Columbus' voyage, it has been suggested, changed the shape of the Old World as much as the New; forced to abandon their maps of the flat Earth, medieval cartographers puzzled over the problem of how to project different continents in parallel to each other. Europeans of the feudal era had long cherished their idea of an enclosed, self-sufficient order buttressed only by an image of Islam as the unassimilated "other," but now, to their chagrin, they found the globe reoriented by other forms of representation involving displacement and abstract relation.[i] It would be like astronomers today discovering a parallel inhabited world within a distant galaxy, so that gazetteers were obliged to remap the universe placing the Earth in relation to an alternative center of civilization.

In 1922, the American artist Man Ray, who one year earlier had arrived in France from New York, produced as the first work in his European career a photographic collage entitled "Transatlantic." This sought provocatively to defamiliarize the map of Paris by placing its established lineaments in estranged relationships with other, seemingly disparate objects. Many of the essays in this book follow a similar principle: Campbell discusses "dialogical encounters" between different cultures in the fiction of Paul Bowles, Desmond analyses the transposition of contextual meaning in relation to the German artist, Joseph Beuys, while other writers interrogate the significance of transatlantic dynamics in areas as wide-ranging as human rights (Edge), nuclear defense (Schrafsetter) and the information revolution (Rampal). All of these authors are concerned with the increasingly problematic status of the nation-state and with the tendency of conceptual categories to exceed national boundaries. At the same time, they do not find themselves impelled to abandon the signifying capacity of the nation entirely; indeed, Transatlantic Studies might be said to situate itself at that awkward, liminal place where the national meets the global. In this, as Machnikowksi and the other contributors to the second section of this book acknowledge, it offers a more materialist counterpart to contemporary discourses on globalization. Whereas globalization in its more utopian (or dystopian) forms imagines a "postnational" world which simply transcends national identity, transnationalism focuses instead upon the frictions and disjunctions brought about by the slow but inexorable erosion of national formations along with the various reactions and tensions which this process produces. According to the essays collected here, Transatlantic Studies takes its impetus from an uncomfortable, highly contested situation where traditional identities find themselves traversed by the forces of difference.

In the 19th century, cosmopolitan figures such as the novelist Henry James and the political scientist James Bryce tended to think of transatlantic travel as an extension of the aristocratic "Grand Tour." For them, it involved fundamentally a broadening of the humanist mind, leading to a more refined capacity to pick and choose among a smorgasbord of cultural options. But in more recent times, under the influence of social and economic changes linked in various ways to the international flow of capital, the transatlantic imaginary has lost many of these more volitional aspects and has become more of a compulsive, unsettling phenomenon which affects issues from language and media to business and international law. In Europe, particularly, debates about the sanctity or otherwise of national borders have become as heated at all levels of society as arguments about the positive or negative influence of American culture outside the territorial jurisdiction of the US. Appropriately enough, the Maastricht Center for Transatlantic Studies is located in a European city where such controversies about relationships of the national to the transnational have a historical and political as well as an emotional resonance. Like Columbus, the Center will inevitably re-imagine the Old World in its scrutiny of the New, and it is poised to become a focal point of contemporary academic inquiry into what Man Ray would have recognized as the paradoxical (and sometimes apparently incongruous) points of convergence, divergence and traversal between local interests and global imperatives.

---

[i] See especially J. H. Elliott, *The Old World and the New, 1492-1650* (Cambridge: Cambridge University Press, 1970), 7-21, and Germán Arciniegas, *America in Europe: A History of the New World in Reverse* (1975), trans. Gabriela Arciniegas and R. Victoria Arana (San Diego: Harcourt Brace Jovanovich, 1986), 9-49.

Preface

Susan Castillo

In the history of the Atlantic world, colonial encounters between Europe, the Americas and Africa have often been theorized as unidirectional, with the European powers imposing their cultural institutions, ideologies, and value systems on passive silent victims while remaining unaffected themselves. It is undeniable, however, that the impact of Africa and the Americas upon Europe has had effects just as long-lasting and radical as those of Europe upon the other populations it encountered. Fortunately, in recent scholarship, there has been a salutary move toward a vision of the relations between the peoples of the Atlantic world as a realm of dynamic interactions and circulating energies, as (to use the expression of Mary Louise Pratt) a zone of contact between diverse cultures where ideas and identities are constantly being articulated, negotiated, synthesized and challenged.

This shift to a more kinetic conceptual model of scholarship, however, is not without consequences for existing academic disciplines. In the Research Assessment Exercise (RAE) which British institutions of higher learning will be undergoing in 2001, there has been considerable discussion of the difficulties encountered in defining Area Studies and of the practical and institutional problems this might create in terms of the disciplinary affiliations of individual researchers. Scholars working in fields such as European Studies, American Studies or African Studies find it increasingly confining to restrict their research to one narrowly defined geographical area or to fit into the have far-reaching implications for the ways in which our fields are conceptualized and our research is carried out in future years.

In many areas, the term globalization has suffered a Procrustean fate, and has come to mean many things to many people. Clearly, one of the dangers of concepts such as the globalization of culture is that, in certain readings, they can often be used to occlude (or be actively complicit with) a neo-colonial extension of Western hegemony over other parts of the world. This groundbreaking collection edited by Will Kaufman and Heidi Slettedahl Macpherson does precisely the contrary, focusing on issues as diverse as migratory movements, human rights, multiculturalism, legal affairs, international news, the history of race, travel literature, dance, and the visual arts. This book is an exciting and innovative initiative both in its theorization of the emerging field of Transatlantic Studies and in its attention to the particular sites in which these dynamic interactions take place.

For their hands-on dedication to the Maastricht Center over the years, our thanks go to Terry Rodenberg, Mr. M. Tsuchida, Fumio Fujimoto, Angela Murphy, Jim Skyrms, and Diana Duvall. We also wish to thank Paul Giles and Susan Castillo for their interest and support, as well as our colleagues at the University of Central Lancashire whose willingness to shoulder increased responsibilities made our study and research leaves possible. Finally, our immense thanks go to our spouses, Allan Macpherson and Sarah Keates, who gave us the support and space to finish this project.

Introduction

Transatlantic Studies: A New Paradigm

Will Kaufman and Heidi Slettedahl Macpherson

> If your concept of world geography was shaped entirely by what you
> read in the papers and saw on television, you would have no choice
> but to conclude that [in relation to Great Britain] America must be
> about where Ireland is, that France and Germany lie roughly
> alongside the Azores ... and that pretty much all the other sovereign
> states are either mythical ... or can only be reached by spaceship.[1]

Bill Bryson's humorous rendition of British geography lessons as
informed by the mass media indicates the primary space accorded to
the transatlantic in the popular imagination of a conspicuously Atlantic
culture. However, if Britain does indeed look towards the US,
conventional wisdom (outside the US) holds that the US is famously
blind to anywhere else, except inasmuch as "anywhere else" can serve
American interests. And, gauging from the bulk of existing literature
under the heading "transatlantic," you'd be forgiven for thinking that
the transatlantic is an exclusively Anglo-American preserve. The
reality, of course, dwarfs this narrow thread—the recent construction of
a "Black Atlantic" linking Europe, Africa and the Americas is just one

indication of an overarching system of connections. Since the Age of Exploration in the 15th and 16th centuries, the encounters between the Atlantic continents have determined the course of history, culture and politics for millions of people of all races: through slavery and the African diaspora; through non-human trade and economic polices; through voluntary migrations; through art and culture. The destinies of Europe, Africa, North and South America have been intertwined to the extent that none of these areas can be said to exist in isolation.

The same might be said for the study of these nominally separate areas. Increasingly, the internationalization of area studies is reflected in movements that attempt to redefine and respond to expanding, globalizing pressures. One highly visible indication of this has been the upsurge of opinion in the past decade over the "future" or "direction" of American Studies. The British scholar Paul Giles's recent work on the reconstruction and "internationalization" of American Studies flags up so many signs of these expanding pressures—"transnational paradoxes," "the ideology of exchange," "comparative perspectives."[2] Giles identifies in the discourse of American Studies the move from a rigid national perspective to a pluralist multinational perspective, and beyond—to the fluidity of the "transnational." In this, he takes his key from Randolph Bourne's provocative essay from 1916, "Trans-National America." In the midst of World War I, with the US embroiled in a global entanglement for the first time in its history, Bourne looked to his homeground and concluded that a monocultural, static conception of America was impossible:

> America is coming to be, not a nationality but a trans-nationality, a weaving back and forth, with the other lands, of many threads of all sizes and colors. Any movement which attempts to thwart this weaving, or to dye the fabric any one color, or disentangle the threads of the strands, is false to this cosmopolitan vision.[3]

Similar signs are visible elsewhere, in other area studies. In the UK, conferences and publications proliferate on the construction of "Britishness"—this during a time of political devolution that contrasts fragmentation with European federalization. Even more narrowly, "Englishness" is constructed through the othering of the Welsh and the Scots, Asians and West Indians. In the opposite direction, Camilo Pérez-Bustillo reminds us in this volume that European Studies faces the same pressure to look outside of itself in order to identify itself. In this case, following E. San Juan and C.L.R. James, he notes that:

the interdependence between the development of modes and forces of production on the one hand, and revolutionary processes on the other, between African peoples and Europe must be understood through the prism of the slave trade and its effects. This is why modern Europe must be at least partly reconceived of as a creation of Africa (and of super-exploited African labor specifically), and ultimately of the struggles of African peoples against slavery.

Clearly, the transatlantic dynamic is an irresistible force of attraction and repulsion, absorption and distinction, between all the continents on the two seaboards. This dynamic has spun an intricate Atlantic web of history, literature, art, technology, dialogue, warfare, human migration—a true diaspora that transcends the boundaries of separate area and disciplinary studies. Rather than "disentangle the threads of the strands," Transatlantic Studies seeks to identify and highlight them in all their entanglement. Its object is to locate the common issues and concerns that necessarily move us beyond disciplinary and monocultural perspectives. Transatlantic Studies results from the inexorable drive towards interdependent and more global perspectives in criticism and education.

This book emerges from the on-going discussions about the development of Transatlantic Studies that have taken place at the Maastricht Center for Transatlantic Studies (MCTS), a consortium-based project in the Netherlands with a mission to encourage and promote a transatlantic perspective through establishing and furthering educational and scholarly links across the Atlantic. Professor Terry Rodenberg of Central Missouri State University was the driving force behind the project. In 1995, he gathered together scholars and teachers from 16 European, Mexican and American universities, with the initial object of establishing an American Studies center in Europe. Almost from the first meeting, it became clear that the commonality of interest and experience lay not in the *American*, but in the *transatlantic* dynamic. In the first days of teaching, it also became clear that what was termed "Transatlantic Studies" could not really be defined in the boardroom. It would only be through teaching at the Center and engaging with like-minded colleagues that this new field would begin to take shape. All the participants accepted that the peculiar relationship linking Europe and Africa to the Americas had been the subject of an established, long-standing debate, but we felt that this debate had too often been atomized or located within rigid nationalist or disciplinary structures. What we sought was an embracing and liberating transdisciplinary framework within which to explore the defining characteristics of the transatlantic dynamic.

MCTS has been successful in its dissemination of Transatlantic Studies to the small cohorts of international students who study there each semester. As participating academics from around the world meet and exchange ideas, Transatlantic Studies takes on even more resonance. With this new collection of essays, we seek to establish it before a wider audience.

The audience is clearly there. The year 2000 sees the first ever conference in Transatlantic Studies, hosted by MCTS. The initial call for papers generated an overwhelming response from interested academics across the globe, with a great host of scholarly disciplines represented. This is a clear sign that a new, inclusive scholarly field is indeed emerging and defining itself.

The present volume, then, seeks to explore the emergent concerns and problems in Transatlantic Studies. In terms of its separate parts, it is a multinational, multidisciplinary collection by scholars from the US, England, Hungary, Mexico, Spain, Poland and Wales, most of whom have taught at MCTS. The contributors hope that this collection will help to set the framework for future discussions about what constitutes Transatlantic Studies It is admittedly the work a small, select, and partially focused team who have embarked on the modest first step of a large and complex critical exercise—what remains is the further critical engagement that will move the focus beyond the multinational and the multidisciplinary, to the transnational and transdisciplinary.

Any conclusions drawn from the first collection devoted explicitly to a particular field must be necessarily tentative. However, even at this early stage it is at least possible to identify some common concerns that transcend national and disciplinary boundaries. In Part 1, questions of citizenship and migration bring together the insights of scholars from legal studies, history, psychology, anthropology, and political science— all concerned with the impact of what John W. Sheets and others refer to as the transatlantic "culture of mobility" that has resulted in social conflicts and debates all up and down the Atlantic seaboards. Camilo Pérez-Bustillo's comparative exploration of contemporary struggles for multicultural citizenship in Mexico and France dovetails with Neil A. Wynn's historical overview of comparative perspectives on race between the US and the UK. Miles W. Williams constructs a paradigm for migration policies in liberal democratic states of the North Atlantic community which, as he says, once "encouraged refugees from the East to 'vote with the feet' and seek asylum in the West," but which "now seems equally committed to *restricting* the migrant flow." The resultant agitation on the streets, courtrooms and legislative chambers of the transatlantic community mirrors the internal psychological struggles of migrants whose "precarious," "threatened" identities are explored by Jane Prince. She asks "how threatened identities can be managed and transitional identities achieved"—a question which, however unformed, may well have been in the mind of one Angus McNeill, an emigrant to Canada from the Scottish island of Colonsay in the 19th century. In John W. Sheets's case study of the Colonsay-Canada migrations, the "Gaelic-to-English trauma" of the McNeills, Mackinnons and others refers back and outwards to the personal and political trauma of so many other transatlantic migrants. Ultimately, as Sheets reminds us, "our understanding of this diaspora falls somewhere between a macrocosm of numerical theory and the microcosms of family history."

The physical migration of bodies and psyches, however, is not the only possible movement in a global context. Other transitions take place across the Atlantic, which either confirm the process of globalization or, perhaps, give the lie to it. Globalization is either a visible fact or an idea. It is either a near-utopian solution or a neo-liberal confidence game dominated by North Atlantic interests—apparently the jury is still out. In Part 2, transatlantic scholars in sociology, philosophy, mass communication and education unite to interrogate and challenge the very idea of globalization, as they analyze transnational movement of knowledge, information, and economic power. Ryszard M. Machnikowski throws down the opening gauntlet in his examination of the ideological interests lying behind the utopian promises of globalization, while Robert Barford argues that the neo-liberal emphasis on property as mere commodity in the global context continues to put a corrosive strain on the foundations of civic republicanism in the transatlantic community. Kuldip R. Rampal analyzes the imbalance of influence and perceived credibility between North Atlantic news organizations and those of the South, further challenging any notion that globalization is synonymous with equality. Neither should globalization be confused with market expansion, as Tamás Kozma warns in his overview of transatlantic changes in the "market" for adult education.

Part 3 embraces aspects of the arts and popular culture in a transatlantic context, focusing on the shared phenomenon of transformation in, perhaps, an initially unlikely combination. John Walton's historical account of seaside tourism in the 19th and 20th centuries reveals the "politics of the beach" in all its power to transform landscapes, lifestyles, and economies, in a comparative exploration of transatlantic sites along Anglophone and Hispanic axes. Transformation figures, too, in literature as in life; but as Heidi Slettedahl Macpherson and Will Kaufman argue in an analysis of transatlantic literary tourism and travel, a fair degree of mythologizing is required to transform the local into the foreign, and the commonplace into the exotic. However, in a case study focusing on the writings of Paul Bowles, Neil Campbell demonstrates that such transformation through literature is not only possible, but carries with it both estrangement and intimate encounter—in this case, between an American writer, the land of his origin, and his adopted Moroccan home. Campbell explores how Bowles's fiction, travel writing and translations "trace varieties of transatlantic experience that begin to map out a sensibility of exchange and dialogue across cultures, ranging from destructive collisions and romantic desires, to hybrid co-presence and collaboration." The transformative process is carried even further, from the beach to the book to the visual arts, as Kathleen Kadon Desmond maps a similar encounter in contemporary art. Desmond's exploration of an "exchange and dialogue across cultures" reveals the European and American artist, curator, and viewer engaged in the parallel aesthetic experience of "destructive collisions and romantic desires" and "hybrid co-presence and collaboration."

It would be a mistake to consider power as an unacknowledged or unspecified force running through these scholarly encounters with the transatlantic, for it is at least implicit in every aspect of the transatlantic exchange. Yet it is made explicit in relation to politics, policy and legislation in Part 4, an arena where sociology, history, law, criminal justice, and human rights meet. Peter W. Edge focuses on transatlantic perspectives on religious rights in the English legal system, highlighting important contrasts between provisions in the US Constitution and the European Convention on Human Rights, and the relative power of each to protect these rights. The transatlantic team of Lesley Hodgson, Andrew Thompson and Donald H. Wallace explores the powers of the International Criminal Tribunal for the Former Yugosalvia, asking whether this seminal institution is indeed "a step forward in extending the scope of international responsibility for violations of human rights and in developing an emergent transnational legal forum for conflict resolution." Javier Maestro offers an historical reflection upon the relationship between transatlantic republicanism and constitutionalism, not only in the context of power struggles between tyranny and free institutions, but also in the face of the potential evisceration of the constitutional republican tradition through the impact of globalization. And finally, a historical investigation of transatlantic power in its most naked incarnation forms the basis of Susanna Schrafstetter's essay on nuclear diplomacy, NATO, and the poker game of deterrence throughout the Cold War.

Transatlantic Studies is an evolving area of study, and it will be through international scholarship that its boundaries will be charted and examined further. If the Maastricht experience is any indication, interested scholars, teachers and students from both sides of the Atlantic have already signaled their desire and intention to view the long history of the transatlantic encounter, in all its permutations, with a critical eye towards definition, rather than impression. There is, admittedly, much to be built upon on here—in particular, through the participation of African and South American colleagues whose voices and analyses are crucial in any discussion of the transatlantic. But as a first step, this collection, we hope, succeeds in establishing the foundations and practice of Transatlantic Studies.

---

[1] Bill Bryson, *Notes from a Small Island* (London: Black Swan, 1995), 32.

[2] See Paul Giles, "Reconstructing American Studies: Transnational Paradoxes, Comparative Perspectives," *Journal of American Studies* 28, no. 3 (1994): 335-58; and "Virtual Americas: The Internationalization of American Studies and the Ideology of Exchange," *American Quarterly* 50, no. 3 (1998): 523-47.

[3] Randolph Bourne, "Trans-National America," *Atlantic Monthly* 111, no. 1 (July 1916): 86-97 (96).

Part One:
Citizenship and Migration

Chapter 1

In Search of Common Ground: Struggles for Multicultural Citizenship in Mexico and France

Camilo Pérez-Bustillo

The French rocker Manu Chao sings a song about an outlaw—a *clandestino*—whose only crime is that he is a foreign worker without papers, "a phantom in the city." His song alludes to the shared experiences of displacement, reaffirmation, and resistance among "illegal" immigrants who embody the "globalization" of labor markets fed by the migration of workers from the "South" to the "North" throughout the world. George Orwell once suggested that the dystopic future he foresaw could best be captured by the image of a boot stamping on a human face. From Chao's distinctively post-colonial perspective, the most representative contemporary image would be a collage of the improvised vessels seeking to carry Moroccans and other Africans "between Ceuta and Gibraltar" to the shores of Spain, Cubans to Florida, Dominicans to Puerto Rico, or inner tubes less miraculous than that of Elian Gonzalez across the river from Mexico to the US.[1]

Chao's song is of particular interest as a point of departure for a discussion on the possible relationship between developing notions of "multicultural citizenship" in Mexico and France, since it urges an affinity among "outlawed" outsiders throughout the world. Chao successively invokes the clandestine reality of undocumented Peruvians, Africans, Algerians, Nigerians, and Bolivians as part of a common weave of globalized marginalization and exclusion. Such a concentrated mix is uniquely Parisian, but could easily be broken down alternatively into the experiences of Peruvian and Bolivian migrants (overwhelmingly "Indian") in "white" Buenos Aires; Nigerians (of multiple ethnicities and religions) in London or New York; and the Moroccan farmworkers whose huts were recently burned down in the contemporary Spanish equivalent of a pogrom in the environs of Almeria. This chapter proposes to outline the basis for a comparative analysis of such social conflicts, public debates, and evolving discourses regarding the impact and desirability of (primarily Arab and African, heavily Islamic) immigration in France, and as to the status of Mexico's indigenous peoples, in light of the debate over the relationship between neo-liberal globalization, multiculturalism, and citizenship.

In France migrants who have come from West Africa, the Mahgreb, Zaire and Haiti are known as the *"Sans Papiers,"* a term initially imposed upon and then adopted by immigrants without papers. The very name they assume as a badge of defiance is a deliberately ironic rendering of the *"Sans Culottes"* sector of the Third Estate who became the social base and symbol for the radicalization of the French Revolution in its initial phases. The label of *"Sans Papiers"* also suggests a link—and an evolution—from the 18th-century demands for transition to a liberal republican regime compelled to respect individual human rights of liberty and property to the 21st-century demand for complementing such rights with those of an economic, social, cultural, and collective character in a multiculturalist framework. What possible common ground could there be between such voices emerging from France's growing African and Arab immigrant population, and that of recently rekindled social movements among Latin America's indigenous peoples? In France the question arises against the background of a profound debate regarding the extent to which its 18th- and 19th-century paradigm of individualist universal citizenship can be reshaped to make room for recognition of the collective rights of non-European immigrant minorities. In Latin American countries such as Mexico, Guatemala, and Ecuador with large indigenous populations, the issue has deep historical roots but has recently re-emerged with great force amidst the wreckage of ostensible democracies hegemonized by neo-liberal economics. "Neo-liberalism" is understood here to be the Latin American version of Reaganomics in the US and of

Thatcherism in the United Kingdom, driven by the "structural adjustment" provisions of the so-called "Washington Consensus" imposed as a condition for debt relief by the joint efforts of the International Monetary Fund (IMF), the World Bank, and the Inter-American Development Bank.

The overall question is inherently transatlantic in scope since its response can be partly constructed in terms of a post-colonial paradigm arising from the "triangulating" effects of Western economic and cultural imperialism on the native peoples of the Americas, Africa, and the Middle East. According to Filipino social theorist E. San Juan, Jr., contemporary notions of "universality" (which I seek to explore here in their French and Mexican elaborations and interactions) must be grounded in a critique of the very concrete manifestations of the contemporary "capitalist world-system." In San Juan's view, analysis of complex phenomena such as the explosive recent re-emergence of social movements among Latin America's indigenous peoples, and of "parallel" movements among France's *"Sans Papiers"* demands apprehension of the "manifold links between [the] national and the international, the local and the global, the singular and the universal."[2] Implicit in this framework is the ethical and epistemological mandate to give due attention to the ways in which struggles for democratic transformation and human rights on the "periphery" of current centers of globalized capitalist hegemony in the US, Europe, and East Asia (e.g. among indigenous peoples in Latin America), or among "peripheral" groups within such centers (e.g. immigrants in France) may have direct and indirect consequences for the expansion of overall notions of democracy, human rights, and citizenship within these "centers."

San Juan carefully traces Trinidadian scholar C.L.R. James's thesis along these lines in his history of the Haitian slave revolt and independence struggle initially led by Toussaint L'Ouverture. James's essential argument in *Black Jacobins* is that the Haitian slave revolt which led to the island's independence from France in effect "completed" the process of human liberation set in motion by the French Revolution itself.[3] San Juan notes that for James, the interdependence between the development of modes and forces of production on the one hand, and revolutionary processes on the other, between African peoples and Europe must be understood through the prism of the slave trade and its effects. This is why modern Europe must be at least partly reconceived of as a creation of Africa (and of super-exploited African labor specifically), and ultimately of the struggles of African peoples against slavery.

James refers to a similar argument made by W.E.B. Dubois in *Black Reconstruction in America* that US modernity is in large part a creation of African-Americans.[4] A further confirmation of the same idea would be the way in which the 1960s' Civil Rights Movement in the US compelled practice (in terms of voting rights and rights of equality more generally) to reflect the unfulfilled constitutional rhetoric. On a broader level, this suggests that no democracy is complete until those most excluded are fully incorporated into it on equal terms. Similarly, it was not until Spanish Christianity grappled with the issue of whether the indigenous peoples of the Americas had souls or not at the urging of Fray Bartolome de Las Casas, that the concept of international law became grounded in a doctrine of universal natural rights which led ultimately to the Nuremberg Trials, the adoption of the Universal Declaration of Human Rights, and more recently the Pinochet Case.

But such a pattern also has implications for redefining issues of identity from the standpoint of "multiculturalism." Is it possible to identify "Americanness" without reference to the contributions of African slaves and African-Americans to what is generally understood to be "American" culture? Similarly what would be left of Mexican identity without reference to its indigenous roots? (Many would argue: Not much, beyond derivatives of Spanish and US culture and some hybrids such as mariachis, Norteño music, and the authoritarian one-party regime of the Institutional Revolutionary Party, in power since 1929.)

Questions of this kind arise in a much different context in terms of France's relationship to Arab and African immigrants, because of the French colonial insistence on a "civilizing mission" and continuing stress on French language and culture as a common ground for shared identity. This stance is ostensibly race-neutral, and sharply distinguishes between state neutrality as to religion and respect for freedom of religious belief in the private sphere. In this context the emergence of new social movements for human rights among both African and Arab immigrants in France (and elsewhere in Europe) and indigenous peoples in Latin American countries, such as that of Mexico's Zapatistas, have certain characteristics in common. In both cases the struggles at issue combine demands for the recognition of rights of identity and autonomy of racial, ethnic, cultural, linguistic, and/or religious minorities—"multiculturalism"—which stretch the limits of liberal individualist tolerance for diversity inherent in the 19th-century model of the nation-state. This model, of course, has its origin in the French Revolution and quickly spread to Latin America in the wake of its struggles for independence from Spain between 1810 and

1824. A broader comparison between the current tensions of this model in Europe and Latin America is more manageable if we focus on two paired examples: in this case, France and Mexico.

This focus on Mexico and France arises from my recognition of the intensity and volume of recent public debates in each country over issues of multiculturalism—bilingual or multilingual voting rights, rights of proportional representation and/or autonomy or decentralization, bilingual or multilingual language policies, education, and mass media. In Mexico, the debates particularly concern the legal, political, cultural, and socio-economic status of the country's indigenous peoples; in France, they concern the status of immigrants from North and West Africa, both black and Arab (many of them Muslim as well).

In both countries such debates have become entangled with long-standing disputes over Church-State relations and over issues of national identity and national self-image, especially as these arise in the context of public education. At another level, the debates in each country have explored issues of the relationship between universalism and particularism, and the complexities of redefining traditional notions of citizenship, nationality, and sovereignty in a "globalized" context. The debate in France over the impact and handling of immigration must be situated against the background of both European integration, and the possible expansion of the European Union (EU) beyond Europe's "natural" boundaries so as to encompass Turkey and Morocco. For Mexico there is the issue both of the impact and implications of its inclusion in the North American Free Trade Agreement (NAFTA) with the US and Canada, and its recent signing of a parallel free trade accord with the EU as well.

The pairing of Mexico and France also makes sense because of the marked influence upon Mexico of French law, political philosophy, concepts and structures of government and aesthetics since the reforms imposed by the Bourbon dynasty governing Spain during the late colonial period, and again as a result of the French imposition of Habsburg Prince Maximilian as "Emperor" of Mexico by Napoleon III in the 1860s. This influence has also been significant elsewhere in Spanish-speaking Latin America beyond that manifested in former French possessions such as Haiti, Quebec, and Louisiana, but has been especially strong in Mexico.

Globalization, Democracy, and Multiculturalism as Matters of Citizenship: The Zapatista Rebellion as a Paradigm

The recent resurgence of an indigenous social movement in Mexico was detonated by the Zapatista rebellion rooted in the most impoverished Mayan indigenous communities of the southeastern state of Chiapas (bordering Guatemala) on January 1, 1994. The revolt was deliberately timed to coincide with the effective date of Mexico's entry into NAFTA. The uprising and its aftermath have drawn widespread (if intermittent) global media coverage and a great deal of scholarly attention. Many analysts have argued that the recent confrontation over issues of globalization at the Seattle summit of the World Trade Organization (WTO) is the most recent expression of a broader debate regarding the inequities of neo-liberalism first triggered by the Zapatistas.

The Zapatista revolt in turn has sparked a wide-ranging public policy debate in Mexico (with immediate repercussions elsewhere in the region) regarding the economic, social, cultural, and political status of the country's—and region's—indigenous peoples. Much of this debate has deep historical roots, but also builds on a continental wave of indigenous social movements which have arisen in the last decade with multiple demands, spurred in part by continental protests of the 1992 Columbus quincentary (and symbolized by the awarding of the Nobel Peace Prize that year to Guatemalan Mayan human rights activist Rigoberta Menchu). Such movements have led directly to efforts to secure constitutional and legal reforms recognizing indigenous rights (with varying emphases and degrees of success) in the late 1980s and throughout the 1990s in Nicaragua, Brazil, Colombia, Mexico, Paraguay, Peru, Chile, Guatemala and Venezuela. Parallel debates have taken place during the same period within various UN agencies and in the Organization of American States (OAS), as steps towards still incomplete universal and American Declarations of Indigenous Rights. In this way indigenous social movements have become important protagonists in the overall processes of democratization in countries such as Mexico, Guatemala, Ecuador, and Colombia. In each of these examples, such movements have demanded both transformations in government policies away from the neo-liberal model which has become dominant throughout the region, and the affirmative recognition of multicultural rights of citizenship.

The region's contemporary indigenous movements thus suggest a basis for exploring the complex interrelationship between processes of globalization, democratization, and the Latin American variant of multiculturalism. The latter aspect is reflected in these movements' demands that indigenous languages and cultures be accorded official status, incorporated into bilingual educational programs and the provision of public services, and in some cases that indigenous groups be recognized as "nationalities" or "peoples" with rights of local self-government (via decentralization or the creation of structures for the exercise of what is often characterized as "regional autonomy") within redefined multicultural or multinational nation-states. My argument here is that such demands are ultimately for the redefinition of Latin American identity and statehood in terms consistent with notions of "ethnic," "cultural," and "multicultural" citizenship originally developed in other contexts by Guillermo de la Peña, Renato Rosaldo, and Will Kymlicka. All of this has important implications for the redistribution of wealth and power throughout Latin America because the region's poverty is most pervasive among its indigenous peoples. Such a redefinition is also a definitive step away from the French-inspired conceptualization of the "nation-state" with a "core" national identity and universalist pretensions (at least within its own public sphere and territory, but often beyond) which transcend all other ethnic, linguistic, cultural, and religious identities.

Latin American poverty is permeated by deep-seated patterns of racism and ethnocentrism which structure its distribution and concentration. These patterns are, in turn, rooted in historical cleavages which are part of the region's legacy of European and US conquest, colonialism, and imperialism, and which have been accentuated by the inequities of contemporary processes of globalization. This is especially true where such processes have been dominated by neo-liberal macro-economic and social policies. As a result, Latin America's indigenous peoples are the single segment of the region's population among whom poverty is most concentrated. In Latin America, in effect, to be indigenous is by definition to be poor, marginalized, and excluded from the enjoyment of internationally recognized civil, political, economic, social, and cultural rights.

Indigenous rights and policy issues in Latin America thus cast a sharp light upon the contradictions between the region's supposed transition to Western-style democracy and capitalist development, and the persistent misery in which the region's vast majorities continue to subsist. Similarly the unequal status of non-European immigrant minorities within "First World" societies such as France poses parallel kinds of questions about the limits of the liberal democratic model of the nation-state which conceives of citizenship as being centered in individualist rights of a primarily civil and political character. Even in a welfare-state context, immigrants are driven to the fringes of this core both by the greater precariousness of their enjoyment of economic and social rights which complement the civil and political dimensions of inclusion, and by their cultural, linguistic, and religious differentiation from the dominant "mainstream."

Movements such as that of the Zapatistas in Mexico also raise important issues about questions of national and personal identity in the region in a globalized, multicultural context—consider, for example, the fact that movement's best-known spokesperson and most "visible" leader, Subcomandante Marcos, is literally and metaphorically masked. The Zapatista movement itself has a social base which is overwhelmingly from Chiapas' poorest Mayan indigenous communities. This base has expanded since the January 1994 uprising to include important sectors of the urban, intellectual left and of Mexican youth, and has helped trigger an even broader, anti-Vietnam-war type of domestic peace movement including non-governmental organizations specializing in human rights defense, grassroots development, environmental and agrarian issues. The Zapatistas have also galvanized those sectors of the Catholic Church closest to currents of liberation and indigenous theology, many of them inspired by Chiapas Bishop Samuel Ruiz, who played a formal role as mediator of the conflict in the region between 1994 and 1998.

The overwhelmingly indigenous character of the movement's base and of its most frequently reiterated demands (recognition of indigenous linguistic and cultural rights and rights of local autonomy) and discourse (as reflected in Marcos's own voluminous collection of communiqués) contrasts, however, with Marcos's own acknowledged non-indigenous origin. If he is who the government has claimed he is (Marcos continues to deny the claim) since he was dramatically "unmasked" on national TV in February 1995, his real name is Rafael Sebastian Guillen Vicente, a philosophy major from the National University and former university professor of media studies who likely did post-graduate work at the Sorbonne, and who speaks relatively fluent French, Italian, and English as well as several of the indigenous languages native to Chiapas. His 1976 undergraduate thesis sought to apply Althusserian Marxist philosophy and Foucauldian discourse analysis to the study of power relationships and their reflections in the texts used in Mexican public schools.

Critics of the movement and of Marcos himself (who seem to be both especially bitter and impassioned and disproportionately available for interviews on Mexican TV), frequently suggest that Marcos's "undue" prominence is indicative of the movement's fraudulent, inauthentic, and/or manipulative character, and proves that there is a hidden agenda at work behind the movement's public image. In the US it would be absurd to imagine a contemporary movement in defense of the rights of African-Americans, Latinos, Asians, or Native Americans led by people who did not share or adequately "represent" the specific group identity at issue.[5] Marcos himself has given three different kinds of responses to such arguments. One is implicit, and includes multiple occasions when he uses "we" and "us" to speak of indigenous peoples and communities in Chiapas or elsewhere in the country, or even slips back and forth between first and third person within the same interview depending on context (or even whim). Second, he stresses his own version of the history of the Zapatistas, saying that he was among its six co-founders in November 1983 who were evenly divided between indigenous and non-indigenous sectors, and that the Zapatistas' much later emergence as a major social force in the region was the result of their "defeat" by the indigenous communities when it sought to impose a non-indigenous paradigm of struggle derived from the Cuban and Central American versions of Marxist-Leninist guerrilla struggles.

In effect Marcos argues that the key to the Zapatistas' eventual successes was due to its ability to transcend its non-indigenous roots and limitations and to find a way to meld its external origin with a virtual assimilation into the region's rich and varied indigenous cultures, traditions of struggle, and organizational strategies. This contrasts sharply with the commensurate failures of guerrilla movements to root themselves successfully in local cultures and settings in Guatemala, Colombia, Peru, and Bolivia under similar circumstances, with tragic and devastating results for all involved (including the death of one of Marcos's most evident heroes and models, Ernesto Che Guevara). I would argue, therefore, that one of Marcos's most extraordinary achievements has been to transcend and reshape his own personal and social identity as a "white" Mexican supposedly born and raised in the Gulf port of Tampico at the other end of the country from Chiapas, and to become more "Mexican" as he has become more "Mayan," reaffirming his own identification with the nation's indigenous roots (regardless of "race," biology, or genetics). In this way Marcos has legitimized an approach to Mexican national identity which suggests that the nation's indigenous roots are the common heritage of all Mexicans irrespective of their ancestry, open and accessible to all who are interested in reclaiming it for themselves. In a broader sense his success has been to embody and prefigure Mexico's own redefinition as a nation whose multicultural character flows from within.

But there is an additional, more "globalized" aspect to the issues posed by the ambiguities of Marcos's identity. His third kind of response to such issues has been a personalized equivalent of the movement's overall alignment with alternative social movements critical of neo-liberal globalization throughout the world, such as those who have gathered over the past year in Seattle, Davos, and most recently for the joint meetings of the IMF and World Bank in Washington, D.C. and then at the Los Angeles convention of the Democratic Party. Who is Marcos anyway, on a global scale? In his own view,

> Marcos is gay in San Francisco, Black in South Africa, an Asian in Europe, a Chicano in San Ysidro, an anarchist in Spain, a Palestinian in Israel, a Mayan Indian, in the streets of San Cristobal, a gang member in Neza, a rocker in the National University, a Jew in Germany, an ombudsman in the Defense Ministry, a communist in the post-Cold War era, an artist without gallery or portfolio, a pacifist in Bosnia, a housewife alone on Saturday night in any neighborhood in any city, a woman alone in the Metro at 10 P.M.... So Marcos is a human being, any human being, in this world. Marcos is all the exploited, marginalized and oppressed minorities, resisting and saying "Enough!"[6]

Multicultural Dimensions of the Public Sphere and of Citizenship

My overall assumption regarding the indigenous peoples in Latin America and non-Western immigrants in Europe is that the formalistic recognition of equal civil and political rights of citizenship for such groups is not a sufficient basis for assuming their successful inclusion in an authentically democratic framework. This is partly because, in practice, for both groups formal recognition has been accompanied by structural patterns of discrimination and exclusion with deep historical roots which render such inclusion incomplete. But it is also because their atomized civil and political inclusion as individuals has been premised in part on the renunciation of cultural rights of identity and autonomy as members of specifically disfavored groups. This is the basis of Will Kymlicka's notion of "multicultural citizenship" as a necessary expansion of the traditional core of liberal rights of a civil and political character. In his view, the failure to expand beyond this individualist core has discriminatory and exclusionary results which frustrate T. H. Marshall's assumption of a triumphal, ascending procession of rights that ends up encompassing the full range demanded by contemporary international human rights law in the civil, political, economic, social, and cultural arenas.

The corollary of such forced recantations of the cultural, linguistic, and religious aspects of membership in such minorities has been the systematic experience of discrimination, at least in part because of their affirmation and expression of such identities. This discrimination in terms of access to and enjoyment of equal opportunities and conditions of education, employment, income, housing, health care, and other fundamental rights itself undermines the supposed inclusion effected by the recognition of rights limited to the civil and political sphere. In a parallel sense, contemporary international human rights doctrine insists upon the universalistic, interdependent, and integral character of the civil, political, economic, social, and cultural rights recognized by international law. Within such a framework, any deficiency in one sphere of rights undermines the efficacy of the model as a whole. But there are at least two other principled bases for questioning the ostensibly democratic character of a state which in effect conditions full membership on cultural assimilation (which both Mexico and France have done as to indigenous peoples and non-European immigrant groups respectively). One critique can be derived from Jurgen Habermas's evolving notion of the critical role played by a healthy "public sphere" in assuring the necessary deliberative space, and thus the structural basis for an authentically democratic society.

According to Habermas, the "public sphere" is the space where "civil society" can become a protagonist by generating and mobilizing public opinion and reason independent both of control by the state and by the market. According to his original view, this sphere had its origin in the press and coffee-house debates of the early Enlightenment. But this sphere must be universally accessible to and inclusive of all potential participants, and if not it is not only incomplete but ceases altogether to be "public."[7] More recently, Habermas has re-examined the concept of the "public sphere" (reformulated in terms of a broader concept of "public space") in light of the implications posed by the increasingly multicultural character of Western European societies. A major emphasis of his most recent reflections about these issues has been on the inherent contradictions in the dual legacy of the French Revolution in terms of the relationship between the nation-state originally conceived of (or "imagined," as Benedict Anderson would have it) in terms of racial, ethnic, linguistic, and cultural homogeneity, and the emergence of citizens characterized by increasing heterogeneity.

The tension Habermas identifies between assumed homogeneity and actual heterogeneity (and thus between nationality and citizenship) leads him to call for the development of a new model of "radical democracy" better suited to contemporary conditions in Europe, and reshaped around an idea of expanded citizenship (understood in terms of the *"citoyennete"* originally invoked in 1789) rather than that of constricted nationality. In his view the original duality between nationality and citizenship has been lost and must be recovered, and a new balance established between them.

The key in his view is to broaden the concept of citizenship by demanding the common ground of a shared political culture reflected in a "constitutional patriotism" divorced from any necessary commonality of national origin, race, ethnicity, language, or broader culture in the anthropological sense.[8] Such a radically democratic multicultural state (or union of states as in the case of the EU and its possible evolution towards federalism) would be justified in demanding, as the "price of admission," not adherence to any specific cultural identity, but rather loyalty to its political culture of participatory deliberation and to the shared framework of democratic rights which make that culture possible. The increasingly multicultural character of such a state would result in the enrichment of its democratic content and horizons. Habermas in fact believes that such a state writ large in terms of Europe could provide the continent with a "second chance" usually denied by history to attempts to forge polities with universalist pretensions. From his perspective, the first opportunity was squandered by Europe's colonialist empires obsessed with economic and cultural domination. The second—democratic—opportunity would be characterized instead by a stress on forging a "non-imperialist" understanding with other cultures and a willingness to learn from them."[9]

Ethnic, Cultural, and Multicultural Citizenship

Habermas's approach is decidedly weak on the devilish details necessary to translate his (moderately) multiculturalist approach into reality. He makes no effort to address the specific extent to which non-European identities, languages and cultures should be affirmatively incorporated into the public sphere and public space of his vision of radical, revitalized Western European democracy. He does not tell us, for example, whether non-citizens should be permitted to vote (although he alludes to the issue), nor whether bilingual educational programs or public services delivered in minority languages should be state-funded or mandatory. My essential argument here is that Habermas provides the necessary principled basis for going the next step, which is provided by Will Kymlicka's notion of "multicultural citizenship" and the related concepts of "cultural citizenship" developed by Renato Rosaldo, and of "ethnic citizenship" employed by Rodrigo Montoya and Guillermo de la Peña. Together their approach breaks with the traditional Western liberal ideas associating citizenship with nationality and a singular national identity derived from the French Revolution—ideas which were adopted in an especially inflexible version by Mexico, with the same pretensions of hegemonic universalism towards the country's indigenous peoples that France itself sought to impose on its colonial subjects, and against which its *"Sans Papiers"* still struggle.

Rosaldo's concept of "cultural citizenship" stresses the idea that no authentically democratic state should require any group to give up their culture and identity as the price of equal entry into its political community. According to Rosaldo and William Flores,

> cultural citizenship refers to the right to be different (in terms of race, ethnicity, or native language) with respect to the norms of the dominant national community, without compromising one's right to belong, in the sense of participating in the nation-state's democratic processes.[10]

The concept was developed in the context of Rosaldo's intellectual leadership within what came to be known as the Latino Cultural Studies Working Group, and rooted in his reflection as an anthropologist and as one of the architects of Chicano Studies in the US.

Guillermo de la Peña frames his use of the concept of "ethnic citizenship" as an expression of Rosaldo's notion but as applied to the recently rekindled struggles of Mexico's indigenous peoples. In his view,

> Rosaldo has successfully used the notion of "cultural citizenship" to analyze the varying possibilities of constructing private and public life which are open, for example, to the children of immigrants to the United States, and also to defend the need to recognize that diversity of possibilities as an essential aspect of the wealth of the human condition.[11]

Here is a Mexican anthropologist applying a concept originally developed to address the cultural exclusion of Mexican immigrants in the US to the cultural exclusion of indigenous peoples within Mexico itself. My argument is that it thus makes perfect dialectical sense to turn this concept back to the immigrant context in France (or anywhere else), and thereby complete the implicit circle traced by de la Peña's reliance on Rosaldo.

In de la Peña's view, the transition towards "ethnic citizenship" is marked by the new insistence of indigenous organizations in Mexico—and elsewhere in Latin America, most recently and explosively in Ecuador, Bolivia, and perhaps Peru—on being recognized by both the state and broader civil society as "interlocutors" on their own behalf, "as ethnicities or peoples and even nations," setting aside decades of corporativist intermediation by official and semi-official entities manipulated by the country's longtime ruling Party of the Institutional Revolution and its captive bureaucracy. It is this transition towards an indigenous social movement bent on speaking for itself (and through "assimilated" spokespersons such as Marcos) that has in turn set the stage for the emergence of the Zapatistas and their widespread social and political impact. De la Peña argues that "ethnic citizenship" in this context means that these movements' demands "are in the process of redefining the rules of social and political participation, which is to say that of the configuration of public spaces."[12]

Rodrigo Montoya defines the concept in terms virtually identical to de la Peña's but applies it more broadly to encompass "the emergence of *ethnic groups* as new subjects with their own voice seeking to reclaim a national political space which had always been denied to them" in Peru and other Latin American countries "with a multiethnic composition," such as Bolivia, Ecuador, Colombia, Guatemala, and Nicaragua. Montoya sees such struggles as having special importance for the West itself, however peripheral they might seem, because they "enrich the Western notion of freedom."[13]

Montoya's suggestion about the implications of "ethnic" and "cultural" citizenship for Western liberalism is taken the next step by Canadian philosopher Will Kymlicka and redefined in terms of his concept of "multicultural citizenship." According to Kymlicka, this concept is applicable generally to societies where collective rights based on membership in a particular group (race, ethnicity, language, religion etc.) permit individuals belonging to such groups not only to be treated as equal citizens, but as citizens whose differential status has been legitimized through legally and officially recognized multicultural practices. The idea is of a democracy built on the recognition, rather than the negation, of difference. Such an approach is more common, according to Kymlicka, than is normally acknowledged by orthodox theorists of Western liberalism.[14] Possible examples range from Canada and the US to the United Kingdom, Spain, Belgium, Switzerland, Norway, Denmark, Israel/Palestine, Ethiopia, Eritrea, South Africa, India, Australia, and New Zealand, to varying degrees, as well as several Latin American countries that have recently adopted or are in the process of adopting constitutional reform measures along these lines in terms of the rights of indigenous peoples. Why not France and Mexico? At the heart of Kymlicka's approach is the argument—much more forceful than Habermas's—that there is no incompatibility between Western liberalism and the recognition of group rights demanded by the notion of "multicultural citizenship," and that, to the contrary, contemporary Western liberalism would be harmfully, perhaps fatally incomplete, and itself potentially threatened by the lack of such a recognition.

According to Stuart Hall and David Held, a "new politics of citizenship" has arisen in the West at the close of the 20th century, rooted in the fact that "from the ancient world to the present day, citizenship has entailed a discussion, and a struggle over, the meaning and scope of membership of the community in which one lives."[15] As Kymlicka argues,

> demands for multicultural rights on the part of immigrant and disfavored groups are, fundamentally, demands for inclusion in order to obtain full participation in the overall society. To consider these to be a threat to stability or to solidarity is implausible, and often reflects ignorance about and intolerance to such groups.[16]

He and Habermas clearly have something to talk about. But Renato Rosaldo gets the last word:

> Citizenship is often understood as a universal concept. In this view, all citizens of a particular nation-state are equal before the law. A background assumption of our work, by contrast, is that one needs to distinguish the formal level of theoretical universality from the substantive level of exclusionary and marginalizing practices.[17]

This is the terrain where the Zapatistas and the "*Sans Papiers*" get to meet, engage in dialogue, and emerge from together.

---

[1] Manu Chao, "Clandestino," Virgin France Records, 1998.

[2] E. San Juan, Jr., *Beyond Postcolonial Theory* (London: Macmillan Press, 1998), 43.

[3] C.L.R. James, *Black Jacobins* (London: Vintage, 1963).

[4] San Juan, 236. Guyanian historian Walter Rodney's book, *How Europe Underdeveloped Africa*, makes essentially the same point, and it has been made exhaustively as to the role played by Mexican and Peruvian gold and silver in capitalizing Europe's development (and distorting that of the Americas) in the 16th and 17th centuries. See Walter Rodney, *How Europe Underdeveloped Africa*.

[5] Though, of course, whites did play a prominent role in both the Abolitionist Movement, and the Civil Rights Movement of the 1960s.

[6] Quoted in Michael Parenti, *Against Empire* (San Francisco: City Light Books, 1995), 19.

[7] Jurgen Habermas, *The Structural Transformation of the Public Sphere: An Inquiry into a Category of Bourgeois Society*, trans. Thomas Burger with the assistance of Frederick Lawrence (Cambridge: Polity Press, 1989), 85.

[8] Jurgen Habermas, *Between Facts and Law* (Spanish language edition, Madrid: Editorial Trotta, 1998), 626.

[9] Ibid., 634-35, 636.

[10] Renato Rosaldo and William V. Flores, "Identity, Conflict, and Evolving Latino Communities: Cultural Citizenship in San Jose, California," in *Latino Cultural Citizenship: Claiming Identity, Space, and Rights*, ed. by William V. Flores and Rina Benmayor (Boston: Beacon Press, 1997), 57.

[11] Guillermo de la Peña, "La ciudadania etnica y la construccion de los indios en el Mexico contemporaneo," *Revista Internacional de Filosofia Politica* 6 (December 1995): 118n5.

[12] Ibid.

[13] Rodrigo Montoya, "La ciudadania etnica como un nuevo fragmento en la utopia de la libertad," in *Democracia y Estado multietnico en America Latina* (Mexico City: La Jornada Ediciones/Centro de Investigaciones Interdisciplinarias en Ciencias y Humanidades-UNAM, 1996), 367.

[14] Will Kymlicka, *Ciudadania Multicultural. Una Teoria Liberal de los Derechos de las Minorias* (Barcelona: Paidos, 1996).

[15] Quoted in Renato Rosaldo, "Cultural Citizenship, Inequality, and Multiculturalism" in Flores and Benmayor, 30.

[16] Kymlicka, 262-63.

[17] Rosaldo, 27.

Chapter 2

Transatlantic Perspectives on the History of Race

Neil A. Wynn

> The problem of the twentieth century is the problem of the color
> line,—the relation of the darker to the lighter races of men in Asia
> and Africa, in America and the islands of the sea. (W.E.B. Du Bois,
> *The Souls of Black Folk* [1903])

If he were alive today, the great African-American spokesman, W.E.B.
Du Bois, would undoubtedly add Europe to the continents listed in his
famous remark. Reports of racist incidents in countries as widespread
as Germany, Spain, France, Sweden, and Britain point to a widening of
the issue; they also suggest that race is likely to be as important in the
21st century as it was at the start of the 20th century. The growth of race
as a global issue led me to develop a course examining aspects of the
transatlantic experience in the belief that comparison of national
experiences might foster a better understanding of this phenomenon. In
contextualizing the US experience, my aim was to show what is unique
to America, and what is part of a broader history—a common heritage
but with different experiences.[1] At the same time, I intended to
foreground an often-overlooked aspect of British history in order to
help understand the present situation in the UK. In summarizing that

taught program here, I will look at three areas which may provide a basis for further research: the common history of racial ideologies and the shared imperial outlook at the end of the 19th century; transatlantic connections through Pan-Africanism in the inter-war period; and comparison of developments in the US and UK in the 1960s with reference to civil rights movements and legislation.

Preparation and Beginnings

Having taught African-American history in British institutions of higher education for some years, teaching a course in the US that compared the American experience of race with that of Britain as part of an international institute posed an exciting and pertinent challenge. It was the first time I had really thought about the history of race in the UK, and putting together the material was in itself quite an education. To my shame I quickly discovered how little I knew about the history of race relations in my own country. More than this, I soon discovered that I was not alone. Little is taught in British schools about the subject, and an investigation of bookshops to find what material was available revealed a remarkable contrast with the situation in the US. In almost any American bookshop, general or academic, there will be a sizeable section on "African-American History" or "Black Studies." This is not the case in Britain. In Cardiff, a city with a not insignificant black population and with a distinct black history, none of the major city-center bookshops has a section on black history or race relations—such material as exists is generally found under "Sociology." This pattern is repeated even in London, where only the more specialist booksellers have a section dealing specifically with matters of race. What does this reveal? Obviously, the subject of race is not of such wide interest on this side of the Atlantic. This is despite the fact that matters of race have been very much the subject of public concern following the investigations into the Stephen Lawrence murder, and the subsequent Macpherson report on racism in the Metropolitan police—events which in some respects paralleled the Rodney King case in Los Angeles or more recent events in New York City.[2]

One obvious explanation for this apparent difference in awareness and interest lies in demography. In the USA, the African-American population comprises some 12% of the population[3]; the black population of the UK is approximately 5%. However, the term "black" is misleading in the British context. The non-white population consists of Afro-Caribbeans (34%), Indians (26%), Pakistanis (16%), and Africans (11%). This population is further divided by culture and religion—Sikh, Muslim, Hindu, as well as Protestant and Catholic. It is also scattered regionally, often with different groups concentrated in particular towns and cities.

Race, then, is often not regarded as a "national problem" in Britain despite national media attention, and it is certainly not thought of as a central issue in British history. Indeed, for most people, race relations became a matter of domestic concern only after World War II with the migration of workers from the Caribbean (which began famously with the *Empire Windrush* in 1947) and with the increase in immigration of people of Asian origin that developed in the 1970s. However, Britain's black population can trace its earliest origins to the Roman armies, and 500 years later there were black faces present at the courts of Henry VII and VIII and of Scottish kings. African slaves were brought into the country from the 1570s onwards, and references to "Mores," "moors," and "Blackamoores" are, of course, well known in Shakespearean literature. Indicative of the early naming of people of African origin as the "other," such terms crossed the Atlantic with the colonists and soon found root in the New World.[4] The first "negars" were landed in Jamestown in 1619, but where the British black population had remained small, the number of Africans in America grew rapidly as the chains of slavery were forged across the Atlantic.

Racial difference soon became one of the integral justifications of and for slavery and the slave trade which linked Britain with the USA from the 18th century on. The famous triangular trade which developed between Britain, West Africa, and the New World not only helped to create wealth for the merchants of Liverpool and Bristol, but also resulted in slave trading in Britain itself, and with this an increase in the black British population. It has been estimated that by 1800, the black population in Britain numbered about 10,000 and consisted of former slaves, seamen, servants, cooks, and performers.[5] This number also included Asians, mainly servants, brought back by employees of the East India Company, and was largely confined to a few major cities and ports, particularly London, Liverpool, and Cardiff.

With the end of the slave trade, the growth of the British black population declined, and it is estimated to have been no more than about 10,000 at the start of the 20th century and concentrated very much in the capital and a few seaports. In America the situation was much different, as the black population grew from one million in 1800 to over four million in 1860, and to 8.8 million by 1900. Most of this population was confined to the southern, cotton-growing states, and even following the demise of slavery, African-Americans only slowly spread out across the US. As late as 1940, more than two-thirds of the black population was still southern, but the black presence, particularly in northern cities, was sufficient to make race a national "problem."

Racial Ideologies—"The Whiteman's Burden"

Although slavery was clearly a racial institution, the demise of the slave trade in Britain in 1807 and USA in 1806, and of slavery itself in Britain in 1833 and the USA in 1865, did not signal the death of racism—quite the contrary. In both countries racist ideology developed with attempts to control and exploit free non-white populations: in the US this was essentially an internal matter, for Britain largely external. The end of slavery coincided with the rise of Empire, and as Peter Fryer wrote, "The golden age of the British Empire was the golden age of British racism too," and he could well have added the US.[6]

The years after 1865 in America not only witnessed the final conquest of the west and the subjugation of indigenous native Americans from New Mexico to Dakota, but also the rise of a system of racial segregation in the southern states which was to survive until the 1960s. The "Jim Crow" system, as it was known, was sustained by the Supreme Court in *Plessy vs. Ferguson* in 1896, when it established the "separate but equal" doctrine. It was also justified by more extreme expressions of race difference that became an implicit part of mainstream values. They included beliefs such as:

1. "Blood will tell."
2. The white race must dominate.
3. The teutonic peoples stand for race purity.
4. The negro [sic] is inferior and will remain so.
5. "This is whiteman's country."
6. No social equality.
7. No political equality.
8. In matters of civil rights and legal adjustments give the white man, as opposed to the colored man, the benefit of the doubt; and under no circumstances interfere with the prestige of the whiteman.
9. In educational policy let the negro have the crumbs that fall from the whiteman's table.
10. Let there be such industrial education of the negro as will best fit him to serve the white man.
11. Only [white] Southerners understand the negro question.
12. Let the [white] south settle the negro question.
13. The status of peasantry is all the negro may hope for, if the races are to live together in peace.
14. Let the lowest whiteman count for more than the highest negro.
15. The above statements indicate the leadings of Providence.[7]

Such views showed the influence of social Darwinist theories of the evolution of races and of "the survival of the fittest" that could be found on both sides of the Atlantic. James Hunt, founder of the Anthropological Society of London in 1863, expressed widely held views when he suggested that "the Negro" was "a distinct species from the European," and closer to the ape. Furthermore, the Negro was an intellectual inferior who could only be "humanised and civilised by Europeans."[8]

In February 1899, in *McClure's Magazine*, the British imperial author and poet, Rudyard Kipling, addressed the American nation in an appeal to take up "The Whiteman's Burden" following the Spanish-American war. As the US Senate debated whether or not to acquire the Philippines, Kipling urged:

> Take up the White Man's burden—
> Send forth the best ye breed—
> Go, bind your sons to exile
> To serve your captives' need;
> To wait, in heavy harness,
> On fluttered folk and wild—
> Your new –caught sullen peoples,
> Half devil and half child.

The rest of the poem outlined the sacrifice and hardship that faced those who took on the noble enterprise of the burden of racial uplift. Behind this appeal was a view which informed much of Britain's imperial expansion: various leaders of the Empire in Africa described the native people as "children," "happy, thriftless, excitable," or worse. G. A. Henty, the popular author, wrote: "The intelligence of an average negro [sic] is about equal to that of a European child of ten years old." In his and other similar writings, African and Asian people were presented as at best exotic, and at worst primitive savages.[9]

Ironically it was precisely a shared view of non-white peoples which led the American southern spokesman and upholder of segregation, Senator Ben Tillman, to oppose imperial expansion. Referring to Kipling's poem in a speech to the Senate on February 7, 1899, he argued:

> [W]e understand and realize what it is to have two races side by side that can not mix or mingle without deterioration and injury to both and the ultimate destruction of the civilization of the higher. We of the south have borne this white man's burden of a colored race in our midst since their emancipation and before.[10]

Speaking of the people of the Philippines, Tillman declared them unready for liberty and unworthy of the loss of American lives that annexation would bring. Despite such arguments, the US did accept the imperial challenge and became involved in a war of suppression as a consequence. Clearly many Americans shared Kipling's racial outlook and with the acquisition of the Philippines, the notion of Anglo-Saxon superiority became part of official US policy. The American South's practice of segregation in turn provided a model for British policy makers in South Africa who, with the Native Lands Act of 1913, began the process of separation which ultimately led to *apartheid*.[11]

In the American South, the notions of "White supremacy" and black inferiority reinforced by a wave of violence which reached horrendous levels at the turn of the century. Between 1870 and 1939, more than 5000 African-Americans were lynched; in one year alone, 1892, the number was 235, and between 1900 and 1917, 1241 black Americans died at the hands of white mobs, often in public spectacles of incredible cruelty. Explanations for the increase in lynching are a matter of debate. It has been associated with social and economic change—the move of African-Americans into urban areas and greater proximity to white populations, increasing industrial development in the South and the consequent social dislocation, and the fear of new political challenges such as Populism. Lynching may also be seen as a "psychic compensation" for defeat in the Civil War and the end of slavery, the poverty of the South, and the sense that the region was falling behind the rest of the US. Given the often sexual aspect of lynching, both in the accusations, suspicions or fears of rape leveled against black male victims, and in the mutilations and tortures often suffered as a consequence, the links between this violence and ideas of masculinity may also be made. Whatever the general explanation, the intention was clearly to educate both races in the nature of race relations—white onlookers saw that black life was cheap, that black men and women were lesser beings; African-Americans were reminded of the penalties of questioning white authority.

Writings such as *The Negro A Beast* (1900), *The Negro A Menace to Civilization* (1907), and Madison Grant's *The Passing of the Great White Race* (1916) suggested a growing apocalyptic vision among some American writers on the matter of race. World War I in many ways exacerbated such fears. The use of African-Americans in the US armed forces and the migration of black workers to centers of war production brought a violent backlash. The war was followed by a "Red summer" of race violence aimed at restoring the racial status quo. Major riots in East St. Louis in 1917, and Chicago, Washington, DC, and several other towns and cities in 1919, an increase in lynching, and a revival of the Ku Klux Klan, all point to heightened white concerns to keep African Americans in "their place."

It is often (somewhat smugly) assumed in Britain that before the 1950s a tradition of tolerance and the small black population in the UK had brought racial harmony. Race conflict, and particularly race riots, are seen as a modern, postwar phenomenon. This was not the case. Not only was there a long established pattern of discrimination and prejudice, but Britain, too, experienced an outbreak of race rioting at the end of World War I. As Britain drew on colonial peoples to serve in the trenches and to man supply ships, the non-white populations of several ports increased considerably both during the war and following demobilization. In Liverpool the black population was thought to be between 2,000 and 5,000 in 1919; in Cardiff it had risen from 700 to an estimated 3,000. Conflict over jobs, housing, and more particularly, women, led to riots in both cities in June 1919. One man died in Liverpool and three in Cardiff. Other, lesser clashes occurred in Barry and Newport in Wales and also in Glasgow, Scotland, and South Shields, Tyneside.

While such outbreaks were part of the general postwar readjustment which brought strikes, protests, and other demonstrations in both the US and UK, several observers located these incidents within a worldwide pattern of race conflict they attributed to a new race consciousness. This consciousness now had a global character that was to manifest itself in new organizations and new militant expressions of race identity.

The rise of the "Colored" Races and Pan-Africanism

World War I had an enormous impact on global race relations. The conflict questioned the belief in white superiority and invincibility in a number of ways. The collapse of European empires and the participation of colonial peoples in the war to make the world "safe for democracy" encouraged black resistance to white domination almost everywhere. The mood of internationalism at the end of the war, as the great powers came together to draw up national boundaries based on principles of self determination and establish the League of Nations, encouraged people of African origin to unite in opposition to colonialism and racism. The rise of Communism also offered a new critique of imperialism and an inspiration for the masses. Throughout the inter-war years, there developed a growing connection between black leaders from the West Indies, the US, the UK, and Africa as new movements and ideas crossed back and forward over the Atlantic. At the center of this development was a growing identification among black people in the diaspora with their African origins, and out of this was to develop much of the future leadership of the movement for African independence.

Pan-Africanism had its origins in an elite network of black leaders, writers, and activists who had established communication at the end of the 19th century. Edward Blyden, a West Indian who emigrated to Liberia in 1850 where he became a newspaper editor and later commissioner to both the US and Britain in the 1890s, was one of the first to call for unity among black people under the slogan "Africa for Africans." In 1900 Henry Silvester Williams, a West Indian-born lawyer living and working in London, called the first Pan-African meeting in 1900. It was attended by a number of distinguished black intellectuals including the American leader, W.E.B. Du Bois, who was appointed chairman of the "committee on the address to the nations of the world." The address the committee produced rejected racial discrimination and called for self-government for African and West Indian peoples. This appeal fell largely on deaf ears and the organization itself soon disappeared. Nonetheless, it established links that were to grow and eventually to have some considerable influence.

Both before and after the war, London was the point where many individuals of African and Asian origin came together to discuss imperialism and the world race situation. As the center of the British Empire, London was obviously a focus of attention, but its universities brought students together from a wide variety of backgrounds. The first publication for and by black people, the *African Times and Orient Review*, was established in London in 1912 by an Egyptian, Duse Mohammed Ali, and was to have a considerable influence on key figures such as Du Bois, Marcus Garvey, and Mohandas Gandhi. Ali was one of the founder members of the African Progress Union (APU) formed in London in 1918. Led by the able politician, John Archer, the APU was largely a student organization, formed to provide a meeting place for "Africans and Afro-Peoples" and to foster the Pan-African sentiments that grew after the war.

The future of the former German colonies in Africa in 1918 focused demands for a free African state and provided the basis for the Pan-African Congress that met in Paris in 1919 under the instigation of W.E.B. Du Bois. Fifty-seven self-appointed delegates, 16 from the US, 20 from the West Indies, and 12 from Africa, gathered to pass resolutions and to lobby ministers from various states. Although little of substance was accomplished, further congresses met in London, Brussels, and Paris in 1921, in London in 1923 and in New York in

1927. While Du Bois and the American civil rights organization, the National Association for the Advancement of Colored People (NAACP), provided much of the driving force for these meetings, black British leaders like Archer and Trinidadian-born John Alcindor were also very active members.

Although dissimilar in certain respects, the leaders of the Pan-African movement—whether American, British, African, or West Indian—shared many of the views of America's first Black Nationalist, the West Indian Marcus Garvey. Garvey was part of London's pre-war black community and a contributor to the *African Times and Orient Review* before he established the Universal Negro Improvement Association (UNIA) in Jamaica in 1914. The aim of the UNIA was the promotion of "race pride and love and self help" under the slogan "One God, One Aim, One Destiny." In 1915 Garvey traveled to the US, and it was there in the aftermath of World War I that his movement grew into a force of influence. Declaring himself Provisional President of Africa in 1918, Garvey called on black peoples to "Rise Up You Mighty Race."

Although ultimately the majority of black Americans rejected his black separatist ideology, Garvey's emphasis on race pride and unity had considerable appeal and one that crossed the Atlantic. His newspaper, the *Negro World*, was published in several languages and was estimated to have a circulation of up to 200,000 worldwide and an influence even in remote parts of Africa. Sadly, poor business practice led to the collapse of the UNIA and Garvey's conviction for fraud in 1923. Following a prison sentence, he was deported in 1927. He briefly visited London in to establish a European base in 1928, and after more years of political activity in Jamaica, he returned to the capital in 1935 and died there in 1940.[12]

Not much appears to be known of Garvey's activities in London, but he certainly continued to have a role among the black émigré community. His influence could be seen in the activities and writings of a group of left-wing Pan-African radicals that emerged in the 1930s. Key members of this group reveal a fascinating pattern of transatlantic connection: George Padmore, born in Trinidad, studied in the US (where he joined the Communist Party) and settled in London in 1935; another Trinidadian, Cyril Lionel James (better known as C.L.R. James), came to Britain in 1932 where he wrote for the *Manchester Guardian* and *Glasgow Herald* before moving to the US in 1938; George Griffith (later known as Ras Tefari Makonnen) was born in British Guiana, educated in the US between 1927 and 1934, and moved to Britain in 1937. All three were active in supporting African nationalist movements and encouraging Pan-Africanism. Padmore, described by James as the "Father of African Emancipation," wrote several influential books on colonialism in Africa, corresponded regularly with W.E.B. Du Bois, and worked closely with Kwame Nkrumah of Ghana.[13] James had an enormous impact as a journalist, theoretician, and historian. His study of Toussaint L'Ouverture's rebellion in Haiti, *The Black Jacobins* (1938), still stands as one of the major contributions to black history. Griffith was more significant as a fund-raiser and organizer of black groups and particularly of the fifth Pan-African congress which met in 1945. Like Padmore, he was a close associate of Nkrumah, and also of Kenya's Jomo Kenyatta, a visitor to London between 1931 and 1946. Influenced by these and other figures, by the end of World War II Pan-Africanism ceased to be an elitist ideal, but emerged instead as a powerful movement that threatened to make the overthrow of empire a reality.[14]

Modern Civil Rights Movements

Pan-Africanism had little direct effect in the US other than to help foster a growing self-consciousness among African-Americans and a sense of race pride and identification with Africa evident in the literary Harlem Renaissance of the 1920s. However, interest in events in Africa continued. While African states attained their independence in the 1950s, the plight of African-Americans and black and Asian people in Britain hardly changed. If the US had once provided the inspiration for anti-colonialism, it was ironic that the African and Indian independence movements subsequently did much to inspire the awakening of the civil rights movement in America. In turn, African-American leaders provided inspiration for British campaigners, and US civil rights legislation offered a model for the UK to follow. There were, however, significant differences in the experiences of the two countries.

The rise of the civil rights movement was probably the most significant development in postwar America. It is a story now so well known only a brief summary is necessary. Encouraged by the gains made during and immediately after the war, and aware of the tide of anti-colonialism that saw 36 African states gain independence between 1957 and 1965, African-Americans were increasingly insistent upon achieving the rights promised them in the 14th and 15th amendments to the constitution. They were further encouraged in 1954 when the Supreme Court declared segregation in schools unconstitutional in *Brown vs. Topeka Board of Education*. When southern whites declared their opposition to this decision, the now famous "Negro Revolt" began.

Building upon a tradition of struggle, African-Americans mobilized, led by the charismatic new leader, Dr. Martin Luther King, and later joined by black and white students in the Student Non-Violent Coordinating Committee (SNCC) and Congress on Racial Equality (CORE). For over 10 years they led protests against segregation in transport and places of public accommodation, against discrimination in housing and employment, and against the denial of the franchise. The battle was fought across the South and then spread to the North as urban ghetto dwellers began to protest against *de facto* discrimination and segregation. As the campaign for equality developed, more militant voices were heard with the rise of Black Power and the influence of Malcolm X. Black anger and frustration spilled over into an eruption of ghetto riots on an almost annual basis from 1965 on. They reached a height in 1968, following the assassination of Martin Luther King. Eventually, however, the force of protest produced a series of legislative measures, notably the 1964 Civil Rights Act, the 1965 Voting Rights Act, and the 1968 Housing Act that together effectively outlawed racial discrimination in America.

British observers watched events across the Atlantic with considerable interest. Despite the long history of a black presence, the issue of race was largely seen as an external one in Britain until after World War II. During the 1950s, the UK experienced an influx of over 125,000 West Indians and almost 60,000 Indians and Pakistanis. Facing dislocations in their home countries, these immigrants were attracted by the job opportunities in transport, public health, and other areas in the rebuilding of postwar Britain. They were further assisted by the 1948 Nationality Act that conferred British citizenship on the people of British colonies or former colonies. Kenyan and Ugandan Asians ejected from the African states joined the earlier immigrants in the 1960s. It was not long before racism in the form of a "color bar" and attacks on non-whites began.

Anti-immigrant riots occurred in Notting Hill, London, and in Nottingham in 1958, and beginning with Oswald Mosely's Union Movement, right wing groups began to demand immigration restriction and repatriation. The immediate result was the introduction of immigration restriction with the passage of the 1962 Commonwealth Immigrants Bill that required an employment certificate and proof of a job or skill. British passport holders living in independent commonwealth countries, such as the Asians in Kenya, were, however, exempt. Race became a central issue in the election in 1964 when the Conservative candidate for Smethwick in Birmingham fought and won on an anti-immigrant platform. In 1966 the National Front, a right-wing anti-immigrant party, was formed and two years later the leading Conservative Member of Parliament, Enoch Powell, projected the issue fully into mainstream political debate when he forecast "rivers of blood" as "the tragic and intractable phenomenon which we watch with horror on the other side of the Atlantic ... is coming upon us here by our own volition and our own neglect."[15]

Despite some considerable opposition, further immigration restriction was introduced with the Commonwealth Immigrants Act (1968) which limited entry to those born in the UK or whose parents of grandparents were born in Britain—in other words, to white people. The Immigration Act that came into force in 1976 added further restrictions and provided for assisted repatriation.

If immigration as an issue separated the British experience from that of America, the almost contemporaneous passage of race relations legislation seemed to offer parallels. There were, however, major differences. In the UK the drive for reform came largely from government rather than from the racial minorities, and was often inspired by the fear of American-style race violence rather than by the example of American civil rights legislation. The Labour government elected in 1964 accepted both the need for immigration control and legislation to prohibit discrimination. A visit to Britain by Martin Luther King helped highlight the need for reform and encouraged the formation of the Campaign Against Racial Discrimination (CARD). CARD had a membership that was 60% white and did not survive beyond 1967. It did, however, contribute to the growing demand for government action. The result was a weak Race Relations Act that banned discrimination in public places and established a Race Relations Board to supervise its implementation. A second Act in 1968 extended the scope to cover housing and employment. While going further than its predecessor, this act, too, was severely limited in its powers, and it was clear that discrimination continued in many aspects of British life.

The civil rights movement in Britain continued to be fragmented and largely ineffective. The creation of the Racial Adjustment Action Society formed following a brief visit by Malcolm X had little impact. Ironically its leader, Trinidadian Michael X (formerly Michael de Freitas), was one of the first people charged under the Race Relations Act for "incitement to racial hatred." Michael X achieved a high profile in the media, but he ended in ignominy. At the end of the decade he disappeared and subsequently surfaced in the West Indies where he was convicted for the murder of two of his followers and executed. A visit by Stokely Carmichael of SNCC in 1967 led to the formation of the Universal Colored Peoples' Association, but this soon faded into obscurity. More important, perhaps, were the Asian groups such as the Indian Workers' Association and the National Federation of Pakistanis Association which, together with workers' organizations, worked at grass roots and shop floor level to effect change. Local actions such as a four-month bus boycott in Bristol also helped to raise awareness of discrimination.

As the black population increasingly found a voice at community level, and as it became more and more apparent that previous legislation had failed, a third Race Relations Act was passed in 1976. Establishing a Commission on Racial Equality, the new measure extended earlier provision to included systemic and indirect discrimination and showed the influence of American affirmative action policies. However, the death of 31 black people in racial attacks between 1976 and 1981, and the outbreak of rioting in black communities in Britain—Bristol in 1980, Brixton (London), Toxteth (Liverpool), Handsworth (Birmingham), and Chapeltown (Leeds) in 1981—suggested that much still needed to be done.

To many observers it appears that even today the legislation in Britain has lagged behind that of the USA, and has been only partially successful in tackling the issue of racial discrimination.[16] But in many respects the situation in the two countries has become more alike. The law *has* been changed in both countries to tackle racial prejudice and discrimination, and many old assumptions and habits have been challenged. The legacies of 19th-century racism and imperialism have been rejected, particularly by younger generations. Nonetheless, recent cases on both sides of the Atlantic, often involving police forces, have made clear the extent of institutionalized racism. Individual examples of racially-motivated attacks such as that on Stephen Lawrence in London or on James Byrd, in Jasper, Texas, in 1998, also reveal the persistence of deep-seated racism.[17] The only encouraging aspect of such cases is the public outcry that followed. Unhappily, however, one has to concede that the color line identified by Du Bois at the start of the 20th century has only partially been erased as we enter the 21st century.

---

[1] This paper is a based on a course entitled "Changing Experiences in Race Relations in the USA and UK" taught as part of the International Summer Institute, Central Missouri State University, 1996, 1997, and 1999. For the fullest account of race relations in Britain, see Peter Fryer, *Staying Power: The History of Black People in Britain* (London: Pluto Press, 1984). The best single-volume history of African-Americans is still John Hope Franklin and Alfred A. Mosse, *From Slavery to Freedom: A History of African-Americans*, first published by McGraw Hill in 1947 and now in its 8th edition.

[2] Stephen Lawrence was the black youth murdered in a racist attack in London on April 22, 1993. The failure to first charge, and subsequently to obtain convictions, of his murderers led to widespread condemnation of the London Metropolitan police. The subsequent public inquiry headed by Sir William Macpherson criticized the police for incompetence and institutional racism in the report issued in 1999. Rodney King, an African-American motorist, was brutally beaten by Los Angeles police in 1991. The trials that followed exposed widespread racism among the LAPD. The acquittal in 1992 of the police officers concerned led to an outbreak of race rioting in Los Angeles. Two police officers were subsequently convicted. In 1997 the New York police were accused of racism following the brutal assault on Abner Louima, a Haitian immigrant.

[3] The population of the US as of 1990 included people of Hispanic origin (9%), Asians (3%), Native Americans (.8%); those of African descent numbered almost 30 million; the non-white population in the UK is 3 million.

[4] "Moor" was later replaced by "Lascar" (actually an East Indian) and "Somali"; similar derogatory racial epithets were to develop on both sides of the Atlantic, but there were occasional differences, e.g. "wog" for "worthy oriental gentleman" in Britain and "coon" in the US, reflecting different aspects of racism.

[5] See Peter Fryer, *Staying Power: the History of Black People in Britain*, (London: Pluto Press, 1984), 68.

[6] Fryer, 165.

[7] Thomas Bailey, *Race Orthodoxy in the South* (1913), quoted in Leon F. Litwack, *Trouble in Mind: Black Southerners in the Age of Jim Crow* (New York: Alfred Knopf, 1998), 181.

[8] Fryer, 176-77, and Douglas Lorimer, *Colour, Class and the Victorians* (New York: Holmes and Meier, 1978).

[9] Fryer, 184-90; see also V. G. Kiernan, *The Lords of Human Kind: European Attitudes to the Outside World in the Imperial Age* (Harmondsworth: Penguin, 1972), especially 242-47. In addition to Henty, authors like Rider Haggard, and later John Buchan among many others, wrote tales of European adventure and heroism in "darkest Africa."

[10] "'The White Man's Burden' as Prophecy," William Jennings Bryan et al., *Republic or Empire? The Philippine Question* (Chicago: Independence Co., 1899), n.p.

[11] See John Cell, *The Highest Stage of White Supremacy: The Origins of Segregation in South Africa and the American South* (Cambridge: Cambridge University Press, 1982).

[12] Details of Garvey and the UNIA's influence can be found in Judith Stein, *The World of Marcus Garvey: Race and Class in Modern Society* (Baton Rouge: Louisiana State University Press, 1986) and E. David Cronon, *Marcus Garvey and the Universal Negro Improvement Association* (Madison: University of Wisconsin Press, 1969).

[13] Nkrumah himself offers an interesting insight into the transatlantic connection—he was educated at Lincoln University, Pennsylvania in the

1930s, and said that America opened his eyes to the true meaning of liberty. It is also worth noting in passing that Du Bois spent his last years in Ghana where he died in 1963.

[14] Paul B. Rich, *Race and Empire in British Politics* (Cambridge: Cambridge University Press 1990), 85-91.

[15] John Solomos, *Race and Racism in Britain* (Basingstoke: Macmillan, 1993), 67.

[16] Solomos, 89-91.

[17] James Byrd was dragged behind a truck until his body literally disintegrated; his murderers were subsequently convicted and sentenced to death in 1999. The Commission for Racial Equality in Britain reported 13,878 racial incidents in England and Wales in 1997-98.

Chapter 3

The New Pioneers: The Psychological Status of Migrants

Jane Prince

Mae hen wlad fy nhadau yn annwyl i mi,
Gwladd beirdd a chantorion, enwogion o fri,
The land of my fathers is dear to me,
Land of bards and singers, famous men of renown
National Anthem of Wales

Prologue

Scranton, Pennsylvania 1890. A young man from South Wales arrives after a journey of some twelve weeks via land and sea. Looking for work and wealth in the anthracite mines of Pennsylvania, he is astounded by the trappings of civilization which surround him. Bars and brothels compete with chapels and choirs for his attention, all calling him in his Welsh mother tongue. The town's population is 10% Welsh; all seem to be speaking to him! His chances of elevating himself in the workers' hierarchy are excellent (as long as he avoids the siren voices of those bars); for each national group there seems to be a place in the pecking order and for the Welsh that place is good. The managerial and superintendent posts are largely occupied by the

Welsh, the foremen mainly Irish and the Poles, while Italians and Slovaks fill the general laboring posts.

Hackney, London. January 2000. A health visitor holds a clinic in a doctor's office. A 20 year-old Kosovan girl arrives with her 11 week old baby. Mother speaks no English but is obviously very concerned about the child who appears to be thriving. The health visitor phones Hackney council's telephone interpreter service. Through the male interpreter the health visitor reassures the mother that the source of her worry—the soft spot on the baby's head—is perfectly normal. The girl knows no one in Britain; between them the health visitor and the interpreter are able to help her contact a Kosovan refugee group in London who can help her adapt to her new country and offer support.

Bordeaux, 1978. A British girl spending a year in France to improve her French chats to the local pharmacist. They share a number of interests and political values in common but the girl is surprised by the hostility and racism in the pharmacist's voice when she talks of the North African communities in nearby Toulouse. Over coffee, in passing, the girl's landlady notes that the pharmacist is "*pieds-noirs* of course." The girl puzzles over her dictionary, finds that *pieds-noirs* is the term for the residents of Algeria of ethnic French origins who fled to France after Algerian independence in the early 1960s. An understanding of what it actually was to *be "pieds-noirs"* eludes her for several more years.

In this chapter I will outline the relationship which exists between personal and national identities and draw attention to the precarious status of the identities experienced by migrants as they make the transition from old nation to new. I will outline some of the ways in which elements of the old nation are used by migrants to a new country to enhance their own status and distinguish them from other (by implication, lesser) immigrants and also explore the ways in which loss—of land, geography, culture and language—characterizes the identity threats which have to be experienced and managed as individuals struggle to accommodate their new host country and its practices into their own sense of self and identity. In so doing I will draw on knowledge from psychological literature to explain how threatened identities can be managed and transitional identities achieved.

During the 19th century millions of people uprooted themselves from familiar environments and emigrated to the Unites States. As we enter the 21st century, such upheaval is still a common phenomenon and the migrations, while involving different groups of individuals moving in a variety of directions, take place for remarkably similar reasons to those which propelled the transatlantic movement westwards in the 1800s. War, economic insecurity, religious and social persecution and the search for adventure, challenge and fortune are the four engines which did and do drive migration. However, for most the leaving of the land of their birth is not easily and painlessly accomplished.

The Welsh immigrants who stormed the coalfields of Pennsylvania, the silver and gold mines of Colorado and California and the farmlands of the Midwest brought with them the Welsh language and literature, their music and songs and their industrial skills. (Conway writes that amongst many immigrants from Wales, there was a belief that where there was a hole in the ground, there should be a Welsh miner at the bottom of it).[1] Jones argues that such aspects of Welsh culture were used by immigrants to elevate their status while other, less attractive, aspects of Welsh cultural life such as drinking were not mentioned.[2] It was the "official" Welsh traits which marked this group out as being natural members of the American community, traits which included morality (better seen in the Baptist Churches than in the Welsh beer-halls) and the possession of a long cultural and linguistic history. And of course since the majority of the immigrants spoke some English, absorption into the Anglo-Saxon Protestant norms of the American white-collar classes was easier for the Welsh than for other immigrants from, for example, Italy, Poland and Lithuania. Of course, if the Welsh had their chapels and *Eisteddfods* [cultural festivals], they also had their criminals and drunks and even their own brothels,[3] but these latter were not elevated to symbolic status as were the former during the successful Welsh attempt to claim the moral and cultural high ground for its immigrant peoples, a success which permitted the Welsh immigrants to make the transition to being American.

Is it really possible to draw an analogy between the Welsh miners, iron-workers, craftsmen and would-be farmers who flocked to the USA in search of not so much fortune as survival and a better quality of life, and the migrants who move round Europe and the USA today? The Welsh were fleeing poverty, unemployment and lack of hope; today's migrants might be fleeing war, political oppression, poverty—or may just want a different lifestyle, swapping the rural backwaters of Britain or France for life in the fast lane in Brussels or Berlin or Boston. What they have in common is their foreignness in a new country, a foreignness marked clearly by their language. (The majority of emigrants in the 19th century, particularly those from rural areas, were

Welsh speaking;[4] they would have been as lost as any other new arrival in the Babel that was New York).

The importance of their "Land" in the hearts of the Welsh-Americans is indicated by the prevalence of Welsh-language newspapers, schools and cultural events in parts of the US. Even now, more than one hundred years after the peaks of emigration, Greenslade[5] lists over a hundred Welsh organizations in the USA and Canada involved in Welsh language activities such as festivals, newspapers, language courses and university programs.

It may be that it was contact with other nationals which made the Welsh in America, and indeed contemporary migrants, more conscious of their own nationality. Morse noted that traditional national symbols (e.g. flags, national holidays or feast days) and contact with people of a different nationality triggered a sense of strong national identity[6]. Twigger-Ross and Uzzell propose that there is a powerful relationship between geography and identity which manifests itself in two ways. First, place might be seen in terms of a *social category*; place identification means a person sees herself as a member of a group defined by geography.[7]

For a migrant this might produce contradictory identities—as, say, a Parisian (by residence) and a New Yorker (by birth). Such transitional identities take on a more complex form when contradiction is further confounded by differences in language or in cultural practices. Thus a British migrant to Kansas City might experience contradictory identities related to geography and culture but not to language. A second way of relating place to identity is to consider that all aspects of identity will have place-related implications and attachment to place functions to support aspects of identity[8] (One manifestation of this is the longing for the home place experienced by migrants—homesickness). Places such as historic sites can play a part in the construction and maintenance of group identity[9] while at the level of the individual's identity the physical environment provides a reference point for continuity between past experience and present identity.[10] Thus migration represents a rupture with past identity (in relation to place) and possibility for new place-related identities. Place identity offers a chance to distinguish between "us" and the other; this distinctiveness is an important element of identity.

Place-identity can also support transitions in identity; a new house marks a new life, a new residential location marks, by its distinction from the location of origin, a change in self and self-related activities. At the same time, sharing a new geographical location with other people from the same country of origin allows for continuity in identity, a link between past and present; this explains why immigrants tend to move to locations where there are others from their own country. English migrants have colonized large parts of the Dordogne in France; Earls Court in London contains more Australians than native Londoners. In London immigrants fleeing religious, racial or economic persecution have tended historically to cluster around the East End where housing and living generally is cheaper, then move out as they became more established. Thus Widgery writes:

> The East End has both shaped generation after generation of migrants and been itself remade by their transitions. Immigrants, émigrés and exiles have stamped the area with a multiracial and nonconformist character which could neither be blitzed nor redeveloped out of existence. Its streets, its argot, its physiognomy and its habits are marked by journeys made across the globe to it and thought it.[11]

Yet even so the East End is not a homogeneous area; there are distinct ethnic communities in distinct geographical locations.

There is some evidence that living in a group of other migrants from the same country of origin provides some protection against psychological health problems;[12] cultural isolation is an enormous source of distress. In general the dispersal of migrants within a host community brings problems for those migrants; this is particularly the case for refugee dispersal.[13]

Identity Conflict

It is probably useful at this stage to consider the ways in which psychology has explained processes of identity development, identity conflict and ways of responding to threats to identity. Identity has been approached through a number of perspectives, which have encompassed views of identity understood with respect to social group membership, as knowledge of self through interaction, a construction historically situated and emerging from social and cultural processes and a set of socially produced knowledges learnt by an individual.[14]

Tajfel's work has focused on the dynamics of inter-group processes. Through the process of intergroup comparison, Tajfel proposed, dimensions (social categorizations) are established through which members of a group both assert difference and learn to value those features of their group which comprise that difference. By internalization of social categorizations characteristic of a group, individuals acquire particular social identities which may have positive or negative value.

Tajfel distinguishes between social and personal identities as being two different (contrasting) levels of self-categorization.[15] If a group identity is particularly meaningful for someone, then the individual traits which mark the uniqueness of the individual become less to the fore of self-representation. In effect, individuals become depersonalized as the values and behaviors stereotypical of the group are internally attributed by the individual group member.[16]

Harré identified three elements of personal-being, the first being the personal (as distinct from the social) sense of identity through which the person conceives of herself as a singular being with a *"continuous* and unique history,"[17] the second being consciousness understood as both knowing and knowing that one is knowing, and hence involving the capacity for attribution or self-reference, and the third being agency, which involves having a theory of self as having the ultimate power of decision and action. Harré believes that in Western cultures (although not universally) self-awareness and agency form the core of a sense of personal identity. Since the practices of the social world communicate themselves through language, he argued, the cultural, ideological and social contexts which constitute language are fundamental to individual understanding of identity .

Gergen, like Harré, views self or identity as being a social construction, historically situated within ongoing social processes.[18] He believes that understanding the dynamics of identity involved focusing not on the individual but on the relationship between individuals, within which the possibility of individual identity is located:

> We speak of persons as having motives, beliefs, understandings, plans and so on, as if these are the properties of individual selves. However, if my arm is positioned above my head there is little that can be said about me as an individual. I am merely a spatio-temporal configuration. In contrast, if another person were before me, crouching and grimacing, suddenly it is possible to speak of me as aggressive, oppressive or ruthless.[19]

Within this approach our identities—our individual characteristics— are primarily products of our proximity to others within specific linguistic, cultural and social contexts.

Mead proposed that an individual acquires a sense of self by taking the attitudes of other individuals towards herself within a social environment or context of experience. For Mead, the agent, the "I," acts on the world; when the action is over it, and its outcomes, are reflected on by the "Me." Thus action and reflection are two stages of the same process and one exists relative to the other as I and Me constantly change position and change into each other. The reactions to the *I* by others inform the reflections of the *Me*—the I as agent acting and the Me as agent-reflecting. Thus gaining knowledge about self is, for Mead, a two-way relationship between a person and her environment.[20]

The acting agent is the "becoming" while the reflecting agent is the "being." Hence Mead formulates a theory of self in which process and being are of equal importance and equally dynamic. Markova takes this conceptualization further. She notes that one can only talk about individuals in as much as they can be differentiated from, or opposed to, their environment.[21] In the same sense the meaningfulness of something is dependent on the meaningfulness of its counterpart. The organization of self is only understood in the context of that which it is not, and "we learn at the same time both what a thing is and what it is not."[22] Thus identity is not based on experience alone, nor solely on a construction based on information transmitted by others. While Markova sees self-knowledge in terms of an agent doing the knowing and structuring of information, she clearly sees identity as being interactional, consequent on practical engagement with the world and a synthesis of processes and knowledges. To know oneself and to have an "identity" requires an acceptance of the presence of contradiction and attempt at its resolution.

Breakwell suggests that identity can perhaps best be understood as a dynamic or rather as a product (continually changing) of a dynamic between the set of current social contexts within which an individual is placed (including relationships, cultural rules, norms and values) and the individual's own history. The social context in which identity is produced is one which can be both host-national and birth-national; hence the identity processes will involve a resolution of any conflict that may occur between the two national identities. For Breakwell the identity through in-group valuation proposed by Tajfel does not take sufficient account of the much wider social and historical context in which individuals are located. In a sense personal identity could be viewed as the more-or-less enduring result of each assimilation to and accommodation of a social identity.

Gergen suggests that identity formation is guided by three principles: continuity across time and situation; distinctiveness or uniqueness for the person; and feelings of self-esteem or personal worth.[23] Thus identity can be seen as a consequence of a series of unconscious and conscious conflicts and the resolution of these, between the existing self and the requirements of a particular situation.

Not only is identity an outcome of actions, but it also directs actions; in search of continuity, self-value and distinctiveness, the individual makes decisions and undertakes acts. Identity is dialectically related to action. In the specific context of a possible challenge to identity, actions will be taken to reduce challenge in some way. Breakwell identifies several strategies for coping with challenges to identity: *Isolation*, a strategy of inaction rather than action, allows the individual to minimize threat by isolating herself from other people, and is particularly effective when the challenge is to self-esteem via stigmatization of an occupation or identity position. *Negativism* entails the tactic of direct confrontation with those who challenge the identities. Apter insists that negativism—at its most basic involving simply saying "No" to other people's attempts to define what a person is when that definition is seen as being illegitimate—is a feature of all of life's transitions; he describes it as a state of mind in which one feels a compulsion to act against pressures from an external source.[24] For example, a migrant may insist on maintaining a traditional dress code; in France this has led to conflict between Muslim parents insisting on their rights to send their daughters to school wearing a head-scarf or veil (for religious reasons of modesty) and the secular State education system which bans the teaching of religion and religious artifacts in schools. Negativism allows for continuity, mentioned above as an important element in identity, in that continuity requires resistance to change in the face of attempts to impose change. It also allows for distinctiveness which is achieved through the rejection of orthodoxies and stereotypes. Furthermore, it enhances self-esteem. However, Apter recognizes a downside to negativism; some people have over-generalized resistances whilst others, in the face of overwhelming external challenges to identity, may turn the anger of negativism inwards on themselves, producing self-damaging behaviors.

The strategy of *passing* may enable an individual to evade a threatening situation through deceit.[25] It normally occurs when the characteristics identifying the challenge to identity are easily hidden. The availability of such a strategy in migrants varies widely from group to group; the Welsh in the US in the 19th century used passing by invoking the similarity between their own values of religion and piety and the values of the early religious settlers, the Pilgrim Fathers. Such an analogy is not always available, particularly when one of the distinctions between migrant and host communities is physical characteristics which are not easy to hide. Even so, a migrant may adopt wholesale the values and cultural practices of the host country; the British-Asian comedy program, *Goodness Gracious Me,* pokes fun at such behavior satirizing a middle-class Indian couple in Britain who insist on English food, express xenophobic anti-Indian sentiments and even insist in being called by Anglicized versions of their real names. Of course, the irony of passing is that while its purpose is to protect a challenged identity, in the process that identity is consigned to the dustbin, or at least is allowed no expression in the social world.

Compliance is a strategy which entails "role-playing" such that the individual conforms to perceived expectations.[26] Stigmatized groups are known to comply with the expected role; such behavior has been observed in, amongst others, hospitalized schizophrenics,[27] and in schoolchildren fulfilling teachers' expectations of poor performance, expectations based on non-academic criteria such as social class and accent.[28] It has been noted in groups who have suffered discrimination and has, for example, been proposed as one factor (albeit a minor one) in the relatively poor performance in school of British children of Afro-Caribbean ethnicity. Compliance has serious implications for psychological health, particularly when the expected role has associations of low level of performance or social desirability. Such associations become integrated into the self-concept and this may lead to low self-esteem and depression.

Managing identities in transition

It is clear that the process of entering a new cultural community will require an adaptation of both personal identity and group identities. Berry recognized the two core elements of the identity decision facing migrants, that of deciding to what extent they wish to retain their original cultural identity and to what extent contact with the host culture can be viewed as desirable. Dependent on the outcome of these two decisions, he argued, migrants would take up one of four acculturation attitudes which he defined as *integration* (positive attitudes to cultural contact with the host culture combined with positive attitude to continuity of identity of origin), *assimilation* (positive attitudes to cultural contact with the host culture combined with negative attitude to continuity of identity of origin), *separation* (negative attitudes to cultural contact with the host culture combined with positive attitude to continuity of identity of origin) and *marginalization* (negative attitudes to cultural contact with the host culture combined with negative attitude to continuity of identity of origin).[29] His assimilation group can be equated with those who adopt the strategy of passing, representing a rejection of the culture of origin and an attachment to the new culture.

Horenczyk argued that a further variable inputting to the nature and stability of identity transitions would be the expectation of emigrants of the host culture's response to them, in particular the extent to which they expected to be required to suppress their own cultural identities. His empirical study of identity reconstruction in Russian immigrants to Israel showed integration to be preferred by both migrants and hosts, particularly in relation to language and culture.[30] This should be reflected, in practice, in an increasing diversity of cultural practices since integration implies both the maintenance *and* weakening of the migrant's culture of origin. Thus a migrant might display different acculturation attitudes for different aspects of life in the new community, such as assimilation in relation to education practices, separation in relation to ideas on gender roles and integration attitudes in the celebration of holidays and festivals.

In real life, however, this expressed desire for integration is not always related to behavior. Other factors, both economic and social, may interfere with the migrant's ability and wish to adapt to the host culture's ways. For example, poor employment prospects in the new country may lead a migrant to rely on connections among other migrants from his birth country for finding work, which in turn could lead to patterns of work (pay, hours, nature of work) which might be maladaptive for entry to the work culture of the host community. Or a need for social continuity might drive the individual into work which has strong cultural links with "home" such as restaurant work. It is one of the apparent anomalies of the *pieds noirs'* experience in the early years of return to France that while their dislike of Algerians as a racial group was strong, many of the migrant *pieds noirs* set up businesses which allowed them to introduce the French to North African cuisine.

In summary it appears that to be psychologically healthy, migrants need to value both the cultural values of the country of origin and those of the host country and to attempt to operationalize those valuations in behavior. How easy this is to do is constrained to a very real extent by individual factors such as language skills, self-esteem and skills, and also by factors such as the host community's value for them and their culture and the extent to which the host community expects conformity to their own values and customs.

Self Esteem and Stigma

Communities are composed of many exchanged signs, some obvious, some not; the person who isn't familiar with the signs, the one who isn't "like us", but a foreign visitor asking to be admitted, is made to understand that the locals do not consider him to be one of them. It is difficult to gain admittance to stable, traditional communities, even harder to become at home in them; it requires the work of several generations. In Europe, one must be an immigrant of several generations to be genuinely at home where one is, but perhaps even that isn't enough.[31]

While continuity of identity is a problem for all migrants, it is particularly problematic for refugees who face not only a sudden disruption of the link between past, present and future but also a stigmatization which at best results in their being viewed as passive victims (for example, Kosovan refugees in the UK in the late 1990s) and at worst stigmatized and reviled for being scroungers, no matter how legitimate their refugee status might be (as for example with the treatment in the British tabloid press of Roma refugees from the Czech Republic in 1999). For such people the maintenance of self-esteem, already noted to be a central part of identity, is particularly problematic. Often the only protection against decreasing self-esteem is a strict adherence to old values, but this can only provide temporary relief since failure to accommodate host country practices is both damaging to self-esteem in the long run and may also lead to stigmatization of the migrant identity. In addition, elements of the old and new cultures may be in conflict.

The presence of racist attitudes in the host community can be reflected in negative identity and stigma attached to migrants.[32] This often manifests itself as a generalized categorization (usually a term of abuse) such as Wop, Paki or Wet-back. Stigma not only diminishes the status of the recipient of the epithet but also denies them their individuality[33] by burying them in a general category (which may not even be accurate). Thus a British Asian girl of Indian descent complains about being called "Paki," arguing that she is "not a Pakistani." The abuse has two levels, firstly in being a term of abuse which the abuser feels empowered to use (and here we can consider institutional legitimization of racism as producing such feelings of empowerment) and secondly in denying the individual identity of the recipient. She has such little status that the question of her ethnic identity is irrelevant—she is foreign, one of "them" and that is sufficient. Racist attitudes and their expression not only stigmatize migrant groups, but they can also serve as a frame for legitimizing consistent exclusion from resources. This legitimacy may be included unconsciously in the individual's self-schema so that he or she accepts lesser rights in the host country. Stigmatizing specific groups by ascribing general characteristics of personality, physique or ability and motivation seriously undermines self-esteem. Thus if an individual defines himself in terms of a collective identity, he will be more sensitive to outcomes for that collective[34] and may find it difficult to dissociate himself from that group when it is challenged and stigmatized, seeking instead to engage in defensive attributions to keep their identities intact when their group's accomplishments are undermined.[35]

The new pioneers? The phrase conjures up an image of robust individualistic idealists, searching for the perfect context in which to establish their new lives. The reality for many migrants, voluntary or not, is of struggle not against the physical elements or a physical foe but against the psychological problem of integrating past and present identities. They are unlikely to be required (or expect) to conquer an indigenous people—rather, the indigenous culture may require them to adapt to the host country's ways. Conflict can be a consequence of failure to maintain self-esteem and continuity; the price paid for such unresolved conflict is likely to be psychological rather than physical— depression, anxiety and isolation. Identity has been shown to be linked to both individual and cultural/group factors and to places; geographical sites have been shown to be an important element of group identity. Difference between host culture and culture of origin can be marked by language, attitudes, religion and values as well as by dress and food.

Perhaps life was easier for the Welsh man introduced in the prologue than for the young Kosovan mother; although facing physical hardship, he was located in a community which allowed him sufficient connection with his Welsh identity to support him in making the transition to being American. The transatlantic migration was, for him, a personal test as well as a quest, but it was arguably a test of his own choosing. Moreover, it took place at a time when westward migration to America was a legitimate journey for a young man looking for a better life, and it had the additional advantage of being made in the company of fellow nationals, supported by familiar customs and language. In any case, it seemed to work out for him; he returned to Wales some 22 years later with a wealth of stories of adventure (but, sadly, no wife); he found he really had made the transition from being Welsh to being American. He stayed in Wales for just over a year then returned to Pennsylvania where life seemed more "normal."

For the Kosovan mother, deprived of any familiarity of language and place and isolated from others in a similar position by language, custom and geography, her future is less certain. Successful relocation for her is tied up with negotiating continuity of identity in tandem with change. Her migration across Europe, though shorter in distance than the transatlantic crossing made by her Welsh counterpart more than a hundred years earlier, has involved more difficulties and possibly even greater physical hardship than did his. Her freedom to return one day to the country of her birth is dependent not on a personal wish and the accumulation of sufficient money to pay the fare, but on wider political struggles conducted well outside her arena of control. The pharmacist in France has also been forced to travel a distance which is far greater in psychological than in geographical distance. Her journey from Africa to Europe is a distance of less than a thousand miles but psychologically her migration was absolute, with no possibility of return. Her transition to a French identity was made easier by a shared language and ethnic identity, but the cultural and social practices which marked her childhood and adolescence continued to exert their influence until her early death in 1996. The polar opposite of our transatlantic Welsh migrant, her psychological migration was never truly accomplished.

---

[1] A. Conway, *The Welsh in America: Letters from the Immigrants* (Cardiff: University of Wales Press, 1961).

[2] W. D. Jones, *Wales in America* (Cardiff: University of Wales Press, 1993).

[3] D. Smith, *Wales: A Question for History* (Bridgend: Seren, 1999).

[4] Conway, 1961.

[5] D. Greenslade, *Welsh Fever: Welsh Activities in the United States and Canada Today* (Cowbridge: D. Brown, 1986).

[6] S. Morse, "Being a Canadian," *Canadian Journal of Behavioural Science* 9, no. 3 (1977): 265-73.

[7] C. Twigger-Ross and D. Uzzell, "Place and Identity Process," *Journal of Environmental Psychology* 16 (1996): 205-20.

[8] Ibid.

[9] A. M. Gallagher, "Social Identity and the Northern Ireland Conflict," *Human Relations* 42, no. 10 (1989): 917-35.

[10] C. McClenahan, et al., "Preference for Geographical Location as a Measure of Ethnic/National Identity in Children in Northern Ireland," *The Irish Journal of Psychology* 12, no. 3 (1991): 346-54.

[11] D. Widgery, *Some Lives! A GP's East End* (London: Simon and Schuster, 1993), 175.

[12] A. Furnham and S. Bochner, *Culture Shock: Psychological Reactions to Unfamiliar Environments* (London: Routledge, 1986).

[13] J. Westermeyer, "Prevention of Mental Disorder Among Hmong Refugees in the US: Lessons from the Period 1976-1986," *Social Science and Medicine* 25 (1987): 941-47.

[14] See, for example, *Differentiation between Social Groups*, H. Tajfel, ed., (London: Academic Press, 1978); G. Mead, *Mind, Self and Society* (Chicago: Chicago University Press, 1934); I. Markova, "On the Genetic Nature of Social Psychology" in *Causes of Development: Interdisciplinary Perspectives*, ed. G. Butterworth and P. Bryant (Chichester: Wiley, 1987); K. Gergen, "The Social Construction of Self-Knowledge" in *The Self: Psychological and Philosophical Issues*, ed. T. Mischel (Oxford: Blackwell, 1977); K. Gergen, "Towards Self as Relationship" in *Self and Identity: Psychosocial Perspectives*, ed. K. Yardley and T. Honess (Chichester: Wiley, 1987); and R. Harré, *Personal Being: a Theory for Individual Psychology* (Oxford: Basil Blackwell, 1983).

[15] H. Tajfel, ed., *Social Identity and Intergroup Relations* (Cambridge: Cambridge University Press, 1982).

[16] H. Marshall and M. Wetherall, "Talking about Career and Gender Identities" in *The Social Identity of Women*, ed. S. Skevington and D. Baker (London: Sage, 1989).

[17] R. Harré, *Personal Being: a Theory for Individual Psychology* (Oxford: Basil Blackwell, 1983). Emphasis mine.

[18] K. Gergen, "The Social Construction of Self-Knowledge" in *The Self: Psychological and Philosophical Issues*, ed. T. Mischel (Oxford: Blackwell, 1977).

[19] K. Gergen, "Towards Self as Relationship" in *Self and Identity: Psychosocial Perspectives*, ed. K. Yardley and T. Honess (Chichester: Wiley, 1987), 61.

[20] G. Mead, *Mind, Self and Society* (Chicago: Chicago University Press, 1934).

[21] I. Markova, "On the Genetic Nature of Social Psychology" in *Causes of Development: Interdisciplinary Perspectives*, ed. G. Butterworth and P. Bryant (Chichester: Wiley, 1987).

[22] I. Markova, "Knowledge of the Self Through Interaction" in *Self and Identity: Psychosocial Perspectives*, ed. K. Yardley and T. Honess (Chichester: Wiley, 1987), 73.

[23] K. Gergen, "Personal Consistency and the Presentation of Self" in *The Self in Social Interaction*, vol. 1, ed. C. Gordon and K. Gergen (Hillsdale, NJ: Lawrence Erlbaum, 1968).

[24] M. Apter, "Negativism and the Sense of Identity" in *Threatened Identities*, ed G Breakwell (Chichester: Wiley, 1983).

[25] G. Watson, *Passing for White* (London: Tavistock, 1970).

[26] E. Goffman, *Stigma: Notes on the Management of Spoiled Identity* (Harmondsworth: Penguin, 1976).

[27] B. Braginski, D. Braginski, and K. Ring, *Methods of Madness* (New York: Holt, 1969).

[28] D. Hargreaves, *Interpersonal Relations and Education* (London: Routledge and Kegan Paul, 1975).

[29] J. Berry, "Psychology of Acculturation: Understanding Individuals Moving Between Cultures" in *Applied Cross-Cultural Psychology*, ed. R. Brislin (Newbury Park: Sage, 1990).

[30] G. Horenczyk, "Migrant Identities in Conflict: Acculturation Attitudes and Perceived Acculturation Ideologies" in *Changing European Identities*, ed. G. Breakwell and E. Lyons (Oxford: Butterworth Heinemann, 1996).

[31] G. Konrad, "The Pitfalls of Community," *Index on Censorship* 2 (2000): 149.

[32] See Widgery, 1993.

[33] See Goffman, 1976.

[34] R. Kowalski and R. Wolfe, "Collective Identity Orientation, Patriotism and Reactions to National Outcomes," *Personality and Social Psychology Bulletin* 20, no. 5 (1994): 533-40.

[35] M. Karasawa, "Towards an Assessment of Social Identity: the Structure of Group Identification and its Effects on In-group Evaluation," *British Journal of Social Psychology* 30 (1991): 293-307.

Chapter 4

Migration Policies in Liberal Democratic States: A Paradigm

Miles W. Williams

Migration policies in Western liberal democracies have undergone a dramatic transformation in the past half-century. In the early years following World War II, immigration was not generally perceived to be a high priority policy issue, although guestworker programs were widely adopted and foreign workers recruited. Not only did that practice end somewhat abruptly in the early 1970s, but today immigration is seen by many as a potential security risk to their region.[1] For most Western liberal states, immigration is largely restricted to refugees and family reunification programs. Even so, by the mid-1990s, the number of foreign-born residents in the various states of the world was estimated at about 125 million and the net flow of migrants between two and four million annually.[2] This coupled with a massive and growing gap between the advanced industrial societies and the "Third World" contributes to a political environment favoring increasingly restrictive migration policies.[3]

During the Cold War, NATO and the North Atlantic community encouraged refugees from the East to "vote with their feet" and seek asylum in the West. The transatlantic community now seems equally committed to *restricting* the migrant flow, and there are a number of factors that might explain this. Two frequently cited reasons are that open immigration poses a threat to the viability of the welfare state, and that society's unique identity and distinctive way of life could be compromised. The formulation of *immigration* policy—the process whereby a government determines how many aliens will be granted residency in a given time period, and the criteria for selecting those individuals—is acknowledged as a state's sovereign prerogative. A state's *immigrant* policy includes the reciprocal rights, responsibilities, and benefits for the alien and the residency-granting state.[4] Logically, immigration policy is influenced by policy makers' perception of the consequences of immigration admission levels on immigrant policy, just as the level of generosity of a state's immigrant policy affects the number of residency requests (the pull factor).

This chapter examines migration policy as the product of the intersection of immigration and immigrant policies, represented visually as a two-dimensional Cartesian coordinate system (see Fig. 1). The policy extremes represented on the intersecting continua reflect clear ideological perspectives on the relationship between the state and the individual as well as between the state and the international system. One might not expect to find such extremes in the real world, but as ideal-types, they are valuable tools for clarifying policy alternatives. Taken together, immigration and immigrant policies offer a paradigm of four discrete ideological and/or policy perspectives. The working assumption is that the empirical expressions of the four ideal types provide a useful basis for policy comparisons and for understanding how states react to domestic and international influences on migration policy.

Figure 1: The Limits of Immigration and Immigrant Policies

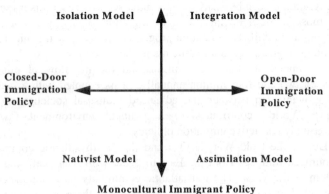

The Theoretical Limits of Immigration and Immigrant Policies

The four quadrants in Figure 1 represent migration policy as any of four ideal types based on the intersection of the x-axis (immigration policy) and the y-axis (immigrant policy). The theoretical range of immigration policy is from *closed borders* in which virtually all immigration is rejected, to *open borders* where state sovereignty is not used to restrict immigration significantly. Garrett Hardin offers the prototypical argument for *closed borders*.[5] Hardin believes that immigration is (or will eventually become) a threat to the state's *carrying capacity* and offers a lifeboat metaphor to explain his case for exclusion. He argues that allowing everyone to board the lifeboat would swamp it, but allowing only a few would mean compromising important values and ideals. Even if there is limited room, the best approach, he contends, is to "[a]dmit no more to the boat and preserve the small safety factor. Survival of the people in the lifeboat is then possible (though we shall have to be on our guard against boarding parties)."[6] In assuming that immigrant and native-born citizens are of "exactly equal quality," he insists that his approach is absolutely not discriminatory. The focus is strictly on quantity, not quality. He does acknowledge that from time to time some "refugees" might be "admitted to the lifeboat," but this does not represent a radical departure from his general position because, as he says, "it is not inconceivable that they might be given proportionately fewer rights than the native population."[7] For example, they might be required to accept population/birth controls.

In contrast, Joseph H. Carens offers perhaps the best-known defense of open borders.[8] "Borders," says Carens, "should generally be open and ... people should normally be free to leave their country of origin and settle in another, subject only to the sorts of constraints that bind current citizens in their new country."[9] He argues that Liberalism permits no other conclusion. "Citizenship in Western liberal democracies is the modern equivalent of feudal privilege—an inherited status that greatly enhances one's life chances. Like feudal birthright privileges, restrictive citizenship is hard to justify...."[10]

For the most part, Carens' 1987 article is an uncompromising moralistic rationale for open borders, yet he does make a distinction between the idealistic and the realistic. In a 1996 article Carens warns that if the gap between the "realistic morality" of "what is and what ought to be" becomes too great, the "ought to be" becomes essentially irrelevant: "[w]hatever we say ought to be done about international migration should not be too far from what we think actually might happen."[11] In a perfect world, borders would be completely open, but as a practical matter that is not going to happen in the foreseeable future and a more realistic approach should be our guiding policy principle. Realistically, the open border criteria might include but not necessarily be limited to the following:

- Membership and full participation[12] in international refugee regimes and regional agreement or accords designed as *burden sharing*[13] arrangements.
- Admissions that are not limited to those qualifying as refugees. For example, the state would admit individuals for family reunification and other humanitarian purposes.
- Immigrant and refugee admission policies that are not discriminatory against individuals on the basis of race, religion, ethnicity, nationality or cultural background.
- Temporary Protected Status (TPS) would used to assist asylum-seekers in need, as part of a group, rather than as a substitute for an open door immigration policy. This criterion is important but admittedly somewhat subjective. TPS can be used to rescue a highly vulnerable *group* in situations where the threat is immediate and the time needed to evaluate the validity of individual claims is not available. Conversely, TPS sometimes becomes the standard procedure for admitting asylum-seekers, and, thus, substituted for an asylum policy.

A closed-door policy would, in all probability, reject most of these criteria.

The y-axis, representing *immigrant* policy, presents a range from total exclusion from the community, a rejection of all citizenship rights—a *monocultural immigrant policy* for those not born into the community to the opposite extreme of a *multicultural immigrant policy*.[14] The *monocultural* extreme corresponds to the position taken by Peter Brimelow, himself an immigrant.[15] In *Alien Nation* Brimelow argues for a return to pre-1965 immigration law and the national origins quotas designed to preserve the Northern and Western European character of the US. Brimelow says "[t]he American nation has always had a specific ethnic core. And that core has been white."[16] Brimelow makes a preemptive strike against those who would label his approach as racist. He says: "Because the term 'racist' is now so debased, I usually shrug such smears off by pointing to its new definition: *anyone who is winning an argument with a liberal.*"[17] Brimelow's approach is classic *nativism.*[18]

George J. Borjas makes the economic argument for limiting immigration: those from Third World countries generally have fewer skills, less education, are generally poorer and therefore more likely to result in a welfare drain than is the general population.[19] In sum, then, in its extreme form, the *monocultural immigrant policy* approaches a *no-citizenship-for-immigrants* policy where welfare benefits are denied and governmental support of minority cultures rejected. The monocultural immigrant policy presumably has the effect of reducing the immigration *pull effect* and, consequently, the level of immigration.

The *multicultural immigrant policy* is based on the principle of equal rights and opportunities for all, the equal worth of all cultures as well as a right of individuals to maintain their ethnic and cultural values and lifestyle. "[M]ulticulturalism," says Dennis J. Downey, "is a strategic component in a broader movement toward social transformation that emphasizes social equality."[20] Will Kymlicka notes that the United Nations' Universal Declaration of Human Rights makes no reference to ethnic and national minorities, although one assumes that ethnic and national minorities are at least entitled to the same human rights protection as ethnic majorities.[21] The shift from group-specific to universal rights avoids the numerous and varied objections of those who might otherwise be counted upon for support. The question posed to those who challenge or oppose multiculturalism is: why not simply treat people as individuals without regard to their ethnicity or national identity? The problem, Kymlicka believes, "is not that traditional human rights doctrines give us the wrong answer.... It is rather that they often give us no answer at all."[22] Simply treating people as individuals, according to Kymlicka, becomes a cover for abuse and injustice. An immigrant policy that fails to affirmatively defend ethnic minorities would, in the view of the multiculturalists, ignore Judith N. Shklar's admonition to never to underestimate the "human propensity for cruelty."[23] It might even be an *illustration* of it.

As a practical matter, a multicultural immigrant policy might include, but not be limited to the following:

- Citizenship based on place of birth (*jus soli*) as well as parentage (*jus sanguinis*).
- Acceptance of dual citizenship
- Constitutional recognition of all ethnic groups as having *equal value* in principle and the enactment of legislative measures to insure that public policy is committed to its realization, including affirmative programs to support cultural preservation and ethnic identity.
- Reasonable and uniformly applied criteria for achieving naturalized citizenship. [24]
- Granting various elements of full citizenship (civic, political, and social) in a timely manner.[25] For example, granting *civic citizenship* immediately, *partial political citizenship* (e.g., the right to participate fully in local elections) at an early stage, and, finally,

granting social benefits equal to those of citizens when the individual's residency status is confirmed.

Figure 2: Migration Policy: A Synthesis of Immigration and Immigrant Policies

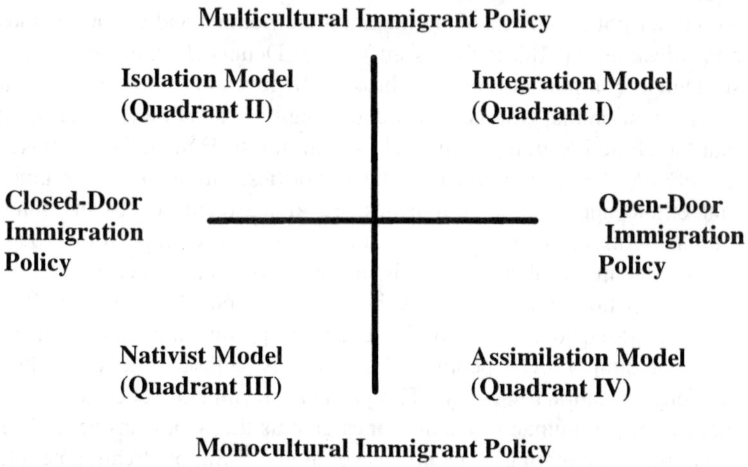

Multicultural Immigrant Policy

Isolation Model	Integration Model
(Quadrant II)	(Quadrant I)

Closed-Door Immigration Policy ———————|——————— Open-Door Immigration Policy

Nativist Model	Assimilation Model
(Quadrant III)	(Quadrant IV)

Monocultural Immigrant Policy

Four migration policy ideal types are: one, the polar extreme of open immigration and multicultural immigrant policies (Quadrant I); two, closed immigration policy and a multicultural immigrant policy (Quadrant II); three, closed immigration policy and monocultural immigrant policy (Quadrant III); and, four, open immigration policy and monocultural immigrant policy (Quadrant IV).

The Integration Model

Quadrant I, a synthesis of open-border immigration policy and a multicultural immigrant policy, is perhaps the ultimate statement of transnational citizenship or post-Westphalian statehood coupled with multiculturalism.[26] Carens asserts that

> ...borders should normally be open and that people should normally
> be free to leave their country of origin and settle in another, subject
> only to the sorts of constraints that bind current citizens in their new
> country. The argument is strongest, I believe, when applied to the
> migration of people from Third World countries.[27]

As a matter of principle, any distinction between *economic* and *political* asylum is blurred. The multicultural state premise is that all peoples and cultures have equal worth and the state's responsibility is to defend that principle. In the Quadrant I migration policy position, the state assumes a responsibility to accommodate immigrants when possible. This will be called the *integration model.* Sweden's migration policy results in an *integration outcome.*

Before World War II immigration to Sweden was rather light. Following the war, an open immigration policy was adopted. In response to a labor shortage, a guestworker program was initiated under the auspices of the Labour Market Board. The policy of consciously encouraging immigration ended in 1967, and since that time, only citizens of Nordic countries are exempt from regulations of movement and employment. Labor immigration ceased five years later, and there has been no significant labor immigration from non-Nordic countries since 1972. Today, approximately 13% of the nation's population is foreign-born or have immigrant parents.

In 1975, Sweden initiated a "permanent residency" policy that embraced a commitment to creating a multicultural society, though Sweden's strong commitment to the integration/assimilation of immigrant predates that. In 1965 a free Swedish language instruction program was initiated; in 1967 a government-subsidized newspapers for immigrants was launched; and, in 1968, special programs for immigrant children were begun. The 1975 permanent residency program was founded on three principles: there should be *equality* between Swedes and immigrants in matters such as standard of living; immigrant should enjoy a *freedom of choice* in their cultural identity; and there should be cooperation and solidarity, a *partnership*, between native Swedes and ethnic minorities. Swedish language instruction was offered to immigrants during their paid working hours; home language instruction is offered immigrant children in the schools;[28] voting rights are granted to foreign nationals in local elections after three years of legal residency in Sweden; and subsidies are given immigrant associations for cultural programs.

In 1985 the government adopted numerous measures affecting refugee policy. For example, both the National Immigration Board— *Statens Invandrarverk* (SIV)[29] and the Labor Market Board were charged with the responsibility for the well being of refugees in Sweden. Their highest priorities were good housing, Swedish language competence, and integration into the local communities. These took precedence even over job placement. To these ends, the SIV negotiates with the 286 municipalities in Sweden to receive and care for refugees; contracts between the SIV and the municipalities cover the refugee for four years. In addition to financial assistance, refugees have the same access to the Swedish health care system as Swedish nationals. However, Sweden's generosity to immigrants in social assistance, housing allowances, and unemployment benefits via transfer payments created something of a backlash as unemployment increased in Sweden, leading the government to initiate a comprehensive policy review.

In June of 1998, the Swedish government created a new central governmental agency, the Integration Office. With the creation of the Integration Office, the role of the Swedish Immigration Board was diminished significantly, at least as a policy priority. In effect, the parliament replaced *immigration* policy with an *integration* policy having the following objectives: monitoring and evaluating integration trends in society; promoting equal rights and opportunities for everyone, regardless of race or ethnicity; and preventing and combating xenophobia, racism, and discrimination.[30] Sweden's immigration policy has tightened significantly in recent years although per capita, Sweden remains among the most generous states in the world towards the admission of refugees. The shift from immigration to integration (from immigration to *immigrant* policy emphasis) is an acknowledgment of a more restrictive admissions policy. Still, rather than making some asymmetrical policy shift based on political expediency, Sweden's migration policy adjustments have been well coordinated and indicative of an ideological commitment to the multicultural state and a realistic integration policy.

If one can generalize about an integration outcome from the Swedish case, it is apparent that maintaining open borders *and* multiculturalism is difficult. The goal is grounded in a humanitarian ideological principle, but practical politics cannot be ignored. As social and economic pressures begin to weigh on policy makers, adjustments are made—either the admission of immigrants decreases, the immigrant policy becomes less generous, or both occur. If a state is to remain as true as possible to its principles, reducing the level of immigration while maintaining a commitment to immigrants seems to be the most reasonable approach. The reverse encourages an exploitation of immigrants.

The Nativist Model

Quadrant III, the *nativist model*,[31] is a synthesis of closed-borders immigration and monocultural immigrant policies and falls at the opposite end of the ideological continuum from Quadrant I, the integration model. Nativism is deeply rooted in the belief that the nation-state has a sovereign right to national self-determination, and those racially, ethnically, linguistically and culturally different from the dominant group pose a threat to society. The threat is believed to come in a variety of forms: overpopulation, a threat to the standard of living enjoyed by the society as a whole, or a threat to our way of life. Regardless of the emphasis, it is "us" versus "them." The nativist model response is two-pronged, involving a common immigration-immigrant approach. Like the integration model, the nativist model's internal consistency is clear. The belief that society's identity is inextricably linked to its ethnic and cultural composition and, like a delicate Eco system, is threatened by change. Immigration would bring this change and borders are closed to avoid that. A closed-borders policy is more easily maintained if the state shuns a generous immigrant policy and the attendant *pull effect*. The symbiosis between immigration and immigrant policies is, therefore, self-conscious. The migration policy of Japan seems to produce this type of nativist outcome.

While Japan falls outside of the transatlantic focus of this chapter, it is helpful to touch on it as Japan would seem to be the quintessential nativist state. Of the nearly 125 million Japanese, 99.4% are classified as ethnic Japanese.[32] In December of 1998, *"The Japan Times* noted that the government had accepted only 1654 applications for asylum since 1982, approving only 225 in that 16-year period. From 1994 to 1997, only one or two persons were granted asylum per year."[33] In 1993 when a Japanese consular official was interviewed by *Forbes* magazine, the anonymous official semi-jokingly said that perhaps three people a year become Japanese.[34] Only about 1% of Japan's population consists of permanent foreign-born residents.

Japanese nationality is based on the citizenship of the parent (*jus sanguinis)* rather than the place of birth (*jus soli).*[35] Beginning in 1955, Japan's Alien Registration Law required compulsory fingerprinting of most resident foreigners 16 years of age and older. Insomuch as the only other group to be fingerprinted was those convicted of crimes, the practice was considered particularly hostile by many.[36] In 1993, a majority of Japanese favored allowing unskilled labor into the country with strict limitations on length of stay, type of work, and the number to be admitted. At the same time, a plurality did not favor increasing the admissions of skilled labor or of allowing foreign workers to have permanent residency.[37]

In the Swedish integration outcome, we saw that a change in social and economic conditions within the country made adjustments in the state's migration policy necessary as a practical matter. Admissions were reduced to preserve the commitment to citizens and immigrants already in the country. The nativist model, and by extension, in states like Japan where a nativist outcome is likely, when social and economic conditions change, there is no need to make significant policy adjustments. Philosophically and ideologically, the state is committed to nativist values and neither an improvement nor a decline in social and economic conditions is likely to change that. Moreover, unlike those cases where a significant ethnic minority does exist and can lobby for a more liberal admissions policy, in Japan there is no powerful immigrant lobby.[38] When things get worse, the expulsion of foreign workers may increase. The *nativist outcome* is, arguably, the most implacable of the four.

The Isolation Model

Quadrant II represents a closed-border immigration policy and a multicultural immigrant policy—an apparent contradiction because it is both pro-immigrant (multiculturalism) and anti-immigrant (closed borders)—the product of pragmatism, not ideology. Rather than a conscious commitment to a policy limiting immigration while promoting multiculturalism, it is more likely that the policy model in Quadrant II is the result of a policy change—either from integration or nativism. While either is possible, a policy originally based on open borders and multiculturalism seems more likely. If a state's policy approximates the integration model and domestic factors force adjustments (e.g., increasing unemployment, population pressures, etc.), maintaining a commitment to the existing population while limiting the admission of others is not unreasonable. Still, even though a state insists on the equal worth of all individuals and groups, by adopting policies that insure permanent minority status for some, the result will likely be minority group isolation. This, then, is the *isolation model*.

The isolationist outcome is the result of a perceived need to limit the admission of immigrants while nevertheless exhibiting support for those who have been accepted. Labeling this outcome as *isolationist* is meant to imply that by limiting admissions of new immigrants, the comparative size of the ethnic groups would likely remain extremely small and their political muscle and cultural impact on the larger society limited at best. The isolationist outcome is not necessarily an *intended* consequence of the resulting migration policy although it could, nonetheless have that effect.

Migration policy in the Netherlands is a case in point. The Netherlands has the highest population density of all countries in the European Union, and yet it also attracts more asylum-seekers, per capita, than any other EU member state. Moreover, the Netherlands' willingness to actually accept refugees has likewise been particularly generous. In 1977 a quota of 550 refugees were invited to take asylum in the Netherlands (a policy that assumed that no more than 250 additional asylum-seekers would be given legal status), but the reality was quite different. The unexpected arrival of Vietnamese "boat people" overwhelmed the system and it became necessary to reduce the quota to 250 per year in 1984.[39] The refugee policy crisis came to a head in 1987 with the arrival of Tamils. The state was forced to wrestle with applications that were disproportionately large compared with neighboring European states, and a reception system that had inadequate housing and other social services. In 1992 a new administrative and reception policy was put in place, and in 1994-1995, special asylum application centers were established on the borders with Belgium and Germany and at Schipol airport in Amsterdam. Further, a TPS policy was initiated to address developments in the former Yugoslavia. Reception policy vacillated throughout the years although it seems that the public was more concerned with the number of admissions than with the reception policy towards those actually admitted. In recent years Dutch admissions amount to one for every 440 citizens compared to one for every 780 in Germany, and, one for every 30,000 in Italy.[40]

In 1998 the influx of asylum-seekers became so great and the administration of the system so overwhelmed that it was necessary to temporarily house hundreds of applicants in tents. A popular outcry ensued and better tents with better heating were found. A policy of generous admissions with generous benefits could not be sustained. Janssen observes that the need to stem the flow of asylum-seekers runs counter to the Dutch liberal tradition regarding refugees, one that dates back to the Dutch golden age in the seventeenth century.

> However, the Dutch are hesitantly acknowledging that something must be done to alleviate the strains on the country's housing, education, health care, social security system, labor market, judiciary system, budget, and public safety.... The government also hopes for greater European cooperation [i.e., burden sharing]. That will almost certainly be futile, as no other country appears ready to volunteer to share the Dutch difficulties.[41]

The dilemma of admissions versus integration is real for the Dutch and goes to the heart of the matter of an isolationist outcome.

The Assimilation Model

Quadrant IV is labeled the *assimilation model*. Like the Segregation model, it is a combination of seemingly contradictory immigration and immigrant policies. Here, the state follows an open-borders policy but also a monocultural immigrant policy. This, too, is likely a pragmatic policy model although it may not be the result of a deviation from either the integration or the nativist model. It is not illogical that a state's policy would be open to immigrants to enter but not to become full participants in society. For example, such a situation could be a calculated policy designed to fill labor shortages while expressly rejecting any policy perceived to affect the culture or national way of life.

In a philosophical sense this migration policy appears to be a consequence of philosophical contradictions. The policy seems to be saying: "come one, come all... but once you get here, we expect you to become like us culturally and attitudinally as soon as possible." While there may be some philosophical basis for the assimilation model, it is not necessary well worked out and is likely, therefore, to undergo considerable change when social, economic, and political conditions change. The US is indeed a nation of immigrants, but attitudes towards immigrants are frequently ambivalent. Rita Simon describes it very well:

> The physical image that seems to best describe the American Public's attitude toward immigrants is that *we view them with rose-colored glasses turned backwards*. In other words, those immigrants who came earlier, whenever "earlier" happens to be, are viewed as having made important and positive contradictions to our society, economy and culture. But ... those who seek entry now, whenever "now" happens to be, are viewed at best with ambivalence, and more likely with distrust and hostility. [42]

Still, all other countries in the world pale by comparison to the number of immigrants admitted by the US. While most countries' immigration policy is really a refugee policy—with some exceptions most liberal democracies long ago stopped an orderly admission of voluntary migrants—the US continues to admit several hundred thousand annually. Their immigrant policy, on the other hand, tends to be "monocultural," i.e., one that would assimilate immigrant groups into the dominant culture rather than adopt policies that recognizes group-specific rights. In the early days of the 20th century, the notion of assimilation in the US was actually a liberal response to the exclusionary rhetoric of nativists who insisted that immigrants from areas other than Northern and Western Europe could not adapt to the American lifestyle.[43] It is sometimes argued that multiculturalism actually leads to separatism and cultural nationalism, not unity and equality.[44] This melting pot notion of a common culture into which persons of diverse cultural backgrounds ultimately blend has attracted both nativists and integrationists who see it as a pragmatic compromise. Thus, in the name of assimilation, one finds a wide range of motives from those who demand that English become the official language, an end to bilingual education programs and perhaps policies that would discourage future immigration, to those whose primary emphasis is on the achievement of equality through an aggressive civil rights movement.

The paradigm presented here assumes that immigration and immigrant policies are best understood as two dimensions of the same policy issue. If the assumption is correct, any effort to understand a state's immigration or immigrant policy decisions outside the context of more general migration policy considerations is likely to ignore variables essential to understanding the policy makers' rationale. The four "ideal types" represent migration policy show a strong philosophical or ideological dimension as well as a pragmatic policy one (see Figure 3).

Figure 3: Migration Policy: Ideological and Pragmatic Dimensions

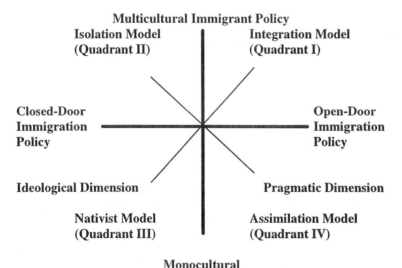

Four states are suggested as possibly representative of the four ideal types. Clearly they are not as extreme as their ideal-type counterparts, merely real-world approximations. They are labeled *outcomes* not *models* to mark the distinction. While suggestive, the selection of case studies was not scientific, as precise measures are still to be determined.

Table 1
Factors Influencing Immigration and Immigrant Policy Outcomes[45]

	Sweden	Netherlands	US	Japan
IMMIGRATION				
Burden-Sharing	Yes	No	Yes	No
Liberal Admissions	Yes	No	Yes	No
Equal Protection	Yes	No	Yes	No
TPS to Help	Yes	No	Yes	No
IMMIGRANT				
Dual Citizenship	Yes	No	Yes	No
Ethnic Equality	Yes	Yes	No	No
Welfare Equity	Yes	Yes	No	No

Several possible conclusions-cum-hypotheses[46] emerge from the examination, including the following: First, *policy outcomes that fall on the ideological dimension (integration and nativism) are less susceptible to public opinion pressures than those that fall on the pragmatic dimension (assimilation and isolation).* Policies on the ideological dimension are more internally consistent and likely to reflect core values within the society. The integration model is particularly generous to "outsiders." Such a policy approach requires some redistribution of the wealth—not because it is seen as a strategy to maintain social order, but because a conscious decision is made that such a policy is consistent with society's definition of what is morally or ethically defensible. At the other end of the ideological dimension, the nativist model, policy decisions are likewise consistent. In this case, however, maintaining the social order probably is the primary consideration. Preservation of the *existing* social order is itself a core value. Such a state may, as Japan has, support the humanitarian objectives of an international regime, but will do so with material assistance to others, not through policies that might change the character of the state. In neither case will the mood of the public, responding to the events of the day, have much of an impact on migration policy. One might expect that policy changes within those states on the ideological dimension will be comparatively minor and not likely to change the basic character of the state's migration policy.

Policies along the pragmatic policy dimension are internally less consistent and not so likely to reflect deeply held beliefs. As a consequence, social and economic changes within the state (unemployment rates, crime rates, etc.) might well influence public opinion and affect the pragmatic-based policy significantly.

Secondly, *to the extent that immigrant policies and immigration policies are correlated, immigrant policy is more likely to be the independent variable.* It is reasonable to assume that the impact of immigration policy is felt less by most residents (citizens and resident aliens) than immigrant policy. Thus, in liberal democracies where public opinion has some impact on policy decisions, immigrant policy is more likely to drive immigration policy than the reverse. The cases of Sweden (integration), the Netherlands (isolation), and the US (assimilation) seem to confirm this. Japan does not have a true immigration policy, although the policy towards foreign labor (temporary residents rather than immigrants) may affect the number of workers admitted rather than the reverse.

Thirdly, *with the exception of states following a nativist model, differences in the level of support for international regimes does not seem to be strongly associated with states' approach to domestic migration policy.* Japan, whose policy outcome was classified as nativist, is a major financial contributor to the United Nations High Commissioner, but grants asylum to virtually no one. Those states fitting the other profiles seem respond to the UNHCR for a broad range of reasons (e.g., membership in the European Union, adherence to the Schengen Accords, domestic opposition to participation in international agreements, etc.). In short, a state's position on international organizations as the appropriate means of addressing international migration seems to be only marginally related to its policies on the reception of immigrants and asylum-seekers.

Liza Schuster says that for states to continue granting asylum, they must believe that benefits outweigh the costs.[47] The calculus of asylum-granting has changed in the post-Cold War era and with it, the extent to which states are willing to receive refugees. Schuster cites economics and the legitimizing force of a liberal democracy demonstrating tolerance, justice and liberty,[48] and without question these factors are highly significant in states' migration policy. Within the transatlantic region, it is also clear that not all states give the same weight to all factors. From the inter-war period to the present, Western Europe and North America have collaborated in a number of venues to address immigration and asylum issues, and have generally been generous in offering asylum to those in need. Even so, widely divergent approaches and outcomes among these liberal democracies[49] are evident and the intent in this chapter has been to construct a useful paradigm for analyzing migration policies and accounting for those differences.

---

[1] Grete Brochmann, *European Integration and Immigration from Third Countries* (Oslo: Scandinavian University Press, 1996).

[2] Philip Martin and Jonas Widgren, "International Migration: A Global Challenge," *Population Bulletin* 51, no. 1 (1996).

[3] The emergence of anti-immigration political parties (e.g., the National Front in France, the Republicans in Germany, the Central Democrats in the Netherlands, the Freedom Party in Austria, the People's Party in Denmark, and the New Democracy party in Sweden) is an indication of the level of public concern. On February 3, 2000, The Austrian Freedom Party joined the government coalition with the strenuous objections of the EU. The Freedom Party had captured 27% of the vote in parliamentary elections, but following the announcement of threatened sanctions by the EU, public opinion polls indicated that 33% of the population would then support the party (*International Herald Tribune*, February 2, 2000).

[4] "Immigrant policy," according to Tomas Hammar, "is the other part of immigration policy and refers to the conditions provided to resident immigrants. It comprises all the issues that influence the condition of immigrants; for example, work and housing conditions, social benefits and social services, educational opportunities and language instruction, cultural amenities, leisure activities, voluntary associations, and opportunities to par6ticipate in trade union and political affairs." See Hammar, *European Immigration Policy: A Comparative Study* (Cambridge: Cambridge University Press, 1985), 9.

[5] Garrett Hardin, "Living on a Lifeboat," in *Managing the Commons* (San Francisco: W. H. Freeman and Company, 1977), 261-79.

[6] Ibid., 263.

[7] Ibid., 277.

[8] Peter C. Meilaender, "Liberalism and Open Borders: The Argument of Joseph Carens," *International Migration Review* 33, no. 128 (1999): 1062-81.

[9] Joseph H. Carens, "Aliens and Citizens: The Case for Open Borders," *The Review of Politics* 49 (1987): 251.

[10] Ibid., 252.

[11] Joseph H. Carens, "Realistic and Idealistic Approaches to the Ethics of Migration," *International Migration Review* 30 (1996): 156-71.

[12] By full participation, I mean that the state accepts and applies, at least at the minimal level, the criteria and practice, admission of asylum seekers at those quotas expected of it by the international and regional organizations.

[13] By "burden sharing," I mean a state's assumption of a "fair share" of the responsibility for accepting legitimate asylum-seekers and refugees. The

concept generally assumes that states recognize that by taking a reasonable number of individuals, protection can be assured and no state will be forced to assume a greater responsibility than they are capable of shouldering.

[14] The *political* expression of multiculturalism might be described as one based on *full citizenship*. See T. H. Marshall, *Class, Citizenship, and Social Development* (New York: Doubleday, 1964), 73 for a discussion of "full citizenship."

[15] Brimelow's argument is actually focused more on a closed immigration policy than an immigrant policy although he makes it quite clear that this is because of his belief that the ethnic composition of the US was and should be essentially Northern and Western European. See Brimelow, *Alien Nation: Common Sense About America's Immigration Disaster* (New York: Random House, 1995).

[16] Ibid., 9.

[17] Ibid., 10-11, emphasis in the original. Brimelow's 1995 book is an expanded version of his 1992 article in *National Review* which includes such observations as "...it should not be necessary to explain that the legacy of Shaka and Cetewayo—overthrown just over a century ago—is not that of Alfred the Great, let alone Elizabeth II or any civilized society," or "...asking people if they want their communities to be overwhelmed by weird aliens with dubious habits is a stupid question" and "...Hispanics, for example, increased from 4.5% of the U.S. population in 1970 to 9% in 1990 because they somehow started sprouting out of the earth like spring corn." See Julian L. Simon, "Public Expenditures on Immigrants to the United States, Past and Present," *Population and Development Review* 22 (1996): 99-109.

[18] The term *nativism* gained great currency with John Higham's work *Strangers in Our Land*. His definition of nativism is "intense opposition to an internal minority on the ground of its foreign (i.e., 'un-American') connections" (Higham, 1970: 4).

[19] George J. Borjas, *Friends or Strangers: The Impact of Immigrants on the U.S. Economy* (New York: Basic Books, 1990). Julian Simon sharply disputes the welfare cost of immigrants. His research indicates that, on balance, immigrants make greater monetary contributions to the welfare system than they take out. See Simon, 1996.

[20] Downey, "From Americanization to Multiculturalism: Political Symbols and Struggles for Cultural Diversity in Twentieth-Century American Race Relations," *Sociological Perspectives* 42 (1999). See also H. A. Giroux, *Living Dangerously* (New York: Peter Lang, 1993).

[21] Will Kymlicka, *Multicultural Citizenship* (New York: Oxford University Press, 1995).

[22] Ibid., 5.

[23] Bernard Yack, ed., *Liberalism Without Illusions: Essays on Liberal Theory and the Political Vision of Judith N. Shklar* (Chicago: University of Chicago Press, 1996).

[24] Again, standards here are somewhat subjective. However, if most countries allow for naturalized citizenship after from two to five years of residency, a

requirement that one be a resident for 15 to 20 years might be considered unreasonable. Further standards should not vary on the basis of an individual's personal characteristics and situation, except for good reason—i.e., a demonstrable threat to the state (terrorist, serious felony convictions, etc.).

[25] See T. H. Marshall, *Class, Citizenship, and Social Development* (New York: Doubleday, 1964) for a discussion of these aspects of citizenship.

[26] Australia, Canada and Sweden have committed themselves to such a society. Australia's multicultural policy, for example, is based on three dimensions of cultural identity, social justice, and economic efficiency (Australian Ministry of Immigration and Multicultural Affairs, 1998).

[27] Carens, 1987, 251-52.

[28] By the mid-1990s, some 70,000 students were receiving this instruction in 126 languages.

[29] The SIV was established in 1969 to administer immigration and naturalization programs.

[30] Lars Jederlund, "From Immigration Policy to Integration Policy," *Current Sweden* 422 (1998).

[31] The term "nativist" or "nativism" is emotionally charged, but it does describe the basic thinking of those for whom it fits—a preference for those considered to be "native" or at the core of society's identity. For a discussion of the concept, see Linda S. Bosniak, "'Nativism' The Concept: Some Reflections," in *Immigrants Out! The New Nativism and the Anti-Immigrant Impulse in the United States* (New York: New York University Press, 1997).

[32] Ronald E. Dolan and Robert L. Worden, editors. "Japan: A Country Study," Federal Research Division, Library of Congress, January 2000, http://lcweb2.loc.gov/frd/cs/jptoc.html.

[33] U.S. Committee for Refugees, "Country Reports: Japan," February 20, 2000, http://www.refugees.org.

[34] Peter Brimelow, "Closed Door," *Forbes* (August 30, 1993): 58-59.

[35] Citizenship criteria were first developed in Japan in the nationality law of 1899. It was based on the principle of *jus sanguinis*, strict rules for nationalization, and strict rules on naturalized citizens. State permission was required for all naturalizations. See Chikako Kashiwazaki, "Jus Sanguinis in Japan: The Origin of Citizenship in a Comparative Perspective," *International Journal of Comparative Sociology* 39 (1998): 278-301. For an examination of indigenous culture and tradition as a basis for nationality in the late 19th century, see Kosaku Yoshino, *Cultural Nationalism in Contemporary Japan* (London: Routledge, 1992).

[36] In August of 1999, the Japanese Diet passed additional laws revising some of the country's immigration and registration laws. Fingerprinting was replaced with requiring a signature of foreign residents. *Xinhua News Agency* (13 August 1999).

[37] Simon and Lynch.

[38] Sassen, "Beyond Sovereignty: Immigration Policy in the Making Today," *Social Justice*, 23 (1996): 9-21.

[39] Philip Muus, "Shifting Borders: The Inclusion and Exclusion of Refugees and Asylum Seekers in the Netherlands," in *Exclusion and Inclusion of Refugees in Contemporary Europe* (Utrecht: European Centre on Migration and Ethnic Relations, 1997): 80.

[40] Joel Janssen, "The Refugee Dilemma: Increasing Number of Refugees in the Netherlands," *Europe* (February, 1999): 43-45

[41] Ibid. The danger, of course, is that such a response will trigger a *spiral of exclusion.*

[42] Rita J Simon, "Immigration and Public Opinion," in *In Defense of the Alien—XVIII* (New York: Center for Migration Studies, 1996).Emphasis mine.

[43] Dennis J. Downey, "From Americanization to Multiculturalism: Political Symbols and Struggles for Cultural Diversity in Twentieth Century American Race Relations," *Sociological Perspectives* 42 *(*1999).

[44] Ibid. Also see R. Bernstein *Dictatorship of Virtue* (New York: Alfred A. Knopf, 1994). Arthur Schlesinger, Jr. believes that assimilation is the best hope of achieving a nation of "one people," which, he assumes, is a good thing. See Schlesinger, *The Disuniting of America* (New York: Norton, 1992).

[45] See text for discussion of the criteria.

[46] The conclusions offered here were arrived at inductively rather than deductively— based on a limited and non-randomly selected sample. Thus, the end product is a hypothesis rather than a hypothesis that has been empirically tested.

[47] Liza Schuster, "Why Do States Grant Asylum?" *Politics* 18, no. 1 (1998): 11-16.

[48] Ibid.

[49]As great as the differences are within the transatlantic community, they pale by comparison with those elsewhere, i.e., Japan.

Chapter 5

"National Culture of Mobility": The Colonsay-Canada Connection

John W. Sheets

An eminent historian of the Transatlantic, Bernard Bailyn at Harvard University, estimates that perhaps fifty million people moved from Europe to the New World during the four centuries after 1492.[1] First from Spain and Portugal, then from the British Isles, the Low Countries, and Scandinavia, emigrants transplanted their languages and cultures to new places where they were transformed, then transmitted, in new contexts. Our understanding of this diaspora falls somewhere between a macrocosm of numerical theory and the microcosms of family history. But the stories all started with a very personal and local decision to "leave home," whether alone or in a group, and Gaelic Scotland, more than many regions, suffered the effects of this accelerating mobility.

For the first *Statistical Account* of Scotland (1791-96), Rev. Francis Stewart of the Parish of Jura and Colonsay in Argyll counted "718 Souls" in 134 families living on the 15 farms of Colonsay and Oronsay islands. He complained that

> in the summer of 1791, a considerable proportion of the inhabitants crossed the Atlantic. Those who remain give out that they are

waiting only good accounts from their relations, and a proper
opportunity.... Pity it is that such numbers should bid farewell to
their native country when there is so great a demand for useful
citizens....

Also in the summer of 1791, King George III approved the Canada Act
which partitioned Quebec into "Lower and Upper" territories, thus
setting the stage for future emigrants from the Highlands and islands to
settle in Ontario.[2] Over the next century people left Colonsay and
Oronsay at different times and for different reasons—opportunity,
recession, famine, religion, work in Glasgow, or land in Canada. Their
transatlantic stories glance at a Gaelic emigration through episodes of
hope, fear, success, failure, return and, in this case, through the eyes of
eminent people "left behind," like Edinburgh University's first Celtic
professor, Donald Mackinnon (1839-1914) from Colonsay.

In 1805 David Wilson surveyed the islands of Colonsay and
Oronsay. Their 20+ square miles contained over 8,650 "Scotch Acres,"
although just 1,740 (or 20%) of these were "Arable and Meadow."[3]
John McNeill (1767-1846) purchased the islands from his cousin
Archibald in 1805 and quickly used his professional education in
agriculture to improve his new estate. He drained meadows, rotated
crops, applied fertilizers, bred black cattle and built roads, bridges,
walls, quays and a parish school. By 1811 the 786 islanders held a
winter stock of 1000 cattle and exported tons of kelp, barley, oats and
potatoes to the Napoleonic War markets of Great Britain. The
affectionately named "Old Laird" created the crofting district of small
farms in "Upper and Lower Kielhattan" on Colonsay's west coast,
which, to one visitor, demonstrated "the fairest specimens of the
industry of these men." Unlike those on the Duke of Argyll's estates on
the Ross of Mull, McNeill's tenants could (and did) subdivide and
sublease their four to six rented acres to relatives and friends.[4] But
despite the laird's improvements and leniency, some individuals and
families still chose to leave Colonsay and Oronsay.

In 1805 Thomas Douglas, fifth Earl of Selkirk, extolled the virtues
of emigration in his *Observations on the Present State of the
Highlands*. The next year no fewer than five emigrant ships sailed for
Prince Edward Island from the "Western Highlands and Isles" and
Caithness. With its 114 passengers, the *Spencer* of Newcastle sailed
from Oban on September 22, 1806. The youngest passenger was three
months old; the oldest was 78. With favorable winds, the journey might
take four or five weeks; under bad weather, it could last much longer.
On board were men, women, and children with Colonsay surnames
such as Bell, Campbell, Currie, Darroch, McEachern, McMillan,

McNeill and Munn. They included young parents with their babies, baptized just seven months earlier in Colonsay's new Church of Scotland building at Scalasaig, within sight of the quay from where they would depart for Oban and the emigrant ship. In August 1808 the *Clarendon* of Hull also sailed from Oban, for Charlottetown. It carried enough biscuits, oatmeal, barley, meat, water and "melasses" for its crew and 188 passengers, all emigrating for "Want of Labour." Half of them came from the Duke of Argyll's estate. Prince Edward Island remained a preference for Colonsay migrants during the first decades of the 19th century. Their presence meant others would follow and go well beyond.[5] Meanwhile, the "Old Laird" needed workers and tenants for his estate, so Colonsay received immigrants from the adjacent islands of Islay, Jura and Mull to replace the departed emigrants. A growing population, crowded crofts, and Baptist evangelism in Mull prompted some families to seek work and worship elsewhere, but not too far away.

By 1830 the population of Upper Canada had doubled to over 200,000. Lieutenant-Governor Sir John Colborne encouraged more and more settlers from Great Britain to stem the tide of Americans into Ontario. He offered them 50 to 100 acre lots, often with no payments for three years, and by 1835 the population increased by another 100,000. In 1831, and possibly with several families from Kilmeny parish in Islay, the adult, unmarried children of Angus and Janet McKinnon from Mull left Kilchattan and Colonsay forever. Charles and Sarah Munn with two young children accompanied Donald, Lachlan, John and Catherine McKinnon to northeast Erin Township in Wellington County of Upper Canada, approximately thirty-five miles north of the port of "Little York," later the Toronto area. The township was surveyed in 1819, received its first settlers in 1820 and became a haven for Gaelic-speaking people from the Highlands and islands of Scotland; the court employed a "Court Interpreter" fluent in Gaelic and English. The census of 1830 recorded "75 householders" scattered on 1,154 acres of cultivated and 12,256 acres of uncultivated land.[6] The McKinnons soon established themselves in the frontier community. Catherine served in the house of James Leslie, later publisher of the Toronto *Examiner*, until she met William Trout from Erin. His father, Henry Trout, descended from London merchants, had settled there in the spring of 1822 and was appointed the first Town Clerk in 1824. The Trout family welcomed the "young Scotch girl that could not speak good fluent English" when she became William's second wife in 1833. They lived and farmed on 120 acres in "Erin and Garafraxa" townships. The land assessment of April 5, 1833 also listed Charles Munn and

"Laughlin" McKinnon, each with 100 uncultivated acres near the Trouts' farm. The next year Lachlan cultivated ten of his acres and purchased two oxen and two milk cows. On December 2, 1834 he married Sarah McKinnon from nearby Esquesing Township in Halton County; her grandparents had migrated from the Ross of Mull in 1805 to New York State. In 1838-39 Donald McKinnon received 100 acres near his brother-in-law, Charles Munn, and his brother Lachlan, who now had 30 cultivated acres, one horse, two oxen, three young cattle and four milk cows to support his growing family. The McKinnons belonged to "Other Denominations" because Lachlan had been "immersed" by the itinerant Baptist missionary, Dugald Sinclair. An early, undated history of Ontario described Lachlan McKinnon as "one of the pioneers who had a share in transforming the wilds of that region into well-tilled farm lands." His last farmhouse still stands a few miles north of Ospringe in Erin Township.[7]

The McKinnons of Erin corresponded with their relatives in Colonsay and Mull where the traditional ways of life faltered. Peace after Napoleon meant open trade and competition from the Continent for Hebridean commodities. Prices for cattle, oats and potatoes plunged; then a cheap substitute for processed kelp, used in making glass, destroyed the seaweed's value. By the mid-1830s the Highlands and islands faced shrinking markets and growing populations. For the first British household census in 1841, Colonsay and Oronsay enumerated 979 residents, or nearly 50 people per square mile. The largest district was Kilchattan with 255 people in 43 households, or nearly six people per household.[8] The year 1846 started ominously when the widowed "Old Laird" died on February 24. The potato famine struck the west of Scotland months later and its lethal effects lingered for over a decade. With it came a new wave of departures from the Highlands and islands to the towns, cities, and points abroad.

In 1846 Angus McKinnon, his wife and four children left Ardtun in Mull for Ontario, and upon arrival 14-year-old Janet contracted smallpox. Her "Uncle John" came from Erin "with a team of horses and wagon and took them home, a journey of 18 miles over rough road and it was too much for her weakened system and she died." Such dire consequences would not deter others from leaving Colonsay, though. From 1841-51 Colonsay lost over 15% of its population size, from 979 to 827 residents. Kilchattan went from 255 to 226 people, by emigration *and* by death. Duncan McNeill (1793-1874), John McNeill's second son, Member of Parliament and the future Lord Colonsay, owned the island but neither his legal nor his political stature could stop its depopulation. Moreover, the increasing number of Baptists in

Colonsay had always aggravated the McNeill lairds, staunch supporters of the Church of Scotland. The "Old Laird" had even refused work for some of the Baptist men. By the 1850s the Baptist movement in Colonsay coincided with the surveying and settling of Ontario lands near Lake Huron, the "Canada West" of Bruce and Grey counties. Lachlan McKinnon in Erin owned lots in Bruce County's Elderslie Township around the Saugeen River, a future and favorite destination for Colonsay emigrants.[9]

Given the pressure of more and more emigrants arriving from famished Ireland and Scotland, the provincial government of Ontario initiated the survey of Bruce County in 1849. It used a 1000-acre sectional system of "100 Acre lots more suitable to immigrant farmers" served by "colonization roads" like the Durham Road from Garafraxa to Kincardine, and the Elora and Saugeen Road to Southampton and Port Elgin. The enumerator of Bruce County's first census in 1851, Hugh Johnston, recorded that "until 1849 it was a wilderness. On Christmas Day of that year Mr. William Johnston (styled King of Brant) left Mr. Buck's tavern in Bentinck on a raft to settle here. I believe there was one man before him...." But the area already had human inhabitants; it was the home of the Saugeen and Newash bands of the Ojibwa Indians. About them, Johnston could "speak from experience having had twelve year intercourse with them," and his opinions resembled American attitudes about the natives on their westward frontier:

> They are better supplied with oxen, cows, ploughs, and all other farming utensils than any other tribe north of London [Ontario] to very little purpose as they are decidedly the laziest set of beings in existence.... They eke out a living by what they call farming, hunting, and fishing and depend too much upon their annual income from the Government.

In 1851, 149 Indians lived on the "Arran and Indian Reserve" with a Head Chief, Methodist minister, schoolmaster, agent and interpreter; nearby Brant Township already had 621 people. Elderslie, on the other hand, listed 14 settlers of three "English Episcopalian" families and one "Scottish Presbyterian" servant. They lived in log houses, had no stock or crops, and anxiously waited for the completion of a saw mill and open roads.[10]

On July 30, 1852, the Crown Lands Department in Quebec announced:

Lands in the Counties of Bruce, Grey, and Huron are now open for
sale.... Ten Shillings per acre, payable in Ten equal Annual
Installments ... occupation to be immediate and continuous ...
cleared at the rate of five acres annually for every hundred acres ...
not more than two hundred acres to be sold to any one person on
these terms.

True to Hugh Johnston's prediction for Elderslie that "settlers have just
commenced flocking in and will increase rapidly," they rushed onto the
land without roads, bridges, schools, doctors or preachers. Two of the
early settlers to cross the Saugeen River were Malcolm McLugash from
Kilchattan and his wife, Euphemia Currie, with their children. In 1852
the brothers Angus, Archibald, and Donald Galbraith arrived from
Colonsay and, like others, rafted down the river to their claims. In
Colonsay, their relative Archibald Galbraith lost his first wife in 1850;
he and three children migrated to Prince Edward Island where he
remarried to a Colonsay descendant, and all came to Elderslie. A leader
of the Colonsay Baptists, the widower Lachlan McNeill in Kilchattan,
sent his son John to Ontario in the early 1850s. John's letters so
encouraged everyone that nine more family members came to Bruce
County in 1852. They settled near the Colonsay enclave, then lost their
patriarch, Lachlan, who died on September 14, 1854. He became one of
the first persons buried in Rusk's cemetery, where his gravestone reads
"Age 69 Native of Colonsay."[11]

In 1854 the government made two decisions which accelerated the
settlement of Elderslie: it negotiated a land treaty with the Saugeen and
Newash and held a land consignment in Southampton to register deeds
for the lots in Bruce County. Donald Blue, a Baptist from
Balerominmore in Colonsay, acquired two 100-acre lots and then sold
one to an Irishman from Cork. Blue became sick and died, but not
before he bequeathed the other lot to his five brothers and sisters in
Colonsay. They immediately emigrated, divided their land into 20-acre
farms, and built identical houses with "scooped out" roof beams, thus
creating what everyone knows today as "Scooptown." News of such
opportunities reached Colonsay people living elsewhere. All of these
Gaelic speakers would travel, settle and cooperate with one another
during their early years of arrival, adjustment, and hardship. Amid
Anglican, Baptist, Catholic, Methodist, and Presbyterian settlers from
England, Ireland, Scotland, Germany, and America, their children
tended to meet and marry one another. For example, Isabella, daughter
of Lachlan McNeill, married Angus, son of Alexander and Flora Munn;
Flora, daughter of Malcolm and Euphemia McLugash, married
Archibald Bell, son of John Bell.[12]

On December 21, 1860, Malcolm McKinnon in Kilchattan, Colonsay, wrote to his uncle Lachlan McKinnon in Erin, Ontario. As the leader of the Baptists of Colonsay after the death of Malcolm Blue in 1858, Malcolm used evangelical language to depict their life on a depopulated, depressed island. About his mother, Mary Currie, he wrote: "[S]he will be found among those who get their sins washed and made them white in the blood of the Lamb.... I know that she was not rightly nourished this long while past...." Like so many still in Colonsay, Malcolm McKinnon wondered if they all should not emigrate to live near their family and fellow Baptists in Ontario: "I am always working by price work and fishing and doing far better than being engaged. I don't think that I shall go to America as long as my mother lives now altho I don't see any way of making a living here...." Neither Malcolm, his wife, mother nor father-in-law ever left Colonsay, but others in their family did. To the embattled Baptist leader who remained behind, there was still in the islands "a great deal of good done by the Lord pouring down of his Spirit among the people and a great [many] of the people turned from darkness to light and from the power of Sin and Satan unto the Lord."[13]

But the laird of Colonsay, Duncan McNeill, made sure the Baptists did not monopolize the Lord's work in his domain. With his insistence and support, on February 27, 1861 the Church of Scotland "disjoined" Colonsay as an ecclesiastical unit from the Parish of Jura and built a new manse for its first minister; on September 26, the Rev. James MacKenzie, from St. Kilda, arrived in Colonsay. According to the 1861 census, he entered a shrinking community of 598 people; Kilchattan had 202 residents with no improvements in sight. Malcolm McKinnon's sister, Janet, her husband Finlay McEachern, their four young children, Mary Currie's youngest sister, Lucy, her husband and children, and others departed Colonsay for Ontario. They reached Elderslie to witness the harsh reality, as well as the indomitable spirit and life cycles of their established kin.

In 1865-66 the McEachern-McKinnon household shifted from Dunblane to the western half of Elderslie's Lot 4, shared with Colonsay's Archibald McNeill and family, near the Williscroft post office and school. Their Gaelic-speaking family and friends were close by. Janet corresponded with her younger brother Donald, who had entered Edinburgh University in 1863 as a 24-year-old "Arts Student." Her letters from Elderslie had an obvious impact upon his studies. He read an essay "Life in Canada" to the Edinburgh University Celtic Society on January 21, 1865 and critiqued another member's essay about "Highland Emigration" on February 18. Perhaps Janet mentioned one of the more towering Colonsay characters in Bruce County, the Baptist preacher Donald McNeill, son of the late Lachlan McNeill and named "Minister *Mor*" for his six and one-half foot height. He began his ministry in the village of Paisley, then took it to the Williscroft people in 1868. Everyone went to the millyard or a schoolhouse to wait for him coming on horseback. He gave his sermons in Gaelic, repeated in English, and, according to local legend, "Woe betide the child who dared to suggest it was too much to sit through two sermons." The Williscroft Baptists erected their first church building in 1875. Likewise, the Colonsay Baptists, under Barbara Munn's brother, James Campbell, erected their first chapel beside the Kilchattan schoolhouse in 1879; Campbell's picture still hangs in its back room.[14]

After his family's annual holiday to Colonsay in the summer of 1887, Professor Donald Mackinnon lamented in the Edinburgh paper, *The Scotsman*, that on his island, "A marriage is a rarer event than a Parliamentary election." Indeed, the populations of Elderslie and Colonsay headed in opposite directions. In 1881 Elderslie peaked with 3,273 people while Colonsay had only 381 residents in 1891. Friends and relatives stayed in touch across the Atlantic, sometimes by the rare trip abroad. In December 1904 "Lachie" McNeill, from Fort William, Ontario, sailed from New York to Great Britain; upon his return the Paisley *Advocate* summarized his Grand Tour. He had visited London, Glasgow and Edinburgh, where "he was the guest of Professor McKinnon, one of the most noted scholars of the British Isles." However, Lachie believed "for living there he would prefer not to. The conditions this side of the Atlantic are better than there, especially among the working class. At present a great many are out of employment...." He chose to spend most of his time in Colonsay, "birthplace of his parents," where "the old Gaelic language is still spoken more than English."[15]

Closer to World War I, when Victorian and Edwardian times yielded to modern conflicts, the end-of-life faced some Colonsay Gaels on both sides of the Atlantic. To a *ceilidh* (or celebration) at Edinburgh's Gaelic parish of St Oran's on January 9, 1908, 69-year-old Donald Mackinnon lamented about "emigration from his native parish upon a somewhat larger scale—friends, neighbours, relatives parting in this world forever. No one who has witnessed the heart-breaking scene is likely to forget it." Colonsay enumerated 273 residents on its 1911 census, about the same number in the Kilchattan area of Mackinnon's youth. In 1908 the old Baptist Church in Williscroft closed and its white-brick replacement opened across the road.[16] The war itself only further propelled death, both in Elderslie and in Colonsay, when both communities sent young men to France, respectively commemorated by monuments in Paisley and at Scalasaig.[17]

Another McKinnon from Ontario, though, would return to Scotland and Colonsay after "the War to end all Wars." Robert Lachlan McKinnon was born in Erin Township, in his grandfather Lachlan's farmhouse, in 1872, ten years after his grandfather's death. He graduated from the University of Toronto in 1895 and became one of Ontario's leading jurists. In 1928, by the King's appointment, he was named judge of the Wellington County Court; in 1935 he received the King George V and Queen Mary Medal. "Judge McKinnon," as everyone called him, held an abiding interest in his Scottish heritage and family history. At Robert's request, in 1902 his father John had written "Cousin" Donald Mackinnon for specific genealogical information. Professor Mackinnon sent them "a jotting regarding the members of your great-grandfather's [Angus McKinnon from the Ross of Mull] family who did not emigrate, in so far as known to me...." But not until July 1936 could Robert and his wife Annie sail from Montreal for Great Britain. On board, they socialized with passengers going to the Olympic Games in Berlin and saw the dirigible "Hindenburg" pass over the ship. They shopped and toured London, and witnessed an attempted assassination of the King on Constitution Hill by a disgruntled journalist.[18]

On the afternoon of August 13, Robert and Annie McKinnon boarded a Glasgow steamer in Oban on its southbound passage to Colonsay. Completing their ancestors' journey in reverse, they unloaded in the rain onto a "tender boat ... with big waves dashing it up and down"; then they met the Mackinnons on the same Colonsay quay at Scalasaig from where Lachlan McKinnon and others had departed in 1831. For eight glorious days they "drove about the island in a two-wheeled cart with pony," met more cousins, walked the hills and paths, collected seashells on the beaches, toured Colonsay House and viewed the crofts of Robert's ancestors in Kilchattan and Miogarus. Giving heart-felt good-byes at the quay, the Mackinnons from Colonsay bid farewell to the McKinnons from Guelph, who reached home on September 12. The next week Robert wrote to a cousin in New York: "It was like going home and the welcome was pure Highland...." But he was worried on the eve of World War II. The day after France surrendered in 1940 he implored his cousin Catherine to leave Edinburgh and come to Guelph; she could "repay me by giving me some lessons in Gaelic that I badly need." Catherine wrote: "I feel I cannot leave Britain till we are at peace once more...." And from Colonsay, his cousin Mary confessed: "[W]ouldn't I love to pack and

run straight to you but—no—we must not be cowards is our motto—
'Fortune aids the brave'—and we *must* be brave and face whatever
comes." Throughout the war the McKinnons in Guelph sent Catherine
and Mary parcels with scarce, rationed commodities such as tea, sugar,
chocolate, coffee, butter, fruits, and bacon. But these transatlantic
cousins, extended over the ocean by emigration, would never see one
another again.[19]

In a 1990-91 Scottish Historical Studies Seminar about "Scottish
Emigration and Scottish Society" held at Strathclyde University, T. M.
Devine, Malcolm Gray, and E .J. Cowan offered examples and analysis
of a "national culture of mobility." Despite Colonsay's tiny size and
remote location, its lairds and emigrants exemplify, if not extend,
aspects of their presentations. After all, John McNeill (son of the "Old
Laird"), as chairman of the board to supervise Scotland's Poor Law,
and his nephew Malcolm McNeill (1839-1919), as Poor Law inspector
for the Highlands and islands, promoted emigration to solve rural
poverty.[20] By 1800 the attraction of higher wages and cheap land in
Prince Edward Island convinced some tenants and laborers to leave
Colonsay despite its prosperity; perhaps the opportunities at home were
not equal for all. These early emigrants braved a long voyage, the
Maritime wilderness, extreme climate, and slow adjustments to forge a
point of entry, settlement, or replenishment for later people from
Colonsay. Like other Scots abroad, they wrote to family and friends. A
Gaelic letter of April 7, 1822 by Malcolm Munn in Kilchattan conveys
all the ambiguity and hesitation of a potential emigrant:

> [T]here are many letters arriving here from others who went over,
> who do not tell the truth—some are praising it while others criticize
> and complain.... I am not too anxious to go to that place to work. It
> would not look too good to me, when strong people with indifferent
> attitudes come home and have left....[21]

Gray captures the essence and spirit of Gaels making the momentous
decision to leave their crofts, cottages, and hearths:

> It is people carefully planning to join earlier emigrants because of
> family and neighbourhood links who sustain the continuity. This is
> to be seen most clearly in the rural context.... The family, in fact,
> was the common unit of planning and it is a particular characteristic
> of Scottish emigration that families were held together. Emigrant
> parties would contain representatives from all age groups from the
> young to the elderly.[22]

Colonsay emigrants aboard the *Spencer* in 1806 and the *Clarendon* in 1808, or Professor Donald Mackinnon's father's siblings gone to Upper Canada in 1831, surely fit this description.

The emigrant groups faced the shock of arrival and the challenges of those first years. They survived in social networks going from their Gaelic village to a ship, to shore and to settlement in a "chain of migration" from Prince Edward Island through Ontario. There were trees to cut, fields to plow, animals to buy, cabins to build, and above all, the winters to fear. In Erin and Elderslie the land available far exceeded any acreage in Colonsay, often ten to twenty times the size of a croft in Kilchattan. The displaced, disoriented islanders did well to clear and cultivate a few acres each year, given the hazards of accident, weather, and disease. Tuberculosis plagued the young adults in Elderslie. Forty-five of the Rusk grave inscriptions between 1860 and 1910—about 20%—record 25 men and 20 women dying between 15 and 35 years old. Of Colonsay's 280 registered deaths for 1860-1910, approximately 18% were young adults aged between 15 and 35; a common cause of death was "Phthisis pulmonalis." Families had abandoned their crowded, damp cottages in Colonsay to build and inhabit crowded, damp cabins in Bruce County, with similar consequences.[23] Even Professor Mackinnon in Edinburgh realized the comparisons (and contrasts), which he conveyed to the Gaelic Society of Inverness in 1887:

> A shrewd observant Highland colonist once informed me that where Celt and Saxon farmer live together on the shores of Lake Huron, the Highlander's "concession" frequently stands first, and is always a good second; but, in a community of Highlanders, one not infrequently comes upon broken fences, open gates, and that general air of negligence and *abandon* so charming to the artistic instinct, but so destructive of good husbandry, which one meets with too often in the old country.[24]

Another irreversible, transatlantic force permeated the emigrants' Gaelic language and culture. Like people of the Scottish Borders transplanted to southern Ontario whose "self-conscious awareness of belonging to a Scottish community seldom extended beyond a generation,"[25] the Colonsay emigrants to Bruce County also encountered linguistically diverse groups of people. Elderslie was an early conglomeration of English, German, Irish, and Scottish enclaves which later dissolved into a mixed population of English speakers, truly a mosaic of its settlement history. "McLugash" from Colonsay changed to "McDougal" in Elderslie, due to the nearly identical Gaelic derivations for "son of Douglas" and "son of Dougal." The families heard both Gaelic and English in church but they read English in school and English on official documents. Learning English in rural Ontario proved difficult for the children of Colonsay parents. Angus Currie McNeill entered "S.S. No 8, Elderslie" in 1868-69. Over 60 years later, Angus still remembered his Gaelic-to-English trauma:

> When my schooling began I could not speak English, and I will never forget the trials I had. If I gave a word the wrong pronunciation, which quite often happened, some scholar would make fun of me, and that was like drawing the red blood from my heart, and any boy who took my part was a friend for life. My heart goes out to any child who is sent to school before he or she can talk the language of the community....[26]

Rusk's cemetery also exhibits this language shift. When the children buried their parents, or descendants later erected a stone, they often inscribed "Native of Colonsay" on the marker, yet omitted any Gaelic notation so common on the cemetery stones in Colonsay.

Cowan regrets that "the Scottish emigrant experience is still somewhat imperfectly understood because comparatively few historians have tried to trace the process across the Atlantic." However, Catherine Wilson at the University of Guelph has studied Scotch-Irish emigration from Northern Ireland to Amherst Island, Ontario, during 1820-60. Like the Colonsay people, they traveled in extended families and "yearned for people and places back in Ireland." Unlike them, they left 20-acre farms to rent 50-100 acres from Irish landlords "even when they could afford to buy." A port of arrival seldom became the Gaelic emigrants' final destination, and records were not always kept on an expanding frontier; the "official statistics of Upper Canada" started in 1825.[27] But the emigrants' children and grandchildren, separated from Colonsay by a generation or two, lived in a New World where they excelled as farmers, wives, husbands, parents, merchants, teachers, preachers, doctors, and lawyers. For them, Colonsay modified through time into a cherished, collective memory.

To learn about those "left behind" in Colonsay, visit the cemetery at Kilchattan where Professor Mackinnon is buried under a Gaelic notation. To witness the same social cohesion among those who departed Colonsay, visit Rusk's cemetery in Elderslie; or visit Wood Islands Pioneer Cemetery, Prince Edward Island, where siblings Angus, James, and Ann Munn, late aboard the *Spencer* in 1806, rest near many of their descendants. Or, visit Coningsby cemetery between Ospringe and Erin in rural Wellington County. Buried almost side by side are

Donald, John, Lachlan, and Sarah McKinnon from the Ross of Mull and Colonsay, together in death as they always were in life. As their nephew, Professor Donald Mackinnon, said seven years before his election to Edinburgh's Celtic Chair: "We consider it a misfortune both for the country and for the people that our Highland peasantry, in order to find a fair field in which they may be able to benefit themselves and their fellowmen, must seek other lands."[28]

This case study of the Colonsay-Canada migrations demonstrates the extent to which Transatlantic Studies is defined by its association with "cultures of mobility." Moreover, the historical figures discussed here share significant patterns of thought and behavior with figures discussed elsewhere in this collection. The propensity to view the transatlantic as a site of conflicting dynamics—of opportunity and loss, home and away, self and other—appears in this story of the Mackinnons and their fellow emigrants, just as it does in other transatlantic engagements in politics, the arts, the social sciences, and the law. In this regard, the transatlantic itself is truly "a fair field" for exploration.

---

[1] B. Bailyn, *The Peopling of British North America* (New York: Knopf, 1986), 5.

[2] *Old Statistical Account XII* (1791-96): 329-30; J. L. Ladell, *They Left Their Mark: Surveyors and Their Role in the Settlement of Ontario* (Toronto: Dundurn, 1993), 9.

[3] "Colonsay and Oronsay ... from an actual survey made in 1804 by David Wilson...." RHP2992, National Archives of Scotland, Edinburgh.

[4] "General View of the Agriculture of the Hebrides" by James MacDonald, 1811, reprinted in *Colonsay and Oronsay*, ed. J. V. Loder, (Edinburgh: Oliver and Boyd, 1935), 274; T. M. Devine, *The Great Highland Famine* (Edinburgh: John Donald, 1988), 281; F. Macalister, *Memoir of the Right Honorable Sir John McNeill* (London: John Murray, 1910), 299.

[5] J. M. Bumsted, *The People's Clearance* (Edinburgh: Edinburgh University and the University of Manitoba, 1982), 226-27, 268-70, 275-80; Colonsay Old Parish Register, 539/2, New Register House, Edinburgh.

[6] Ladell, 119, 123; "County of Wellington" in *The Guelph Mercury* (13 and 18 September 1906); C. J. McMillan, *Early History of the Township of Erin* (Cheltenham: Boston Mills, 1974), 25; H. L. Mack, *The Twelve Townships of Wellington County* (Guelph: Ampersand, 1977), 75-80.

[7] *Trout Family History* (private), 52, 132-34; Assessment and Census of Erin Township for 1833, 1834, 1839 and 1840, Wellington County Archives, Elora and Fergus; McKinnon Family Papers; "The Province of Ontario" under "Angus McKinnon, M.D."; *Country Home* (May 1993): 40-45.

[8] 1841 and 1851 Census for Colonsay, New Register House.

[9] G. Yuille, ed., *History of the Baptists in Scotland* (Glasgow: Baptist Union, 1926), 115.

[10] Ladell, 123, 135; 1851 Census, Ontario, Canada West, Bruce County, Bruce County Museum and Archives.

[11] *Canada Gazette*, 14 August 1852; N. Robertson, *The History of the County of Bruce* (Toronto: William Biggs, 1906), 366; Yuille, 115-16; Catalogue of Rusk's cemetery, Elderslie Township, "Recorded by Mrs. Barbara Adolph, 1972," Bruce County Museum and Archives. I thank Bell, Campbell, Galbraith, McLugash, McNeill and Munn descendants in Ontario for information about their Colonsay ancestors ("Digging for Roots in Bruce," Owen Sound *Sun Times*, 24 April 1995).

[12] *A History of Elderslie Township, 1851-1977* (Chesley: Elderslie Historical Society, 1977), 69-72, 296-98.

[13] Letter of 21 December 1860, McKinnon Family Papers.

[14] Paisley *Advocate*, 8 January 1914; 16 June 1866, List of Voters for Elderslie Township, Bruce County Museum and Archives; Minutes of the Edinburgh University Celtic Society, Special Collections, Edinburgh University Library; *A History of Elderslie Township*, 161; Yuille, 116.

[15] D. Mackinnon, "Lonely Colonsay," *The Scotsman*, 23 August 1887; Paisley *Advocate*, 9 March 1905; "Our McNeill Ancestry" by Douglas and Audrey MacDonald (private).

[16] "The Melancholy of the Gael," Mackinnon Collection B1(7), Special Collections, Edinburgh University Library; Letter of 10 January 1944, McKinnon Family Papers; Colonsay Death Register, 1914/539/2/7, New Register House; Paisley *Advocate*, 1 October 1908, 8 January 1914, 7 January 1915, 4 February 1915, and picture in *A History of Elderslie Township*, 276.

[17] McKinnon Family Papers; "Descendants of Alexander Munn and Flora McPhail" by Lorna Irwin (private). Dr. Duncan Mackinnon is buried in the Meteren Military Cemetery, Nord, France, Grave Reference IV.H.794; Dr. Malcolm McKechnie is buried in Vignacourt British Cemetery, Somme, France, Grave Reference V.A.6 (Commonwealth War Graves Commission, www.cwgc.org).

[18] Diary page-copies, Mackinnon Family Papers; *The Times*, 17 July 1936.

[19] Letters of 1933-44, McKinnon Family Papers.

[20] T. M. Devine, ed., *Scottish Emigration and Scottish Society* (Edinburgh: John Donald, 1992), 1-15, 16-36, 61-83, 84-103; W. Norton, "Malcolm McNeill and the Emigrationist Alternative to Highland Land Reform," *Scottish Historical Review* LXX, no 188 (1991): 16-30.

[21] Courtesy of Kevin Byrne, Colonsay.

[22] Gray, in Devine, 28, 34.

[23] Among those in Rusk's cemetery: "Tuberculosis was a dreadful disease in the early years, and claimed many of the victims buried there. We are told of one plot filled with eight graves all from one family, all died of tuberculosis with no stone to mark them. Deaths of many more of those buried there were caused by TB. This disease, when it struck a home, not only claimed the lives of those living there then, but the germs seemed to live on, ready to attack others who moved in later. To burn the house and contents seemed the only way to destroy the disease..." (*A History of Elderslie Township*, 178).

[24] D. Mackinnon, "Language as an Index to Character," *Transactions of the Gaelic Society of Inverness* XIII (1886-87): 335-52 (reprint in the Carmichael-Watson Collection, 492-496 [15], Special Collections, Edinburgh University Library).

[25] Cowan, in Devine, 75.

[26] "History of S.S. No 8, Elderslie" by J. D. Grant and R. McKelvey, issued for the re-union held August 3, 1935 (courtesy of Marnie Vogel).

[27] Cowan, in Devine, 61; C. A. Wilson, "The Scotch-Irish and Immigrant Culture on Amherst Island, Ontario" in *Ulster and North America: Transatlantic Perspectives on the Scotch-Irish*, ed. H. T. Blethen and C. W. Wood (Tuscaloosa: University of Alabama, 1997), 141-42; M. Flynn, ed., *Scottish Population History from the Seventeenth Century to the 1930s* (Cambridge: Cambridge University Press, 1977), 449.

[28] D. Mackinnon, "Olim Marte, Nunc Arte," *The Gael* 4, no. 39 (1875): 89.

Part Two:
Globalization

Chapter 6

The Ideology of Globalization, the Globalization of *the* Ideology

Ryszard M. Machnikowski

> Globalization is what we in the Third World have for several
> centuries called colonization. (Martin Khor)

Written in the early part of the 20th century, Karl Mannheim's famous
book *Ideology and Utopia* has made a huge contribution to the
sociology of knowledge in that it has helped to define both of the main
terms of his title. Mannheim's theory of ideology and the sociology of
knowledge acknowledges the interconnectedness between thought and
social structure, and further analyzes the *interdependence* between
knowledge and the social environment in which this knowledge is
created.

According to Mannheim, ideas—whether everyday,
"commonsense" ideas or consciously structured academic ideas—can
be much better understood if we try to trace the links between them and
the social positions and/or political interests of their producers or re-
producers. Mannheim clearly follows Marx in this regard; however, he
did not limit his analysis to social classes, but extended it to strata,
generations and other social groups. Also noteworthy is Mannheim's
hostility towards a deterministic interpretation of his thesis, as he

understood it in a hermeneutical, not causal, sense. One should remember these constraints, in order to perceive properly Mannheim's notions of "Ideology" and "Utopia."[1]

Mannheim argues that the concept of "ideology"

> reflects the one discovery which emerged from political conflict, namely, that ruling groups can in their thinking become so intensively interest-bound to a situation that they are simply no longer able to see certain facts which would undermine their sense of domination.[2]

Conversely, utopian thinking relates to oppressed groups who may, by wishing to see the destruction of a particular social order, be unwilling or unable to see any positive aspects of the current situation. Thus,

> Their thought is never a diagnosis of the situation; it can be used only as a direction for action. In the utopian mentality, the collective unconscious, guided by wishful representation and the will to action, hides certain aspects of reality. It turns its back on everything which would shake its belief or paralyse its desire to change things.[3]

Ideology in this sense plays a conservative role in the society, trying to defend the existing social and political status quo, whereas utopia is a revolutionary thought, expressed by the oppressed groups in the society, showing the ideal state of affairs which should supersede the current order. Ideology tends to portray the status quo in bright colors, neglecting the existence of any serious disadvantages of a system, while utopia prefers to magnify all these disadvantages, deliberately ignoring any positive aspects of the existing system. As Mannheim properly observed:

> What in a given case appears as utopia, and what as ideological, is dependent, essentially, on the stage and degree of reality to which one applies this standard. [...] The representatives of a given order will label as utopian all conceptions of existence, which from their point of view can in principle never be realized. According to this usage, the contemporary connotation of the term "utopian" is predominantly that of an idea which is in principle unrealizable."[4]

However, we can observe some utopian projections that have become, after their practical institution and intellectual transformation, ideologies in the Mannheimian sense: liberalism and Marxism are perhaps the best and most widely known examples.

These "classical" concepts of ideology and utopia provide the starting point (and the frame of reference) for my thesis, that the contemporary concept of "globalization" includes both ideological and utopian functions as Mannheim describes them.[5] This concept is not solely ideological because it aims at a global and radical (if not revolutionary) restructuring of apparently separate economic, social and political systems rather than the preservation of an existing status quo. But neither is it predominantly utopian, as it expresses ideas of dominant social and political groups rather than the oppressed (the possibility of realizing such perceived globalization is not itself under discussion now).

The concept of "globalization" has become a catchword for journalists and politicians, losing in the process some of the nuances of its academic meaning. It has been, and still is, used to cover a vast array of new phenomena in social, cultural and economic life and to describe some of the most important changes shaping contemporary society. It has both analytical and descriptive functions in politics, economics and sociology. Academic disagreements over this term center on what aspects can be considered the major elements of globalization, as well as whether it is a recent—or even real—phenomenon. The result is that this term is extremely ambiguous, even vague, as there are so many definitions and understandings of it. While this state of affairs is quite normal in the social sciences, it does create problems, since the term has been adopted rather cavalierly by newspapers and politicians. Therefore, it is useful to underscore some of the most common uses of the term in academic circles. Anthony Giddens argues that globalization "can be defined as the intensification of world-wide social relations which link distant localities in such a way [that] those local happenings are shaped by events occurring many miles away and vice versa."[6] Similarly, Spybey defines globalization as "the tendency for routine, day-to-day social interaction to be imbued with patterns that are to an increasing extent shared across the planet."[7]

More metaphorically, Kanter links the term to the image of "a global shopping mall in which ideas and products are available everywhere at the same time."[8] No definition is without bias, of course, and the potentially contentious issues surrounding globalization are often evident from the commentators' words. Dunkerley, for example, is concerned about the way in which "events of happening on a world-wide scale affect individuals, groups and whole societies in almost deterministic fashion such that the latter have little control over their own destinies."[9] Similarly, Cox notes that globalization potentially involves making sovereign states into little more than "agencies of the globalizing world."[10] Waters argues that the "constraints of geography" become less apparent in globalization, and that individuals are attuned to the changes that result from this.[11] Clearly, globalization incorporates many potential conflicts, as nation states determine their own hierarchies in a "world without borders."

The effects of globalization are many and varied. They include the emergence of a truly world economy and an interdependent financial market. Within this "global economy" transnational companies (TNCs) are increasingly powerful. Global traders and speculators transfer money around the globe with the speed of light. The result is that most states cannot control their economies, so national strategies of economic management are becoming increasingly irrelevant. A second effect of globalization is the presumed demise (or at least powerlessness) of nation states and their slowly decreasing functions and policies. Globalization means the decline of the sovereignty of states in the increasingly interconnected world.

Along with monetary change comes a revolution in the communications and mass media, which results in instant access to information. Events in one location can be immediately observed and copied everywhere (provided, of course, one has adequate electronic equipment). Mobile and satellite phones, interactive TV and the Internet have changed human lives significantly—at least for those with access to them. This factor more than others highlights the uneven and unequal nature of globalization.

But what has exercised critics the most about globalization is the potential homogenization of culture. With the disappearance of borders, time and spatial boundaries, the old ideas of geographical space and chronological time are no longer relevant, due to the speed of communication. Thus—potentially—people around the world will become "identikit," taking on the most dominant characteristics of this new global culture. This results in the emergence of a "postmodern" culture defined by its consumerism, commercialism and relativism. A more positive spin, adopted by some critics, suggests that the concept of world citizenship may have some lasting benefits as people begin to think of themselves as part of a global solution to problems that individual nation states cannot tackle alone—such as pollution, the thinning ozone layer, global warming, AIDS, financial crises and nuclear war.

While I do not claim to have rehearsed *all* the arguments about globalization and its effects (indeed, to do so would require several thousand more words, if not an entire book), I have tried to present the most common viewpoints. Clearly, there is at least the same level of disagreement as the level of consensus within academia. As a result, and following classical Mannheimian definitions, the concept of globalization cannot solely be "ideological." Nevertheless, the term "globalization" has penetrated the language of politicians and media commentators, and some of them are either not aware of the compound structure of both the concept and the processes described by it, or they have chosen either to conceal or to over- or underestimate it. For the sake of journalistic and political "clarity," high hopes have been enhanced and the risks and dangers minimized in political speeches and newspaper articles. Transatlantic political and economic elites embrace globalization gleefully. The question is, should the rest of us?

Transatlantic "spin doctors" promise four things: greater and smoother financial flow; increased access to culture; global trading; and new forms of government. But are these factors equally attractive to all states? And what are the potential negative consequences that may obtain?

Due to the liberalization of trade and finance (the collapse of the so-called Bretton Woods system), communication and media revolution (the spread of the Internet and the other global media), and the expansion of the high-tech industries, people of the whole world *are* living in the *real* world society, based on the *real* global economy (often called "the New Economy"). Global financial capital circulates around the globe, penetrating even the most "noplacevilles" of the world, seeking highest gains. This financial flow brings the global civilization and advanced technology to the most distant regions, giving them peace, stability and a new way of life—or does it? In previous centuries, European colonists convinced themselves (and others) that they were bringing the natives good news; today these colonists are superseded by the TNC representatives. The positive spin of TNCs is that they make the local economies competitive, increase wages, make new goods and products available to the local population, and incorporate local markets into the global economic system. Whatever economic role TNCs play, they also play a social and cultural one, as their representatives introduce new standards of work and lifestyle. These standards are perceived as desirable and are copied by the local "young urban professionals," the prospective elite of the region. In this way, a standardized professional and domestic culture is spread and reproduced all over the world. Regional economies, and then societies, become increasingly identical and interdependent, thanks to the deregulation and suppression of all economic barriers of trade and investment. As the economic and domestic culture is thus affected, so too is the political culture. This encourages some to claim that nation-states themselves are obsolete and will soon disappear, becoming merely one type of a social organization (a relatively short-lived accident in the history of social institutions). It is not clear what kind of new institutions would acquire their responsibilities—whether it would be the "substate" or "suprastate" global governance, or whether the whole problem of governance would be marketized and captured by the private sector.

As one can see, a positive or negative reading can be applied to most aspects of globalization. A popularized view of globalization tends to be much more certain about the progressive consequences of this profound social change, neglecting to a large extent possible threats which these processes may bring in. This powerful vision suggests that all the world's people will be members of a single, global village. They will have instant and free access to information about events taking place in their little community—the world. Most of the people will share the values of an overarching culture comprised of a vast range of local cultures. They will be picking up products, images and ideas from a global, cultural shopping mall. They will observe the almost "natural" decline of a nation state, and along with that they will say farewell to all the wars caused by particular interests of the states. In this sense globalization may lead to "the end of history," where market economy and liberal democracy conquer the world (as one of the most famous prophecies of the early 1990s suggested).[12] Particularly attractive in this vision is the hidden promise of an egalitarian society, where human performance depends solely on individual abilities and is no longer determined by the place of birth and social status. In this sense globalization is the French Revolution, realized.

In the popularized, transatlantic view, the means of achieving globalization are relatively simple: liberalize further trade and investments; eliminate still existing economic barriers; do not hamper high-tech development; accept the powerlessness or eventual elimination of the nation-state—it seems that never in the history of humankind could so many can gain so much by doing so little. This vision is the genuine "utopia" for the 21st century. However, this is more than utopia; it is also ideology. Its persuasive rhetoric is powerful, and its promises are far-reaching and impressive. It gives poor societies the hope that they will benefit in the near future, provided they are competitive enough and expose themselves to the power of globalization. This vision (in a Mannheimian sense) obscures the real condition of a given society and hides certain aspects of reality, especially the way in which the dominant groups (power elites, big business) and not the oppressed (unemployed, socially-excluded Third

World societies) can extend their control and powers. It presents a distorted view of reality and does so in favor of the privileged groups of society within the dominant civilization—in other words, the transatlantic elites. The term "globalization" conceals Western political, economical and cultural dominance and American military hegemony over the rest of the globe.

At the same time, however, globalization is obviously progressive rather than conservative since it does not intend to preserve the existing status quo; thus, in Mannheimian terms, it is also utopian. It is "utopian" because it portrays new challenges and opportunities for people all over the world, bringing them hope for a better life in the future. In total, then, the concept of globalization is a set of ideas used by the economically and politically dominant groups of the Western world—primarily the powerful nations of the transatlantic community—to promote their interests and to create the global system which would be compliant to their will and secure their dominance in the future. Thus globalization is the transatlantic bloc's ideological utopia of the next decade. But what does the West hide from the rest?

- *That the salutary role of uncontrolled global financial circulation is exaggerated.* It certainly can bring many benefits for local economies, but due to its chaotic nature it can be transformed into the awesome force devastating regional economies; consider Mexico (1994), East Asia (1997) and Russia (1998). Because the economic game is never ending, the balance is always open for disastrous change. Some commentators even question the existence of a "New Economy" based on the high-tech sector and fueling the global financial flow,[13] although the adherents are triumphant as long as the American economy continues to grow. However, this attitude may change—as happened after the Asian crash of 1997, before which many had believed that Asian corporate values promoted economic growth. Afterwards only a few maintained this view.
- *That genuine TNCs, as Hirst and Thompson have persuasively argued, are relatively rare—most of them are national companies trading internationally.*[14] The majority of these national companies are of transatlantic (American, European) or Japanese origin. Their net profits replenish corporate pockets while, thanks to favorable taxation and accountancy loopholes, even the societies in which they originate do not uniformly benefit from them. Moreover, some of the biggest

global players are established through "mergerization" processes, definitely profitable for their CEOs, but not necessarily for the ordinary workers facing redundancy.[15] Hirst and Thompson claim that "globalization" in fact means the "triadization" of the world economy, as most trade, investment and financial flows are concentrated in and between "the triad" of the EU, the US and Japan. This suggests that there is no major shift of finance and capital flow from the developed to underdeveloped countries.

- *That global communication is not really global; it is still determined by the level of welfare of the local society.* Because the majority of the world's population lives in poverty, and the social inequalities are increasing rather than diminishing, it is difficult to call this process truly global. By focusing attention on the absolute numbers (e.g., the quantity of computers, mobile phones, TV sets sold), one disregards the increasing problem of social injustice and inequalities within national economies, the growing gap between the rich North and the poor South, the pauperization of many societies, and such consequent social problems as crime and drug-trafficking.
- *That "global culture" is primarily a culture of the US-dominated transatlantic elites.* The biggest media and show business companies are American, as are their products (study cinema and television schedules, and try to find any Zambian films; study record store hit lists and try to find any Bolivian artists). As far as culture is concerned, globalization *means* Americanization.

When transatlantic politicians and top rank managers talk about globalization, they tell us only a part of a whole story. They tend to conceal factors such as who are the prospective winners and losers of these processes. It therefore comes as no surprise that the term "globalization" evokes strong emotions and radical actions, which were observed on the streets of Seattle in December 1999, and Davos in January 2000. In these places the institutions perceived as the agents of globalization were vilified, and hostile demonstrations and protests were met with pepper spray, arrests, and curfew.[16]

Globalization is a complex social process, with both attractive and destructive consequences. Celebration of the transatlantic, through new courses of study, a new discipline, and new academic interests, should not obscure the "real" effects of globalization—and the way that it can be used by the powerful against the weak. As public protest demonstrates, at least some people are paying attention to this message; it will take some time, though, before we can look back upon "globalization" and be sure we can assess its impact properly. It is important, in any event, to remove the solely "ideological" slant given globalization by politicians, media moguls and corporate agents. Otherwise, as Karl Mannheim has taught us, we can expect even more social unrest and intellectual anxiety.

---

[1] One should not confuse this meaning of the term "ideology" with a different one—"ideology as false consciousness." The question whether "ideology" (or "utopia") is "true" or "false" is secondary and not under investigation here.

[2] Karl Mannheim, *Ideology and Utopia* (New York: Harcourt, Brace, Jovanovich, 1991), 40.

[3] Ibid.

[4] Ibid., 196.

[5] As I do not feel entitled to introduce a new English term "ideopia" (ideology + uto-pia), I use these two "classical" Mannheimian terms, although they are not exact in this context.

[6] Anthony Giddens, *The Consequences of Modernity: Self and Society in the Late Modern Age* (Cambridge: Polity Press, 1990), 64.

[7] T. Spybey, *Globalization and World Society* (Cambridge: Polity Press, 1996), 168-69.

[8] R. Kanter, *World Class: Thriving Locally in the Global Economy* (New York: Simon and Schuster, 1995), 18.

[9] D. Dunkerley, "The UK and the Emerging World Society—Socio-Economic Aspects," in *The Role of Great Britain in Modern World*, ed. K. Kujawinska-Courtney and R. M. Machnikowski (Lódz: Lódz University Press, 1999), 111.

[10] R. Cox, "Multilateralism and the Democratization of World Order" (paper presented at the International Symposium on Sources of Innovation in Multilateralism, Lausanne, May 26-28, 1994), 3.

[11] M. Waters, *Globalization* (London: Routledge, 1995), 3.

[12] Francis Fukuyama, *The End of History and the Last Man* (London: Penguin, 1992).

[13] "How Real is the New Economy?" *The Economist*, 24 July, 1999.

[14] See P. Hirst and G. Thompson, *Globalization in Question: The International Economy and the Possibilities of Governance* (Cambridge: Polity Press, 1996).

[15] As the recent merger of Deutsche Bank and Dresdner Bank shows—15,000 jobs were lost.

[16] As William Pfaff observed: "'The New Woodstock' in Seattle this week, as it has understandably been called, reacts against what widely and accurately has become seen as a program to transfer power over society from governments—the enterprises and institutions of individual nations—to international corporations, most but no means all of them American [...]. The drive for generalized deregulations is an ideological crusade, commonly

called globalization, which many serious people severely criticize or oppose."
"Globalization, Alas, Is About More Than Tariffs," *International Herald Tribune*, 3 December, 1999.

Chapter 7

Property, Neo-liberalism and Transatlantic Civic Republicanism

Robert Barford

This chapter is devoted to an analysis of how the current globalization process impacts on national and international politics, in particular between the US and Europe. It is generally agreed that globalization evolved as the solution to the world-wide economic stagnation of the 1970s. Beginning in the early 1980s, a regime of laissez-faire capitalism (often referred to as neo-liberalism) was put into place by the Reagan and Thatcher administrations, calling for the dismantling of the welfare state, the weakening of labor unions, the deregulation of markets, tax cutting, and the embracing of supply-side economics. When Ronald Reagan took office, the Heritage Foundation, a think tank with billion dollar yearly budgets largely funded by American corporations, presented the administration with a 3,000-page document recommending reductions of government activity, 61% of which were adopted. And in England Margaret Thatcher took the same cues from the Centre for Policy Studies. Thus was the role of the state radically redefined, abandoning the progressivist and Rooseveltian triad of capital, labor, and government in cooperative interconnection devoted to promoting social welfare, full employment policies, strong labor unions, and regulated markets.

Two different conceptions of the relationship between the state and capital are exemplified here. The first, laissez-faire capitalism, goes back to 17th-century England and the Glorious Revolution of 1688. The victory of parliament over the crown did away with the traditional power of royalty and deposited political power into the hands of the landed aristocracy and the emerging business class. Effectively it established the power of capital over the state, the political order in the service of capital. In the words of Fernand Braudel, "Capitalism triumphs only when it becomes identified with the state, when it is the state."[1] The philosophical and political legitimacy of these developments were formulated by Thomas Hobbes and John Locke in the framework of what we now call "neo-liberalism."

In contrast is the long tradition of social welfare and concern for the common good, latterly exemplified by the New Deal and the Rooseveltian reforms. Politics rooted in the idea of the common good goes back to the classical era and the Middle Ages, especially as laid out by Aristotle and Thomas Aquinas. Here we can say that the economic order is subordinated to the political order as guarantor of justice, equality, and welfare of the citizens.

The difference between the two historical forms of the relations of state and economy are best viewed in terms of the meanings of private property. Neo-liberalism is property as commodity, as negative freedom, that is, freedom-from—in this case, as the immunity of the private realm from interference by the political order. This is the Lockean tradition championed by Alexander Hamilton in the US constitutional period. Three additional characteristics are "[t]he moral and political priority of the individual over the community; the subjectivity of values; the market as the primary mechanism for mediating individual preferences within society."[2]

The other, progressivist form is property as propriety, described by Gregory Alexander as follows:

> According to this view, property is the material foundation for creating and maintaining the proper social order, the private basis of the public good. This tradition ... has continuously understood the individual human as an inherently social being, inevitably dependent on others.... This irreducible interdependency means that individuals owe one another obligations, not by virtue of consent alone but as an inherent incident of the human condition.[3]

This form of property fits the Rooseveltian model and is a basic feature of writers during the US constitutional period, especially as emphasized by Thomas Jefferson. It promotes the priority of the political over the economic order.

It being the case that neo-liberalism—property as commodity—is the base for globalization, the traditional nation-state as the center of political life is under severe pressure, owing to the flexibility of capitalist expansions both of world trade and of finance mechanisms seeking profitable investments. The development of trans-national organizations such as the World Trade Organization (WTO), the International Monetary Fund (IMF) and the World Bank are added components to the mixture of powers which put into question the viability of the political order. The maintenance of domestic tranquility and world peace on the international level is all the more difficult for nation-states. In what follows I shall examine first the outcomes in the world economy based on globalization rooted in property as commodity.

For the most part, my focal point will be the US as the most powerful and leading state, the model and pace-setter for the world economy. Ever since the 17th century, the competition for wealth and power has been located in the state, the wealth of nations. The nature of this inter-state competition gives rise to a hegemon, a leading power— witness the Dutch supplanting the Italian city states (17th century); the British supplanting the Dutch (18th century); and the US supplanting the British (late 19th century) and still the world hegemon.

A major theme of the World Economic Forum in Davos, Switzerland, in February, 1996, was the need for an ethical dimension to globalization. One report summarizes the tenor of the meeting as follows: "the globalized economy must not become synonymous with free market on the rampage, a brakeless train wreaking havoc"; "capitalism is doomed unless it develops a heart."[4] The ensuing years since 1996 have given us ample evidence of this "brakeless train wreaking havoc." The Asian meltdown of 1998 is one example of the "free market on a rampage," in this case within the financial markets themselves. Developments in technology have allowed instantaneous financial transactions on a massive scale, taking place with destabilizing speculative raids on national currencies, as happened to Asia in 1998. As recently as 1975, currency trading stood at 80% involved with the real economy of imports and exports. In 1998 only 3% was involved with the real economy and 97% given over to speculation.

Global economic inequality has grown apace as follows: 20% of the world's most wealthy receive 86% of the world's GDP; the middle 60% receive just 13%; while the poorest 20% have 1%. The income gap between the top 20% and the bottom 20% is now 74 to 1, while in 1960 it was 30 to 1. Assets of the world's wealthiest 200 more than doubled between 1994 and 1998 to over one trillion dollars.[5]

Other factors that need to be mentioned include the use of sweat-shop labor on a global scale. In El Salvador, for example, women work seven days a week, sometimes 15 hours a day, are fired if they become pregnant, may use the bathroom once in the morning and once in the afternoon, and are paid wages that meet only one-third of the cost of living. Women are paid 84 cents for sewing a Liz Claiborne jacket which retails for $198—a labor cost of 0.4%. There are about 65,000 total sweat-shop workers in El Salvador without one union to represent them.[6] Sweat-shop labor is one example of how multinational corporations operate, putting into effect what is called "flexibility of labor markets." This connotes the ability to export jobs from the advanced economies to the sweat shops, giving rise to such phrases as "downsizing," "outsourcing," and "re-engineering" among others. Economist Lester Thurow describes what the labor market has become:

> Downsizing is a way of life even in good times. In a global economy, if skills are cheaper somewhere else in the world, companies will move there to lower production costs. They aren't tied to any particular set of workers.... Something is happening in the world that has never happened before.... In the past if a company was going broke, it always laid people off—that's the American way. But we didn't have people laid off and downsized in profitable companies until the 1990s. Today, about 800,000 Americans a year lose their jobs despite the fact that their companies are profitable and they are personally doing good jobs.[7]

Careers and job stability are thus becoming a thing of the past. Formulating educational plans for working careers has become a matter of guesswork and often futility, again demonstrating the "flexibility of labor markets." These job losses impact with particular severity in the case of unskilled labor. For example, the industrial boom after World War II allowed those African-Americans who emigrated to the North to find work in factories. Thousands became blue-collar workers, and gradually their children made it into the middle class. Though before the Civil Rights era (1954 to 1976) only about 5% had done so, the number increased to 25% by the 1980s.[8]

The globalization process has put an end to this upward mobility via blue-collar work for many working poor. In 1998, 29% of all American workers were in jobs paying poverty-level wages. At the same time as these instabilities in the labor markets were taking place, calls for the elimination of the welfare state were coming forth from the think tanks funded by corporate America, especially the Manhattan Institute. According to Charles Murray in his book, *Losing Ground*, welfare rewards sloth and causes moral degeneracy of the lower classes, pervasive illegitimacy, and urban violence. He appeals to the "civilizing force of marriage" as the remedy for "young black men who are essentially barbarians."[9] Needing to soothe the fears of the upper and middle classes—that is, those who vote—a whole program of so-called "zero tolerance" in regard to social behavior was put into place across America. Police forces were vastly expanded and law enforcement assumed a hyper-aggressive profile in regard to even the slightest misdemeanor, fighting crime "inch by inch" and adopting slogans such as "a broken window is the first step" and "he who steals an egg, steals an ox."

As a result, the US has now the largest prison population (2 million) of any country in the world, recently surpassing Russia. One in every 138 Americans is behind prison bars, with 80% of black youths in ghetto areas involved in the criminal justice system at some level.[10] Extolling the so-called booming economy in his recent State of the Union address, President Clinton waxed triumphant with the statements: "We are fortunate to be alive at this moment of history," and "never before has our nation enjoyed, at once, so much prosperity and social progress."[11] These statements could hardly be extended to many of the poor and working poor in America, many of whom are languishing in prison. The prison population in the US has tripled in the past 15 years, a level 10 times higher than in the European Union, although, having adopted the neo-liberal policies in economics and state politics, the EU is beginning to put in place the "zero tolerance" methods mentioned above. These methods are sure to increase incarceration in Europe.

A prison archipelago stretches across America, at a $70 billion construction cost over the past 10 years, with a $35 billion annual incarceration cost. We have now a situation of decreasing education budgets and increasing prison budgets; a 30% increase for prisons and a 19% decrease for education. As a result, the California university system saw its share of public funds slashed by $250 million and between 1983 and 1995 had to reduce its higher-education workforce by 8,100.[12] Though demanding that China stop the exporting of prison labor, American corporations are using American prison labor as even cheaper labor than overseas sweat shops. Again, "prosperity and social progress"? The particular brutality of the prison system is well documented, especially concerning the "boot-camp" type of "discipline learning" for young prisoners, which has become so brutal toward youth that it is being disbanded throughout the country.

I believe it is safe to say that the globalized economy in the year 2000 has indeed become a "free market on the rampage" and "a brakeless train wreaking havoc." This is not to deny that significant economic growth and prosperity has taken place in many parts of the world. The economist Joseph Schumpeter has described the dynamics of capitalism as "creative destruction."[13] In other words, economic expansion comes at a cost: the dismantling of traditional economic, social, and political structures and interests.

In this light I turn to the idea of property as propriety. In many ways this view represents certain key ideas of socialism or, in the case of Roosevelt, social democracy. The analysis of propriety takes us to basic distinctions in ethics and philosophical anthropology. The leading idea is the priority of the community over the individual. According to Aristotle, the state is prior both to the family and the individual because the individual is not self-sufficing. In the *Politics* he asserts that the state is not an artificial creation—it belongs to nature, and the human being is by nature a *zwon politikon,* a political animal.[14] Politics, for Aristotle, is primarily an ethical enterprise, how to create a society of virtue and moral goodness. He writes: "Justice is the bond of men in states, for the administration of what is just, is the principle of order in a political society."[15] And in the *Nichomachean Ethics* he writes: "Justice alone of the virtues is thought to be the good of the other because it is related to our neighbor, for it does what is advantageous to another."[16] But perhaps his most famous criticism is that of the endless accumulation of money and of the unlimited desires which drive the consumption of goods and services. He writes:

> Some persons are led to believe that getting wealth is the object of household management, and that the whole of their lives is that they ought to increase their money without limit, or at any rate not to lose it. The origin of this disposition in men is that they are intent upon living and not upon living well; and, as their desires are unlimited, they also desire that the means of gratifying them should be without limit.[17]

The core of civic republican thought in 18th-century America held that private interest should be subordinated to the common welfare. This viewpoint derives from the classical tradition, as pointed out above, and Thomas Jefferson was its most insistent advocate. Gregory Alexander points out that for civic republicans, the common good was the only objective of government. Cultivation of the moral good was essential as transcending private interests. Liberty of the individual was recognized, but always in the context of the public meaning of liberty. The central idea of government was not protecting individual freedoms from governmental encroachments (as in commodity property), but it was rather protecting the public rights of people against aristocratic privileges and power (as in proprietary property). And in this latter case, it is matter where protecting the political liberty of the collective people protects individual liberty. This is a central idea, for it shows on the one hand how commodity property is more or less a kind of oligarchy of wealth in which government is viewed as a threat to be held in check and chiefly put at the disposal of private interests. In the light of Aristotle, in order to carry out the program of civic republicanism in America, it was necessary to cultivate a moral character among the citizens—that is, the overcoming of selfishness and greed. This involved a constant practice of the virtues. Virtue was defined as creating in the citizens a willingness to subordinate individual wants for the well being of the whole polity. Jefferson distinguished between an "aristocracy of virtue" and an "aristocracy of wealth," the one rooted in virtue, equality, and liberty, and the other in corruption, privilege, luxury and servility.

But how does property actually relate to civic republicanism and the common good? In the case of property as commodity, which I shall denominate as possessive individualism, the private sphere and property ownership are categorically separate from the public sphere. As I have pointed out above, its meaning of freedom is *freedom from* the public sphere. On the other hand, for civic republicanism ownership of property—that is, proprietary property—is necessary for self-governing citizens. It provides the basis for civic virtue and enables the citizens to pursue the common good. Proprietary property is a form of liberation, *freedom to* own property, so as to avoid a split in the civic domain between those who own property and those who are dependent on and subject to the power of others who own property. Being dependent on others, they will lose the freedom and autonomy to develop the virtues necessary for the flourishing of the public sphere. Autonomy is a necessary condition for virtue. Fee-simple ownership of land was the preferred model of Jefferson. According to Jefferson, "dependence begets subservience and venality, suffocates the germ of virtue and prepares fit tools for the designs of ambition."[18] Hence the evils of wage labor, that is, the work of unpropertied subjects who had lost their autonomy in having to put themselves under the power of

private interests—the system that had been in place for over a century
in England as the new form of the market society.

But it is commodity property, the basic form of neo-liberalism,
which is the model for the current globalization process. In classical
economics, commodity property (and its possessive individualism) is
the practical field for the explanatory theory of economic relations. One
can say that a radical departure from the ancient and medieval views of
human nature, society, and property are at play here. With commodity
property we are, in effect, at the beginning of modernity. The anchor of
this social and economic vision was the emergence in England of a
market society for the first time in history. This is quite different from
simple market exchanges, which have always existed in traditional
societies. In a market society all power is based on a possessive
individualism. The individual is not viewed as a moral being, nor as
owing anything to society, but rather as a proprietor of power.[19] A
whole new conception of human and society came into being. Writing
in 1651, Thomas Hobbes observed that there is "a general inclination of
all mankind, a restless desire for power after power," not only because
of a hope for "more intensive delights" but because "he cannot assure
the power and means to live well, which he has at present, without the
acquisition of more."[20] This leads to a competition for power which
Hobbes describes as "a war of every man against every man."[21] Those
with an eminence of natural power are able to maximize that power by
exercising it over others. Power turns out to be a commodity which is
alienable and transferable in a market for power, based on the idea that
"[t]he value or worth of a man is, as of all other things, his price—that
is so much as would be given for the use of his power.... And as in all
other things, so in men, not the seller but the buyer determines the
price."[22] In other words labor itself is a commodity and society is an
interconnection of market relations in which each individual seeks the
maximization of power.

With respect to society, Hobbes rejects outright the classical idea
that the human beings are *by nature* political animals. Hobbes sees all
human intercourse as based on utility. He writes, "[A]ll society is either
for gain or for glory, that is, not so much for love of our fellows, but as
for the love of ourselves."[23] Humans by nature seek dominion over
others rather than society. Benefits of this life, though promoted by
mutual help, are "better obtained by dominion rather than society."[24]
The natural war of every human against every human can only be
ended by universal agreement to give all power over to the sovereign, a
commonwealth likened to a "mortal god."[25] Hobbes was positing his

viewpoints not so much philosophically as through observations on the modalities of power in the emerging English market society.

It is really John Locke, writing in the late 17th century, who provided the basis for the form of liberal democracy still in practice today. He had particular influence over the founding fathers of the American republic. The foundation of property as commodity is well laid out in Locke. He makes the basic distinction between man in the state of nature and man in civil society.[26] These two are essentially separate structures. In the state of nature, property rights are based on natural rights and natural law. In accordance with natural law, he asserts that the earth and its fruits are given to all in common. All men are equal to one another and have a natural right to the possessions necessary for self-preservation. Appropriation is rooted in the labor of my body and hands, making it my own and giving me the right to dispose of it as I see fit. Acquisition of property is limited in that one must leave as much and as sufficiently good property for the needs and use of others.

But the invention of money overcomes the natural law's limits on appropriation, allowing for unlimited accumulation. Money accumulation is not the useless hoarding up of more than one can make use of in miserly fashion. Money is a commodity and functions as capital. Locke is putting money into a mercantile framework of promoting trade and return on investments. The nation's wealth is drawn from capital accumulated by private industry and commerce. It is the unequal distribution of money that fuels all of this. Both land and money are capital, for the unequal distribution of money brings a tenant for my capital and the unequal distribution of land brings forth a tenant for my land. According to Locke, the consent to money is *made independent of and prior to the consent establishing civil society*:

> ... it is plain, that Men have agreed to disproportionate and unequal possession of the Earth, they having by a tacit and voluntary consent found a way, how a man may fairly possess more land than he himself can use the product of, by receiving in exchange for the overplus, Gold and Silver, which may be hoarded up without injury to any one.... This partage of things, in an inequality of private possessions, men have made practicable out of the bounds of society, and without compact, only by putting a value on gold and silver and tacitly agreeing to the use of Money.[27]

This rather astonishing claim is an attempt to justify the unequal distribution of wealth by creating a state of nature that justifies inequality simply by the introduction of money *before* civil society is created. Locke is here asserting that everyone *consents* to the unequal distribution of wealth. This is to ensure from the beginning that the political order can have no jurisdiction over the question of property rights and justice in regard to distribution.

Civil society is a political structure which, as Hobbes declares, all citizens must accept, a handing over of power to the majority. Why is a civil society created at all?—because of the difficulties of enforcing the consent given to money in the state of nature. Civil society appears as a policing entity—law enforcement—rather than a system of policies that enhance virtue and promote the public good. Civil society has to enforce the natural-law principles present in the state of nature. Civil society cannot override natural law. Locke, like Hobbes, does not see human beings as political beings by nature. This is because the political order is an artificial construct introduced to pacify disputes. Locke's view of the working class is rather severe. Children of the unemployed over the age of three were considered a burden on the society and they should be set to work and made to earn more than their keep. All this was justified on the explicit ground that unemployment is due to moral depravity—a view which apparently anticipates that of Charles Murray.

The views of both Hobbes and Locke had significant influence on ideas of property as commodity in America. Alexander Hamilton is to this view what Thomas Jefferson is to civic republicanism. Hamilton, like Hobbes, assumes that selfishness is basic to human nature, virtue only fit for a kind of artificial utopia. But it is necessary to point out that the idea of virtue was increasingly in low repute in European philosophy because it seemed impossible to stem human passions. According to Albert O. Hirschman, in the 17th century it was thought that normative and moralizing philosophy could no longer be trusted to restrain the appetites and destructive passions of humans.[28] Seeking man "as he really is" became the wisdom of the day. Thus the vice of greed was gradually laundered into its replacement, namely, rational self-interest. Love of gain is rehabilitated as predictable economic activity capable of sublimating and pacifying the passions.

Alexander Hamilton was well conversant with these ideas. He rejected outright the civic republican meaning of property in favor of a commercial one. He writes:

> As riches increase and accumulate in few hands; as luxury prevails in society; virtue will be in a greater degree considered only as a graceful appendage to wealth, and the tendency of things will be to depart from the republican standard. This is the real disposition of human nature.[29]

Hamilton embraced totally the Lockean mercantile view which extended the economic power of the state into the international context, that is, in competition with other nation-states. He recognized a new set of virtues such as energy, ambition, innovation and capability, with the power to stem the destructive passions.

All this relates to the impact of globalization on the relationship between the US and Europe. First, one should recall that the current recourse to commodity property in its neo-liberal form began almost simultaneously in the US and Great Britain. The distance between Ronald Reagan and Margaret Thatcher, conservatives, on the one hand, and Bill Clinton and Tony Blair, denizens of liberal politics, on the other, is not very great. Both sets are adherents to neo-liberalism and commodity property—that is, the political order largely abjuring propriety. Here and there one hears talk of the "Anglo-Saxon disease," what I have called possessive individualism, having priority over the common good. Baroness Thatcher coined a term which has led us to believe that there is no other recourse to the neo-liberal program—the TINA principle: There Is No Alternative. There is no doubt that in the US, the Democratic party, the party of Franklin Delano Roosevelt, has wholly and entirely abandoned the proprietary idea, has adopted the neo-liberal program, and is indistinguishable in this regard from the Republican party. As jokesters are saying, what is needed in the US is not a third party but a second party.

Across the Atlantic the situation is different. There are some clear splits concerning neo-liberalism. An enduring socialist tradition in nearly all the European countries requires a more nuanced approach to globalization. Given the undeniable material facts of competition forcing social and economic changes, policies need to be carried out in some way faithful to what the citizens of those countries expect from a moderate socialist regime. What has emerged is the reformulation of an old idea: the "Third Way" of Tony Blair and the "New Middle" of Gerhard Schroeder—that is, something between "brakeless train" capitalism and state socialism. A previous third-way effort in this direction was the welfare state from the 1950s to the 1970s. It came to an end for a simple reason: the moderation shown by capitalism in relation to labor, social welfare, and progressive taxation was not a *structural* change but *conjunctional*, fitted to the concerns of capital in the immediate post war era (fear of communism, strength of unions and the potential for open class struggle).

The matrix of the Blair-Schroeder program combines the following: new technologies; market driven incentives; higher production and greater competitiveness; supply-side entrepreneurism; innovation; responsibility rather than welfare; equal opportunity as the answer to inequality; increased income for all rather than redistribution.[30] James

Petras has presented a thoughtful critique of this third or middle way. He points out that social inequalities have increased rather than abated; class divisions have weakened labor; tax reductions have flowed to the wealthy; monopolies have skewed competition; families are overworked to compensate for downsizing; political choice is stagnant; budget cuts have impacted negatively on education and job training.[31] In short, globalization has taken the world back to the 19th century in terms of social organization—to a new kind of social Darwinism.

Of all of the European leaders, two stand out as critics of neo-liberalism. Lionel Jospin of France has insisted on maintaining what he calls "the precedence of the state over the economic."[32] This is a theme that has run through this chapter. And Vaclav Havel, the President of the Czech Republic, looks out at the West and sees a "dictatorship of money, of profit; a plundering of the earth; materialistic obsessions; a flourishing of selfishness, etc." He believes that the West should undertake a "moral self-examination," and hopes that perhaps what he learned under the totalitarian regime of the former Czechoslovakia—that politics is doomed if it does not respect moral dilemmas—can be embraced by the West.[33] To my mind, a gulf is opening between Europe and the US, the latter being completely devoted to neo-liberalism based on commodity property, and the other somewhat forced in that direction but trying to maintain some idea of propriety property. Efforts to bridge any gulf must be developed. The possibility of world conflict is real—a Eurasia and the West in opposition. Europe and the US need to rethink their relationship in such a way that they create a world leadership based on moral norms that pertain to the well-being of all nations.

---

[1] Fernand Braudel, *After Thoughts on Material Civilization and Capitalism* (Baltimore: Johns Hopkins University Press, 1977), 64-65. Actually the union of capital and the state goes back to the Italian city states of the 15th century and the United Provinces (Holland) of the 17th century.

[2] Grant S. Alexander, *Commodity and Property: Competing Visions of Property in American Legal Thought* (Chicago: University of Chicago Press, 1997), 3.

[3] Ibid., 2.

[4] D. Shniad, "Globalization Backlash is Serious, Klaus Schwab and Claude Smadja," *Futurework* (futurework@csf.colorado.edu) 17 February 1996: 1-5.

[5] Thad Williamson, "The Real Y2K Crisis, Global Economic Inequality," *Dollars and Sense* 227 (January/February 2000): 42.

[6] Charles Kernaghan, "Sweatshop Blues, Companies Love Misery," *Dollars and Sense* 222 (March/April 1999): 19-21.

[7] Lester Thurow, *The Jobs Letter, 109,* http//.jobsletter. org, (October, 1999).

[8] Richard Barnet, "Lords of the Global Economy," *The Nation* (19 December 1994): 754-57.

[9] Loic Wacquoant, "Penal 'Common Sense' Comes to Europe," *Le Monde Diplomatique-The Guardian Weekly,* 10 April 1999, 11.

[10] Joel Dyer, *The Perpetual Prisoner Machine: How America Profits from Crime* (Boulder: Westview Press, 2000), 1-6.

[11] President William J. Clinton, "The State of the Union Address," *The New York Times,* 28 January 2000, A16-17.

[12] Dyer, 256.

[13] Joseph Shumpeter, *Capitalism, Socialism and Democracy,* 3rd ed. (New York: Harper and Brothers, 1950), 81-86.

[14] Aristotle, "Politics," in *The Basic Works of Aristotle,* ed. Richard McKeon (New York: Random House, 1941), (1153a2-4) 1128-29.

[15] Ibid., (1253a37-39), 1130.

[16] Aristotle, "Nichomachean Ethics" in *The Basic Works of Aristotle,* ed. Richard McKeon (New York: Random House, 1941), (1130a 4-6), 1004.

[17] Aristotle, "Politics" (1257b38-1258a3), 1139.

[18] Thomas Jefferson, *Notes on the State of Virginia* (1785; reprint, New York: Harper Torchbooks, 1964), 157.

[19] The term "possessive individualism" stems from the work of C. B. Macpherson, *The Political Theory of Possessive Individualism Hobbes to Locke* (Oxford: Oxford University Press, 1964). This book is indispensable for understanding the origins of the market society in Britain.

[20] Thomas Hobbes, *Leviathan* (Indianapolis: The Library of Liberal Arts press, 1958), 86.

[21] Ibid., 106.

[22] Ibid., 79.

[23] Thomas Hobbes, *Man and Citizen (De Homine and De Cive)* (Indianapolis: Hackett Publishing Co.,1991), 110-13.

[24] Thomas Hobbes, *Man and Citizen,* 113.

[25] Thomas Hobbes, *Leviathan,* 142-43.

[26] "Man" is used in this instance because in Locke's day, women were not generally considered in relation to property rights (except perhaps as property themselves) [ed.].

[27] John Locke, *Two Treatises of Government* (New York: Hafner Publishing, 1947), 145.

[28] Albert O. Hirschman, *The Passions and the Interests, Political Arguments for Capitalism Before its Triumph* (Princeton N.J.: Princeton University press, 1977), 14-15.

[29] Quoted in Alexander, 74.

[30] See James Petras, "The Third Way: *My and Reality*" in *Monthly Review* 51, no.10 (March 2000): 19-35.

[31] Ibid., 31-35.

[32] Roger Cohen, "Triumphant, The Left Asks What Else It is," *The New York Times on the Web*, 21 November 1999, 4.

[33] Vaclav Havel, "Paying Back the West," *The New York Review of Books* XLVI, no.14 (23 September, 1999): 54.

Chapter 8

North Atlantic Information "Soft Power" and the North-South News Flow

Kuldip R. Rampal

At the dawn of the 21st century, serious questions are being raised by governments, academics and average citizens about the implications of the Information Revolution for the worldwide flow of news and information. For the world long used to an established and predictable pattern of news and information mostly flowing from the developed North Atlantic bloc to the developing South, the Information Revolution was expected to serve as an equalizer in this unequal flow of information. After all, the most revolutionary component of the new information technologies, the Internet, was seen as a truly democratic medium, allowing anyone to disseminate information worldwide with practically negligible transmission costs. Six years after the Internet seeped into people's consciousness across the globe, it is commonly recognized that while it is greatly easier to transmit one's point of view to the other end of the world, how seriously and credibly that point of view is taken is an altogether different matter. In other words, the mere availability of information previously not within reach is not a sufficient factor for it to compete effectively with other information on a common issue. The new information must also be seen to be competing with existing information within the realm of credibility before it can hope to make any significant impression on the information consumer.

The same argument can be made regarding the competitiveness of news and information purveyed by another major component of the Information Revolution—international satellite television. Ever since its live coverage of the Gulf War in 1990, the global popularity of Ted Turner's Cable News Network (CNN) has spawned scores of satellite television channels by many countries interested in taking their view of events to people regionally and globally. But does China's CCTV, seen in the US via satellite television dishes, carry the same credibility that, say, the BBC World Service does across the world? Can the news service of the international channel of Egyptian television compete well with the one provided by Germany's Deutsche Welle TV?

Even when the political factor contributing to the credibility problem is removed, can we say that news programs from satellite channels of two democratic countries—for example, the US, a superpower, and India, a developing country—will carry the same credibility to the global audience? If the answer to these questions were to be "no," then we have to ask the question: What *are* the factors that contribute to the appeal and credibility of information purveyed by international news organizations? This chapter will address this question and examine the implications of the new world of communication unleashed upon us by the Information Revolution.

This revolution began with the introduction of the fax machine in the early 1980s and has progressed through the stages of cable and satellite television, cellular telephony, and the desk top computer-based Internet, with its multi-media appendages such as voice e-mail and digital radio and video. The European Union has recently surpassed the Americans, pioneers in information technologies, by pushing forward to introduce Internet-protocol-based devices such as cellular phones with screens and personal digital assistants that, when combined with Internet access services, effectively allow users to manage their communications any time at any place. With the impending severing of the Internet umbilical cord from the desk-top computer, the Information Revolution is about to come of age.

Because of the ideological and economic appeal of the North Atlantic bloc, and the established credibility of its news organizations, the new information technologies provide additional "soft power" to the North to further its ideological objectives in the developing South.

"Soft power," as defined by Joseph Nye, Jr., a Harvard University international relations theorist, is

> the ability to achieve desired outcomes in international affairs through attraction rather than coercion. It works by convincing others to follow, or getting them to agree to, norms and institutions that produce the desired behavior. Soft power can rest on the appeal of one's ideas or the ability to set the agenda in ways that shape the preferences of others.[1]

Theories of International News Flow

Several studies have identified and explained the factors that influence the flow of news and information globally. Galtung found that there is a "center-periphery" pattern in the flow of international news where news flows mostly from the "center," or dominant countries, to the "periphery," or dependent areas. These theoretical constructs are related to communication and cultural interactions between nations, and Galtung points to vertical interaction as the major factor in the inequality of nations, a division reinforced by "feudal networks of international communication" dominated by nations in the "center."[2]

A study by Kariel and Rosenvall supported this theory by concluding that the "eliteness" of a nation as a news source was the most important criterion for news selection.[3] The authors referred to Schramm's definition of elite nations as a "group of highly developed countries which are also dominant in world politics."[4] The term "elite" also describes the relative standing of a nation in the eyes of others.[5] Kariel and Rosenvall found a statistically significant correlation between the amount of trade between two countries and the number of news items about the two countries in each other's media, as well as between the gross national product of a country and the number of news items appearing about that country in another country's media. But the highest correlation was found between the elite ranking of a country and the number of items about that country appearing in the media of nations ranked lower on the scale. The authors described this correlation as both statistically significant and substantively important.[6]

A study by Hester concluded that at any given time, the nations of the world have designated places in an international pecking order. Perceptions of positions in that order partially determine the flow, direction and volume of information. This study also noted that strong economic relations or cultural affinities increase the flow of news among nations, as does the perception of threat between any two nations.[7] Another theory suggests that news flow is vertical from developed countries (the North Atlantic) to developing countries (the South), with supplemental horizontal flows within the North and within the South, although flow within the latter is substantially lesser in volume. Also, while a good deal of news flows from South to North, it tends to be significantly less in volume in comparison with the flow from North to South.[8]

These theories would place the US, the major countries in the European Union (Germany, Great Britain, France and Italy), and— outside the North Atlantic bloc—Japan as the elite countries for political and economic reasons in the hierarchy of nations. Keohane and Nye, Jr. argue that ideological and material success of a country makes its culture and ideology attractive.[9] They note that America's popular culture, with its libertarian and egalitarian currents, dominates film, television and electronic communications. Germany, Britain, France, Italy and Japan reflect the same attributes, although to varying degrees. When the "language" factor is added to the factor of elite standing, the US and Britain acquire particular significance. Clearly, English is the most widely spoken international language in the world, which facilitates and promotes the spread of values and culture from these two countries. It is no coincidence, therefore, that the standards and architecture of the new information systems, like the Internet, are built around the English language.

The use of the French language in several parts of the world would similarly enables France, another of the elite North Atlantic nations, to spread its values and culture. The language factor may inhibit the media "soft power" of Germany, Italy and Japan around the world, something that at least Germany is very much aware of in view of the fact that one-third of its daily programming on DW-TV for the global audience is broadcast in English.

Theory of Information Credibility

Much research has been done over the years to determine the factors associated with credible information. After more than 50 experiments, Yale University's Program of Research on Communication has identified and explained several factors which contribute to information credibility.[10] They are: a) The communicator, b) The message, c) The audience, d) The interaction. Some of the key findings are as follows.

A credible communicator is one who is seen to be "trustworthy," "expert" and "likeable," and a communicator who is perceived to have had a history of providing credible information will have an edge over a new communicator. Unsurprisingly, communicators or information sources perceived to be biased and unfair have low credibility. Presenting both sides of an issue is more effective with those who are well educated or initially opposed, and it makes little difference whether the pro or con arguments are presented first. In fact, two-sided presentations tend to inoculate against future counterpropaganda. Moreover, audience interaction is a much more effective way of changing opinions than passive participation, such as merely listening to a program on a radio or reading a news story or editorial. Klapper, in his study on the effects of mass media, concluded that all face-to-face contact is more persuasive than radio, which, in turn, is more effective than print. Television and films probably rank between face-to-face communication and radio, but this latter point has not been empirically demonstrated.[11]

Elite Standing, Credibility and Media Dominance

It is easy to understand within the framework of these news flow theories and information credibility factors why dominant media players in the world have been, and continue to be, from the major North Atlantic countries. The elite position of the US, Great Britain and France is clearly a factor in the global dominance of print, audio and video news services from these countries, but what needs to be explained is why other elite nations—Japan, Germany and Italy—do not have international news organizations with a similar level of presence. After all, Japan and Germany are stronger economically than Britain and France when measured in per capita income levels, and Italy is economically strong enough to be a member of the G7 group of industrial nations.

One explanation to this anomaly in media presence could be offered within the context of one measure of credibility discussed earlier—that a communicator with a history of providing credible information will have an edge over a new entrant in the marketplace of ideas. Up until the end of World War II, Japan, Germany and Italy all had controlled and officially directed media systems, which were known globally more for their propaganda activities than for any credible journalistic endeavors. The US, Britain and France, on the other hand, have had long-standing pluralistic democratic political systems predicated on the values of rule of law, human rights, and religious freedom, among others. The media systems that emerged within the framework of these values showed commitment to the journalistic values of accuracy and objectivity sooner rather than later, which contributed towards consolidating their credibility. In the US, for example, journalistic objectivity has been a tradition for almost 150 years, while the BBC, under the direction of John Reith, built up a world news service in the late 1920s under tenets of objectivity[12] amidst propaganda from fascist and Nazi movements in Europe. This same news service has been called "Britain's gift to the world" by UN Secretary-General Kofi Anan.

Since the perceived elite standing of a nation combined with the perception of credibility of a media organization from that nation are the necessary factors to the attractiveness of that news organization globally, we can see why North Atlantic news organizations are dominant while those from other major countries are only marginal players. It will take a long time for the media of Russia, a one-time elite nation in the form of the "superpower" Soviet Union, to get over the legacy of Marxist propaganda that was the hallmark of the Soviet media, including TASS, its global news agency. China may be an up and coming economic power, but its media are still state owned and used to purvey only the government version of domestic and world affairs, just as the media did in the old days of the Soviet Union. Democratic India's media are doing much better in the realm of objectivity, but India is a developing country so its media do not yet have the appeal or financial resources to compete with the news organizations of "elite" states. Indonesia, another large country, has only recently emerged as a democracy from more than 30 years of authoritarian rule, so it will be a long time before its media make an impression globally.

Indeed, even as the democratic wave has spread around the world since the collapse of the Soviet Union, less than half of the world's nations had democratic political systems in 1999. The New York-based Freedom House, which annually publishes a report on the status of civil liberties and press freedom around the world, said in its 1998-99 report that 88 of the world's 191 countries (46%) were rated as "Free," meaning that they maintain a high degree of such freedoms. Although this is the largest number of free countries on record, the remaining 54% continued to deny or substantially limit political and civil rights, and personal and press freedoms to their people.[13]

Given that educated people around the world are interested in accurate and reliable information on domestic and international issues, they are likely to turn to international news providers when their domestic news organizations cannot provide such information because of limited news gathering resources or government controls. Keohane and Nye, Jr. note that news organizations in the US, Britain and France have capabilities for collecting intelligent information that dwarf those of other nations. "Information power flows to those who can edit and credibly validate information to sort out what is both correct and important.... Brand names and the ability to bestow an international seal of approval will become more important."[14] North Atlantic news organizations have both the brand names and the international seal of approval because of the elite positions and credibility factors mentioned before. To reach such a status, emerging news agencies will have a lot of catching up to do before they can compete with the established North Atlantic news agencies such as the Associated Press (US), Reuters (UK), the BBC, Agence France-Presse, The *New York Times* News Service, and CNN International, among others.

The "Soft Power" Factor in North Atlantic Media Dominance

At the surface level, it would appear that news organizations from the North Atlantic are dominant globally because they have the financial, personnel and technological resources to provide news and information services that countries in the South cannot provide. On a more substantive level, however, the dominance of North Atlantic news organizations has to do with their coverage of international affairs in a fairly unbiased manner within the context of their countries' pluralistic, liberal and secular values. Conflicts over competing ethnic, religious, or national identities often escalate as a result of propaganda campaigns by demagogic leaders around the world, who also go to great lengths to suppress dissident political movements. News organizations from the North typically strive to provide unbiased reportage on these issues and expose false reports. They also promote the values of democracy and market economies, and frame the coverage of international issues in a manner that promotes these ideals and other Western interests. Such coverage historically has been able to engage the suppressed people from the South whenever they have had unrestricted access to North Atlantic news organizations. That is where the "soft power" dimension of these news organizations lies.

For example, Lawrence E. Magne, the editor of *Passport to World Band Radio*, attributed the BBC's "vast international audience" to its "objective news." He added that "one reason it's so powerful is because it is credible."[15] Indeed, when a sample of secondary-school educated people in four Egyptian cities were asked, "How believable is the BBC's coverage of international issues?", the results confirmed widespread credibility. The answer "Always" received 39%, while "Usually" received 58% and "Seldom" received a mere 2%.[16] Even in democratic India, audience research has shown the BBC's strong appeal as a news source. A 1986 study in Calcutta found that the BBC was considered to be the best source of news, as compared with all home and other foreign stations.[17] Indeed, studies have shown that in several countries, BBC news is held in greater credibility than the native radio newscasts. The Voice of America also has a significant credibility abroad. For example, in China, the VOA audience, which is typically about 17 million daily, went up to an estimated 100 million during the 1989 Tiananmen pro-democracy movement because of its extensive and reliable coverage of the movement.[18]

North Atlantic news organizations are also the suppliers of most of the non-local news appearing in the media of the South. The AP, Reuters and AFP control the bulk of the world's news flow, with their daily output of about 25 million words. The next five leading news agencies account for only 1.09 million words daily.[19] Several academic and professional studies since the 1960s have shown that the South depends on the news agencies from the North, both print and broadcast, for over 75% of the general world news and even news of geopolitical regions in the South.[20] As a result, people in the South are forced to see each other, and often even themselves, through the medium of news agencies from the North Atlantic.

Many critics in the South say that the North Atlantic media dominance confines judgments and decisions on what should be known, and how it should be made known, into the hands of a few news organizations. However, the South's efforts to develop its own viable newsgathering organizations with global appeal have not amounted to much because of a lack of financial and professional resources, as well as political ideologies that are not always conducive to purveying accurate, objective and impartial journalism.

The ability of the dominant media of the North Atlantic to set the agenda on what issues are important and how these issues should be framed has been a source of its soft power for many years. Coverage of the Gulf War provides a relatively recent example. Keohane and Nye, Jr. argue that when Iraq invaded Kuwait in 1990, the fact that CNN was an American company helped to frame the issue worldwide as aggression. Had an Arab company controlled the world's dominant TV channel, perhaps the issue would have been framed as a justified attempt to reverse colonial humiliation.[21] The agenda set by the North Atlantic media was said to be largely responsible for creating public opinion worldwide, including practically all of the Arab world, in favor of the US-led invasion of Iraq to reverse the "aggression."

By the same token, the Kosovo situation in Yugoslavia was framed by the North Atlantic media primarily as a violation of Muslim Kosovars' human rights by Christian Serbs, setting the stage for NATO's unilateral intervention in early 1999 even though no such move was endorsed by the United Nations. The Yugoslav government had viewed the Kosovo Liberation Army as a terrorist separatist movement bent on snatching away a part of its territory. In a clear recognition of the soft power of the North Atlantic media, Dr. Cedomir Strbac, the Yugoslav ambassador to India, wrote, "The very idea of the two channels with the widest reach in the world [CNN and the BBC World Service] being the tools in a war game is profoundly disturbing."[22]

A 1999 research study gives credit to the Voice of America, the BBC World Service and, especially, US-sponsored Radio Free Europe and Radio Liberty stations for keeping the spirit of democracy alive during the Cold War in the Eastern European satellite states and the Soviet Union. This study also notes that during the Tiananmen Square massacre in 1989, democracy activists hooked VCRs to hotel satellite feeds and taped CNN's images to circulate across the country. Fax machines were used for communication with the outside world despite the efforts of a powerful state apparatus.[23] The Communist government in Beijing was also concerned enough about the influence of the BBC World Service channel on its people that it forced Rupert Murdoch to end this service, provided through his Hong Kong-based STAR-TV, in 1994 in return for a commercial concession. A year earlier, Murdoch had told a shareholder meeting that satellite television was "an unambiguous threat to totalitarian regimes everywhere."[24]

In January 1998, four days before Pope John Paul was due to leave for a visit to Cuba, both the BBC World Service and CNN highlighted a story of 15 Cuban dissidents brought to Rome by an Italian human rights organization. The dissident group reminded the Pope to keep Cuba's human rights abuses on his agenda in his talks with President Fidel Castro. Castro released about 300 prisoners, including more than 70 political prisoners, as a goodwill gesture after the pontiff's groundbreaking trip to the island.[25]

Another example of North Atlantic media framing global issues in such a way that it advances Western objectives comes from the coverage of President Bill Clinton's trip to South Asia at the time of this writing. Even though in their separate interviews with *Newsweek* magazine in early March 2000, Indian Prime Minister Atal Bihari Vajpayee and Pakistani leader Gen. Pervez Musharraf ruled out the possibility of nuclear confrontation between the two countries,[26] practically every major North Atlantic news organization was warning of such a danger. The lead focus of stories on Clinton's trip, even before the president had made any statement upon his arrival in India, was on the necessity of India and Pakistan to curb their nuclear weapons programs and sign the Comprehensive Test Ban Treaty. Such a focus by the news organizations was presumably influenced by the concerns of Western governments ever since the testing of nuclear devices by India and Pakistan in 1998. Meanwhile, US Secretary of State Madeleine Albright, who has been one of the major critics of India and Pakistan's nuclear programs, raved about India's knowledge economy in a speech to the Washington, D.C.-based Asia Society on March 14, 2000, four days before Clinton left for India. She went on to describe India as one of the unreported economic success stories of the 1990s.[27]

Conversely, Nye, Jr. and Owens explain what can happen when the North Atlantic does not actively use its soft power to deal with crisis situations, such as that occurring in Rwanda in 1994, when mobs of the Hutu majority led by soldiers and militia systematically put to death up to a million minority Tutsis and politically moderate Hutus. They argue that information campaigns to expose hate propaganda in Rwanda could have prevented one of the most intense bouts of killing in history:

> A few simple measures, such as suppressing extremist Hutu radio broadcasts that called for attacks on civilians, or broadcasting Voice of America reports that exposed the true actions and goals of those who sought to hijack the government and incite genocide, might have contained or averted the killing.[28]

"Soft Power" in the Age of the Internet

The Internet has revolutionized the instrument of soft power and the opportunities to apply it for the elite nations of the North Atlantic. There are several reasons for this development. First, unlike the traditional mass media, which could be barred from entering countries hostile to information campaigns from the North Atlantic, the Internet is practically impossible to control. Blocked Web sites can simply change their Web addresses. Internet users in a country imposing controls can also dial into a server outside their country and access the desired information. Given the global nature of the Internet, content can be published from anywhere in the world. When a government tries to prosecute a content provider or force the withdrawal of material, there are others around the world prepared to copy or mirror the information on their own sites, in countries where the information is legal.

Secondly, although costs are negligible for anyone wishing to disseminate existing information via the Internet, the collection and production of new information often requires costly investments. The US, Britain and France have capabilities for collecting quality information and intelligence that are rarely within the grasp of other nations. Thirdly, the massive amount of information available in cyberspace may not have much credibility for an educated individual unless it is processed and packaged professionally, and has a seal of approval associated with internationally-known and valued information suppliers, most of whom are based within in the North Atlantic power bloc. Editors, filters, interpreters, and cue-givers become more in demand, and this is a source of power for the North.[29]

Fourthly, the very low cost of information transmission has opened the field to networks of non-governmental organizations and even individuals. These networks are particularly effective in penetrating states without regard to borders and using domestic constituencies to force political leaders to focus on their preferred agendas. The democratic, elite states of the North Atlantic find these networks natural allies in promoting their ideological and other objectives abroad.[30] Finally, whereas the traditional media provide only a one-way communication to the receiver of information, the Internet, as the only true interactive mass medium, allows the receiver to choose information selectively to meet specific needs and provide immediate feedback. Interactivity allows for the development of new virtual communities—people who imagine themselves as part of a single group regardless of how far apart they are physically from one another—and helps coordinate action across borders.

These attributes of the Internet combined with its explosive growth over the last several years make it a formidable instrument of soft power for the North Atlantic, and, to varying degrees, for other countries of the world. In February 2000, about 200 million people worldwide were subscribing to the Internet, including 100 million in the US.[31] One billion people—one-sixth of the humanity—are expected to be using the Internet by the year 2005, two-thirds of them outside the US. A key reason for the Internet's rapid growth is that countries rightfully see it as an important tool for strengthening their economies and reaching out to their populations in the 21st century. Therefore, it will become difficult for authoritarian regimes to reconcile political controls with the increasing role of the Internet in the future.

It is not surprising then that among the first to use the Internet were human rights organizations in the North Atlantic bloc. They include Human Rights Watch, Human Rights Internet, Human Rights Interactive Network, the Carter Center, Amnesty International, the Institute for Global Communications, and NetAction, among others. These Web sites are powerful tools for increasing human rights awareness around the world and collecting signatures to launch worldwide campaigns. The San Francisco-based Institute for Global Communications, for example, offers to host Web pages and e-mail addresses for human rights activists. Its mission is to advance and inform movements for peace, economic and social justice, human rights and environmental sustainability around the world by promoting the strategic use of appropriate computer networking technology.[32] Another human rights group, the New York City-based Human Rights in China, posted a comprehensive report on its Web site in September 1999, revealing a nationwide system of arbitrary detention in the country. The report made a number of recommendations to the international community, including the UN, to express concern about the use of arbitrary detention in China.[33] At the time of this writing in March 2000, the US was getting ready to sponsor a resolution at the UN meeting on human rights in Geneva condemning China's human rights record.

Several examples illustrate the support provided by the North Atlantic governmental or non-governmental organizations for activities promoting human rights and democracy around the world. In June 1997, Chinese dissidents founded *Tunnel*, a Chinese language journal of dissent managed and edited in China. Once an issue is ready to be published, it is secretly delivered to the US and then e-mailed back to China from an anonymous address. "Thus its staff remains safely hidden in cyberspace, and all of its contributors, both in China and abroad, write under pseudonyms."[34] In Indonesia, bypassing the government-controlled television and radio stations, dissidents shared information about protests by e-mail, inundated news groups with stories of President Suharto's corruption, and used chat groups to exchange tips about resisting troops and bringing democracy to the country. After more than 30 years of authoritarian rule, Indonesia finally turned democratic in 1999.[35]

During the Kosovo crisis in 1998-99, a pro-democracy radio station in Belgrade, Radio B92, was shut down by the authorities. The station put its programming on the Internet through RealAudio, using a Dutch service provider. Radio Free Europe, the Voice of America, and Deutche Welle picked up the station off the Internet and rebroadcast it back into Serbia, where it served as the source of independent reporting and a focal point for democratic opposition. Faced with this strategy, the government allowed the station back on the air.[36] This example also illustrates the creative ways available on the Internet to disseminate information around the controls of censors.

US-sponsored Radio Free Europe and Radio Liberty, which have long campaigned for democracy via the airwaves, now also use the e-mail to disseminate information to a dispersed audience very inexpensively. In Brazil, when an Indian tribe was threatened, the Internet carried news of the threat and sparked pressure on the Brazilian government that generated a change in policy. Similarly, US-based non-governmental organizations supporting rebels in Chiapas used the Internet to forestall the bloody reprisals they expected from the Mexican government.

Other computer-assisted approaches, such as fax-casting and e-mail, are also being used effectively by individuals and interest groups to engage in political discourse. As of August 1998, one service identified 29,000 Internet Relay Chat (IRC) channels, 30,000 Usenet newsgroups, and 90,095 mailings lists—each one representing a network of individuals worldwide interested in a particular subject. An overwhelming majority of these discussion groups were conducting their activities through North Atlantic Internet servers.[37]

Authoritarian and semi-authoritarian governments, worried about the effects of freewheeling political discussions by Usenet groups on their people, have taken steps to stem the tide of such discourse. *The New York Times* reported in early 1999 that in China, "Hundreds of agents are reportedly being trained to sniff around inside companies and universities for objectionable Web sites and subversive messages."[38] The government has used firewall technology to try to block access to scores of Web sites it deems objectionable, including *The New York Times* and CNN. "But savvy users here know how to use proxy servers or other techniques for circumventing the firewall," the news story said. On February 1, 2000, the Chinese government strongly criticized a White House report on US global leadership objectives in the 21st century. "To lead the world is the same thing as seeking global hegemony," a Chinese government spokesman said, adding that

> America would achieve its goals through the use of 'soft forces'—the Internet, film, television, books, capital and consumer products—which would be backed up by the 'hard forces' of its military seen in the 1991 Gulf War and the bombing of Yugoslavia last year.[39]

Two important conclusions emerge from the foregoing discussion. Firstly, a nation's appeal to people around the world and its influence in world affairs is dependent on its elite standing, meaning its ranking in the pecking order of nations. The elite standing itself is dependent on the ideological, economic and military strength of a country. Either because of their inherent appeal or because of their proven success, the ideological and economic values that have emerged as having the strongest appeal around the world are pluralistic democratic political systems and market economies, such as those of the North Atlantic bloc. It is also obvious that strong countries built on these values manifest quite liberal social and cultural values as well, which further add to the attractiveness of such nations.

All of these factors converge to establish the elite standing of a nation, a necessary prerequisite to meet before its say in world affairs can carry a significant weight, or "soft power." The US, Britain and France have been the pre-eminent large elite nations in view of their long-standing commitment to liberal ideological, economic and socio-cultural values, and their military strength. It is little wonder, then, that the largest export from the US is its information and cultural products, bringing $60.2 billion in revenues from abroad in 1996. This writer, having traveled to some 25 countries, has seen first-hand the huge presence of American, British and French information and cultural products. As other countries reach the level of development of "elite" nations, no doubt, there will be greater competition for "soft power."

Secondly, those who had assumed that the Internet would have a leveling effect on the unequal flow of information between the North Atlantic and the South are finding that it will take more than just a heavier flow of information from the South to the North to address the imbalances. The South must also match the credibility associated with major news and information suppliers from the North Atlantic before it can hope to see an equitable international communication order it has advocated for years. And, as we have seen, credibility is rooted in a firm discipline of information gathering and packaging, a discipline that can be developed only in democratic nations with press freedoms.

---

[1] Joseph Nye, Jr., *Bound to Lead: The Changing Nature of American Power* (New York: Basic Books, 1990), 15-16.
[2] Hamid Mowlana, *Global Information and World Communication* (New York: Longman, 1986), 24-26.
[3] Herbert G. Kariel and Lynn A. Rosenvall, "Factors Influencing International News Flow," *Journalism Quarterly* 61, no. 3 (Autumn 1984): 509-516.
[4] Wilbur Schramm, *Mass Media and National Development* (Palo Alto, Calif.: Stanford University Press, 1964), 58-59.
[5] Kariel and Rosenvall, 511.
[6] Ibid., 513. These figures are, respectively, 0.586, 0.469, and 0.845.
[7] Al Hester, "International Information Flow," in *International and Intercultural Communication* (New York: Hastings House, 1976), 248-49.
[8] Mowlana, 25.
[9] Robert O. Keohane and Joseph S. Nye, Jr., "Power and Interdependence in the Information Age," in *Foreign Affairs* 77, no. 5 (September/October 1998): 86-87.

[10] Shearon A. Lowery and Melvin L. DeFleur, *Milestones in Mass Communication Research*, 3rd ed. (White Plains, NY: Longman, 1995), 165-88.

[11] Joseph T. Klapper, *The Effects of Mass Communication* (New York: Free Press, 1960), 108-9.

[12] Roger Milner, *Reith: The BBC Years* (Edinburgh: Mainstream Publishing Co., 19830), 158-251.

[13] Adrian Karatnycky, "A Good Year for Freedom," in *Freedom in the World: The Annual Survey of Political and Civil Liberties* (New York: Freedom House, 1999), http://www.freedomhouse.org/survey99/essays/karat.html.

[14] Keohane and Nye, Jr., 88-89.

[15] "Candor Becoming a Staple of Shortwave," *The New York Times*, 19 March 1989, 18.

[16] USIA Research Report, *Media Use by the Better-Educated in Four Egyptian Cities,* (Washington, D.C.: Office of Research, USIA, 1984), 40. The other possible answers were "Never" and "Don't know."

[17] Kuldip R. Rampal and W. Clifton Adams, "Credibility of the Asian News Broadcasts of the Voice of America and the British Broadcasting Corporation," in *Gazette* 46, no. 2 (1990): 101.

[18] "The Voice of America Has Won the Ear of China," *The New York Times*, 9 May, 1989, 4.

[19] Howard Frederick, *Global Communication and International Relations* (Belmont, CA: Wadsworth Publishing Co., 1993), 128.

[20] Mowlana, 28-29.

[21] Keohane and Nye, Jr., 91.

[22] Cedomir Strbac, "Rebirth of Goebbels," in *The Hindustan Times*, New Delhi, India, 10 April, 1999, 5.

[23] Akshay Joshi, "The Information Revolution and National Power: Political Aspects," in *Strategic Analysis* 23, no. 6 (September 1999): 1004-1052.

[24] China Welcomes Murdoch in From the Cold," in *The Age*, Australia, 12 December 1998, http://www.theage.com.au/daily/981212/news/news16.html.

[25] "EU Welcomes Prisoner Releases in Cuba, Seeks More," Reuters news story, 24 February 1998, URL http://www.fiu.edu/~fcf/eunion22498.html.

[26] "Tense Words, Tough Talk; India's Prime Minister Atal Bihari Vajpayee," and "Tense Words, Tough Talk; Pakistan's Gen. Pervez Musharraf," in *The Washington Post*, 12 March, 2000, B01.

[27] "Remarks by Secretary of State Madeleine K. Albright to the Asia Society," DC, 14 March 2000, http://www.asiasociety.org/speeches/albright3.html.

[28] Joseph S. Nye, Jr., and William A. Owens, "America's Information Edge," in *Foreign Affairs* 75, no. 2 (March/April 1996): 32.

[29] Keohane and Nye, Jr., 89.

[30] Ibid., 83.

[31] BBC World Service, "World Business Report," 14 February 2000, http://www.bbc.co.uk/worldservice/worldbusinessreport/.

[32] "About IGC Internet," http://www.igc.org/igc/gateway/about.html.

[33] Human Rights in China Web Site, "New Study Reveals Nationwide System of Arbitrary Detention," September 1999, http://www.hrichina.org/reports/cleanup.html/Recommendations.

[34] Regardless of Frontiers Web Site, "Global Internet Liberty Campaign," http://www.cdt.org/gilc/report.html, 9.

[35] Ibid.

[36] Ibid.

[37] Ibid.

[38] "In China, the Internet Is Double-Edged," in *The New York Times*, 10 February 1999, 1.

[39] "China Accuses U.S. of Seeking to Dominate the World," in *The Hindustan Times*, India, 2 February 2000, http://www.hindustantimes.com/nonfram/020200/detFOR02.htm.

Chapter 9

"The Fourth Stage": Transatlantic Changes in Adult Education[1]

Tamás Kozma

"Globalization" has been a catchword in the educational and education policy literature throughout the first part of the 1990s. In Eastern Europe, however, it is more than a catchword. "Globalization" has become an umbrella concept in the education policy discourse that has collected various influences—some of them contradictory—and has channeled them into the transition debates. Educational conservatives use "globalization" to point out unacceptable changes such as identity crisis, demythologization of (national) histories, and overflow of international capital that destroys the former (socialist) welfare systems. Fundamentalists, therefore, suggest an educational policy of recentralization with state controls on curriculum and student flow. Conversely, education liberals use "globalization" as the signal for necessary modernization in education and the educational system. They interpret it as a sign of all necessary and positive changes in education and society. The positive interpretation covers privatization, market incentives, decentralization, and competitiveness. Those ideas lead the education systems into further expansion and growth.

Globalization or Expansion?

The term "globalization" was first used by economists, and adopted by educational studies in the late 1980s. By the mid 1990s it had already become the focus of attention, with educationalists often arguing that there is a causal relation between global education and economics. According to this viewpoint, the globalization of education is the most intensive where it overlaps with the global economy. This is especially visible in vocational training. The relation is obvious: internationally standardized technologies need internationally standardized modes of production. Workers in a global economy must have the same educational background, which means that vocational training should be the same in all parts of the global economy.

Some have concluded that, while we might identify differences in the vocational *training* of different countries, we will find none in the *results* of vocational education. Differences may originate from the varied cultural backgrounds of the workers, but the basic, preparatory stages of vocational training must somehow connect these varied cultures with the standardized modes of global production. An international standard will necessarily influence the forms of education that prepare for vocational training—namely, primary and secondary education. Thus, in a great chain reaction, global standardization in vocational training impacts upon elementary education all over the world. Just as, at the beginning of the 19th century, the culture of colonizers influenced and unified educational systems in the underdeveloped parts of the world, at the end of the 20th century the technologies of globalized production have had the same influence. Local labor markets likewise connect to each other and—gradually and spectacularly—become unified. The globalized labor market has led to the assimilation of local cultures into one another, aided by the rapid globalization of information, communication, and transportation. Local cultures fade away as the vocational and non-vocational cultures gradually become similar.

The scenario outlined above became well formulated in the past decade. It can be argued, however, that such conclusions are based more upon speculation than upon research. The story has advanced to such an extent that analysis or follow up seems unnecessary; perhaps this is why there are so few empirical studies or statistical analyses to support such conclusions. One might well *believe* that education is under the process of globalization, but one can scarcely document it.

There is one area, however, where there *have* been basic studies for 20 years, and this is in the *expansion* of education. Some researchers have closely related it with globalization, as if expansion were the inevitable result of globalization. Others—especially those who had identified expansion in education before the 1980s—tend rather to consider the expansion of education a self-controlling phenomenon that occurred (or would have occurred) regardless of globalization. Those of the latter view—myself among them—have long thought that education expands because it produces its own "market"; that is, we ourselves educate people who "further consume" the products of education. Expansion has already been defined in several ways—entering different stages of education, credentialism, "overconsumption" of educational products, "overeducation," and so on. Studies by such scholars as J. W. Meyer et al., J. E. Craig, M. S. Archer, and Ferenc Jánossy[2] all indicate that expansion in education preceded most of the rhetoric of globalization.

As higher education in particular develops into mass education, it has closer and closer connections with the whole educational system of a country. This process is revealed etymologically: the aristocratic and reserved university was once considered "higher education" in educational discourse; today, it is promoted (or degraded) as "tertiary education." The ongoing transition from elite into mass education suggests that, in the future, expansion will not stop with the "conquest" of the tertiary stage: the market will create its own "fourth stage."

The Definition of Adult Education

In the 1990s the transatlantic estimation of adult education changed radically. Studies such as Savicevic's comparison of European and American systems reveal an image of adult education as a kind of alternative education.[3] In this sense adult education is a matter of justice, compensating for exclusion from education by a selective and elitist school system.[4] This function of adult education, at least in Europe, has a long history and is rooted in the political schools of the labor movement. The studies of the 1960s and 1970s clearly reflect the alternative character of adult education as education of the oppressed.

Another definition is "community" education, which began in the US in the 1930s. Community education integrates adult education with the social, economic, and political problems of the community, and the resolution of these problems.[5] The trends of urban education connected adult education with alternative education. For example, deschooling movements, such as those in Latin America, have concentrated on adult education and reject forms of institutional and governmental education that indoctrinate the young. Alternatively, some European movements consider adult education as *integrated* into lifelong learning.[6] They show how the traditional forms of adult education (in-service education, civil movements, initiatives of the church) constitute one continuity. In this sense the role of adult education is not compensation and justice, but rather a lengthening of the formal school system.[7] While community adult education in the 1930s was organized around the institution of elementary education, today, to our surprise, the locus is not an elementary or secondary school, but often the university or college of the region.

At the end of the 1990s there is an urgent transatlantic question: to what extent is the university, or higher education in general, open to adult education? European forms of adult education have started to integrate in one system—their radical, oppositional character is diminishing but their pragmatic and integrative features are more evident—hence the common European governmental policies that aim towards integrating the traditionally isolated forms of adult education into a national system, or recasting them as "lifelong learning."[8] I want to emphasize that these processes of expansion in higher education do not necessarily mean the expansion of traditional institutions. The great mass of people do not head for the universities in the most developed areas of the Atlantic region, but rather towards other forms of post-compulsory, post-secondary education. These two trends—the expansion of the non-traditional institutions of higher education and the integration of adult education into lifelong learning—really do coincide. In this sense the "fourth stage" is an emerging reality.

The Fourth Stage

Mass education, then, will continue to expand beyond the frame of formal education and, following the tertiary stage, will involve a fourth stage, which is now the most varied section of adult education on both sides of the Atlantic. The fourth stage may take on numerous definitions: the traditional "adult education"; "layered education" (alternating periods of work and education regularly); "recurrent education" (returning to education again and again from work); "lifelong learning"; "continuing education" (meaning that education would be permanent in the adult age). Recurrent education was formulated in Sweden, continuing education has conservative roots in France, and lifelong education was introduced by the British Labour Party. Thus, the aim of these forms of education was originally to complement, equate, or at least efface the memories of discriminatory educational systems. My object is not to investigate the differences of meaning between these terms—they are only mentioned to illustrate how diffuse and diverging this emerging interest has been. Undoubtedly, a new element of education has appeared: education out of school, besides school, parallel with it, or following it. In one sense the phenomenon is not new; but it has not yet been related to the expansion occurring in national systems of education.

In Europe, at any rate, the attributes of the welfare state and expansive policies of education, healthcare and social care seem to have come to a standstill as a consequence of neo-liberal economic policy. In such a corporate climate, adult education has attracted increasing interest under different names such as "personnel and in-house training," "in-service education," and "workplace education." In the 1980s the impression was that in-service training might take over some of the educational budget of the impoverished "welfare states" which had traditionally supported continuously expanding education (however under-funded, per capita). For the first time since World War II, international finance experts were seriously proposing tuition fees for secondary education. While this never came to pass, tuition fees became more common in tertiary education, especially in the European state sector. Curiously enough, "adult education," which had nearly been forgotten since the 1970s, met with renewed interest in the 1990s, and not only in theory. In Eastern Europe, for instance, alongside the educational expansion that was integrated with economic and political restructuring, in-service training started to flourish as never before. Clearly, then, the market for training and education is expanding in most North Atlantic countries. Here students represent demand—they are clients and the tutoring institution or person is the supplier. While the actors in politics and experts try to match diminishing state resources with the continuously growing needs of citizens, this network formulates the new stage of education: the fourth stage, owing to the functioning market of education.

One great problem in gathering evidence and statistics concerning the fourth stage is that most educational statistics are based on institutions rather than on the participants of education. In addition, evidence about the fourth stage will not generally be found in the educational statistics but rather in different databases, such as those in human resources; and of course their aim in gathering information is not the analysis of trends in education. As a result, my data is necessarily partial, and more research needs to be done at a broader level. However, it is useful to analyze some illustrations below.

Figures 1 and 2, taken from an ongoing European study, illustrate the number of participants on Ph.D. programs in Hungary and Finland. The S-curve (logistic curve) can be clearly seen representing the first, stagnant phase of growth. In each country the curve formulates in the same way, in spite of the numerical differences for the given years.

These two figures point to my supposition that in the next two decades postgraduate education will follow a similar trend to that of tertiary education, which has already become mass education.

Fig. 1.   **The numbers of new Ph.D.s in Finland**

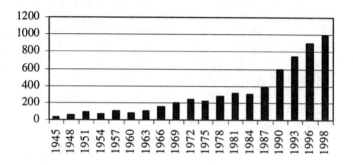

Fig. 2.   **The numbers of Ph.D. students in Hungary**

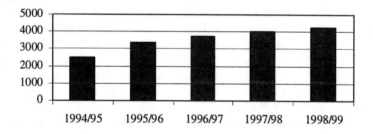

The second illustration (Figure 3) shows participation in adult education in a chosen year: 1997. This data is taken from an OECD publication on human resources (*not* on the institutions of education). It represents only one chosen year so it is inadequate in forecasting trends. Because the information was not gathered from the field of education, the structure of information is different, and countries are different. It must be said that questions concerning education in human resources were not common among researchers in this field until the last decade. Nonetheless, this example well illustrates the phenomenon of fourth stage expansion.

Fig. 3.

Participation in adult education according to certification of education (%)

Source: OECD - Human Resources Canada,
Paris 1997.

- ☐ elementary
- ▨ lower intermediate
- ■ upper intermediate
- ■ post secondary
- ■ university

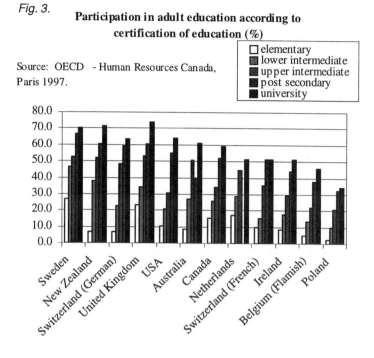

Figure 3 shows the qualifications of participants in adult education in different countries, that is, what percentage of people with elementary, secondary, or higher education certificates participated in adult education in a given country. I have divided secondary and tertiary education and separated those with "lower intermediate education" from those who obtained the certificate of secondary education; furthermore, I have separated those with a university diploma from those with a certificate of some other form of higher education. The figure shows data of 12 countries on both sides of the Atlantic—seven European and five non-European countries.

We can see the following: the higher the level of education in a country, the higher the rate of participants in adult education. The statistics of four North Atlantic countries (Sweden, Switzerland, Great Britain, and the US) separate quite clearly from the others in this sense. Conversely, in countries where a larger proportion of the population share a lower level of education, there is less participation in adult education.

As I have said, at the end of the 1990s both the role and the character of adult education changed on both sides of the Atlantic—at least in the developed countries. Previously it had a kind of complementary or compensatory role, to do justice for those who had been rejected from an unjust or elitist system of education, whether for social or economic reasons. The above data suggests that adult education has this complementary role even today, especially in countries with high rates of immigration. Nevertheless, the complementary and equating function of adult education has visibly diminished today. Since the late 1990s, the character of adult education is that it is dominated by participants with higher education. The data of the above mentioned developed countries makes this clear. We can see that the character of adult education in the North Atlantic region is basically different from elsewhere. The rate of participants with higher education in adult education is growing; the rate of less educated participants is decreasing. The main function of adult education is no longer to complement formal education, but to continue and complete it.

When one considers the earlier function of adult education, one might expect the opposite. If the function of adult education is to compensate for social injustice—and given the democratic reforms whereby secondary education becomes general and higher education expands—it is reasonable to expect a decreasing role for adult education in developed countries. There is no evidence of this in my statistics. On the contrary, we can see adult education flourishing, continuously expanding throughout the whole of society as the level of education increases. These statistics, then, lead us to the conclusion that in parallel with the expansion of higher education, a new stage—a fourth stage—is formulating in education. The prototype of it is what we still call "adult education."

If we turn to the case of the less developed countries of the Atlantic region, we see that, here, both functions of adult education— compensation for educational injustice *and* extending education—are present. The evidence of Poland is a case in point (see Figure 3). Of all the countries shown here, participation in adult education is at its lowest in Poland (the Flemish community of Belgium shows similar results). Here, too, the highest number of participants in adult education have already gained some form of higher education. It is clear, as well, that the proportion of those with secondary education is higher than that of those with elementary education. On the basis of this data, we can conclude that the rate of participants with elementary or secondary education has recently changed in Poland. If this conclusion is correct, it means that the data of 1997 shows different countries at different levels of the same trend: Sweden or Switzerland have gone further than Ireland or Poland down the road of formulating a new type of adult education. But the trend itself is undeniable: adult education is less likely to be the activity of people who only have an elementary education; increasingly it aimed at people with higher education.

The data from Hungary completes this explanation (Figure 4). The data shows how both the number of participants in out-of-school courses (that is, those not organized through the state education system) and the inhabitants' level of education change in Hungary between 1949 and 1996. The figure shows that the inhabitants' level of education increased dramatically in this period. In Hungary, illiteracy is around 0%; 20% of the population have completed secondary education; and more than 10% have completed higher education. It is clear as well that the number of course participants rapidly increased between 1960 and 1982. The data from Hungary does not contradict, but rather validates the claim that the increasing level of education there is due to an increasing number of participants in adult education. Statistical data regarding course participation also shows that adult education swallows up people with higher education, even if some forms of adult education are not necessarily or originally designed for them.

Figure 5 shows how the tendency of these processes changed in Hungary between 1960 and 1980. Mass participation in course education emerged in Hungary around the 1970s (and it is similar to the tendencies elsewhere in the Atlantic region). Figure 5 is especially significant in that it shows how the educational rates of self-employed workers and paid employees changed in the period. In 1960 obviously more workers participated in training courses, but by 1970 the rates had reversed. Yet as the rate of course participation increased among active earners, so too did the rate of employees increase. (In 1982 nearly all employees took part in training courses, and the rate of workers decreased to some extent). The reason for the changes in the rates of participation in adult education was not the retention of more and more workers, but rather because more and more employees participated. The character of the training courses and the target groups changed in Hungary, too, between 1960 and 1980.

Again, this data is necessarily incomplete, but it is sufficient to illustrate my supposition that in the Atlantic countries where secondary and tertiary education have expanded, a new, further stage of education is formulating. At the moment we conditionally call it "the fourth stage" of education in the future.

Fig. 4.   **Level of education and the numbers of course participants**

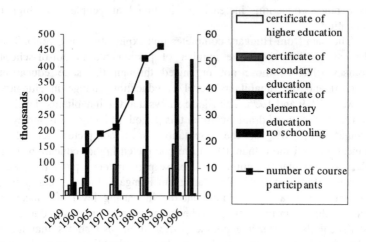

Fig 5. **The rising proportions of active earners completing training courses between 1960 and 1982**

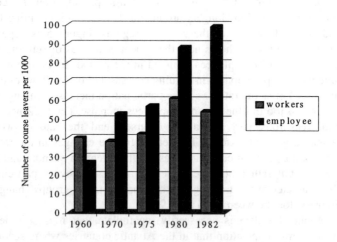

A Dynamic Process

The development of the fourth stage is accelerating. The expansion of elementary education took centuries in the European societies; 150 years passed until elementary education became general and illiteracy was restricted on the continent. The labor movement demanded the expansion of secondary education for the first time around World War I (they argued for eight years of compulsory schooling instead of four or six years). These demands became general on the continent between the two world wars, but the general expansion of secondary education did not occur until after World War II. In the end it took only half the time that was necessary to expand elementary education and restrict illiteracy. In Eastern Europe, the expansion of the higher education began in the 1960s; in Western Europe, the 1970s. The expansion of tertiary education has reached the East (at present, about 40% in Hungary) while in the West the tertiary stage has effectively expanded into general education. It has taken about 40 years. Furthermore, if my supposition is right, expansion of the fourth stage is coming. If the cultural and pedagogical ideologies of adult education in the 1970s are the prototypes, then it has taken twenty or thirty years.

Supply and demand in the education and training market determine the real structure of the system. This means that adult education, on the supply side, is developing from a movement into a profession, while on the demand side, it is becoming a regular station of one's career life, rather than merely a personal achievement. The formation of the fourth stage is perhaps driven by the fact that vocational training is extricating itself from the formal system of education whilst at the same time increasing in educational status. Initially, vocational training was the poor relation in secondary education; now it is somewhere between secondary and tertiary education, and it is visibly moving closer and closer to the tertiary stage. As a result, the role of the institutions of traditionally tertiary vocational education—high schools and colleges— is changing. As they become preparatory and theoretically founding institutions, they have less opportunity to fulfill the role of developing up-to-date knowledge and skills. Moreover, they are no longer expected to do so by students or the economic actors. Instead, both expect high-level preparation (foreign languages, information technology and the like), and this can be the basis for the employer to train the employee in what is necessary for the actual job.

The changes in life and work how the fourth stage is being structured. These changes affect many Atlantic countries and their speed is accelerating. Basic features include decreasing population numbers, the fact that the economically-active period in one's career life is getting shorter, while at the same time people are living longer and generally experience better states of health. If we consider these facts from a traditional point of view, we might consider them some of them as problems (loss of population, the crises of traditional communities and families, fewer children, growing numbers of the elderly, new needs for social care, new needs for spare-time activities, typically old-age health problems like depression, etc.). Yet it is possible to see new uses and functions for education in such a restructured transatlantic society. In the traditional societies of the 19th and 20th centuries, the most important role of school was the socialization of children and the preparation for their involvement in the distribution of work. Now school has an increasingly important role in keeping and activating the older generations. In the past, for societies on both sides of the Atlantic, the child or the youth was the prime "human capital"; increasingly, the lengthened life career and the accumulation of experience will be important resources, and thus the reactivation of the elderly will be key.

The impact of immigration is also an important issue, one that will demand extensive consideration elsewhere. We might ask how the expansion of education will change in the future, if, for instance, a country like Hungary is to encounter mass immigration, as is predicted. This leads to a further question: what will be the relation between the fourth stage in particular and a nation's basic immigration policy? There would be not only children but young adults, as well, among the immigrants—people who are active earners. They will have to get acquainted with their new economic, political, and cultural surroundings. Under these conditions there will be a clear need for the fourth stage of education not only because the level of education increases, but also because—and this will be more important—the cultural background of a nation's immigrants will be only partially adequate for what they have to know in their new location. If this prediction comes true, the social need for the fourth stage of education across a range of countries will be stronger than ever before. Here in Hungary, as elsewhere in the Atlantic region, we await the answers of educational policy.

[1] This chapter is based on a research project sponsored by the National Scientific Research Fund of Hungary (OTKA T-20246). The author wishes to thank Tamás Híves, Gabriella Pusztai, Imre Radácsi and Gabriella Zsigovits for their contributions. However, the author alone remains responsible for the contents of this chapter.

[2] See J. W. Meyer et al., "World Expansion of Mass Education, 1870-1970," *Sociology of Education* 65 (1992): 128-49; J. E. Craig, "The Expansion of Education," *Review of Research in Education* 9 (1981): 151-213; M. S. Archer, ed., *The Sociology of Educational Expansion: Take-off, Growth and Inflation in Educational Systems* (London: Sage, 1992); and F. Jánossy, *A gazdasági fejlodés trendvonala és a helyreállítási periódusok* (Budapest: Közgazdasági, 1966).

[3] J. Reischmann et al., *Comparative Adult Education* (Ljubljana: Slovenian Institute for Adult Education, 1999).

[4] M. Mayo, *Imaging Tomorrow: Adult Education for Transformation* (Leicester: National Institute of Adult Continuing Education, 1997).

[5] F. Colley, "Community Adult Education" (Conference manuscript: ERIC ED361491, 1993); and B. Brennan, "Fourth Education Sector" (Conference manuscript: ERIC EJ1498527, 1994). The latter author inspired the title of this chapter.

[6] P. Jarvis, *Adult and Continuing Education: Theory and Practice* (New York: Routledge, 1995).

[7] Woodrow and Crosier in P. Alheit and E. Kammler, *Lifelong Learning and Its Impact on Social and Regional Development* (Bremen: Donat Verlag, 1998).

[8] U. Giere, *Adult Learning in a World at Risk: Emerging Policies and Strategies* (Hamburg: Unesco Institute of Education, 1996).

Part Three:
Popular Culture and the Arts

Chapter 10

Seaside Tourism in the 19th and 20th Centuries: Some Transatlantic Comparisons[1]

John K. Walton

The seaside holiday or beach vacation has been a great British cultural export, almost on a par with soccer. It was an invention of the 18th century which spread from its island home to mutate into diverse variations on its central theme in different settings across the world, becoming big business and promoting cultural change, social conflict and environmental problems wherever it went.[2] As befits a phenomenon with transforming powers over lifestyles, landscapes and local (if not regional and even national) economies, seaside tourism has attracted its historians, despite the condescension of those (on both sides of the Atlantic) who remain wedded to a traditional agenda based on high politics, diplomacy, the "great thoughts of great men" and those aspects of big business which produce goods, massage markets and generate direct conflict between the forces of labor and capital.

Geographers, sociologists, economists and anthropologists were quicker on the scene, however, and form the backbone of a fledgling "discipline" of Tourism Studies which in turn pays little heed to the past, except where theme-park allusions to nostalgic or titillating aspects of it can be harnessed to the remaking of tired old resorts at the wrong end of the product cycle.[3] The history of the seaside and its associated health and pleasure regimes has been pursued mainly on a country-by-country basis, too, with a strong and (in practical terms) understandable bias towards local case studies. Thus, international comparisons are in short supply, despite the still-growing importance and ubiquitous nature of beach tourism at the turn of the millennium; transatlantic ones are rarer still, although opportunities present themselves promisingly in both Anglophone and Hispanic settings.[4] As a result of this gap, this chapter focuses on comparisons between seaside tourism in Britain and the US and in Spain and Argentina between the early 19th century and World War II.

The timing of beach resort development varied between countries and within them, as the sea-bathing fashion spread outwards from England and changed its form and expression as it became assimilated to differing cultures. This set of practices was promoted by entrepreneurial British medical men from the early 18th century, and from the 1750s onwards it spread rapidly to affect scores of places along the extensive English coastline by the early 19th century. The growth of a summer holiday "season," ostensibly focused on therapeutic sea-bathing, brought new life to decaying ports and fishing settlements and stimulated the founding of new, purpose-built bathing-places. The visiting public expanded from aristocrats and landed gentry to embrace growing numbers from the proliferating middle ranks of commercial and industrial Britain, while the speed and cheapness of rail travel from the 1840s helped to extend the market still further. Growing numbers of the industrial working class were finding their way to the coast in the second half of the 19th century, first as day-trippers, then as visitors staying for a week or more. England and Wales alone had perhaps 150 seaside resorts by the World War I, and expansion continued through the inter-war years, with growing emphasis on sunshine, fresh air and exercise alongside the "pleasure palaces" and fairground amusements which had been proliferating in the larger popular resorts since the late 19th century.

The sea-bathing fashion took hold rather later on mainland Europe, beginning on the North Sea coast in France, Belgium and the Netherlands from the 1780s, with considerable direct British influence. The French wars interrupted its progress, but bathing resorts were taking root across northern Europe as far north as Sweden by the turn of the century. Southern Europe was slow to follow suit, and medical orthodoxy recommended the strong, cold, invigorating waves of the North Sea and Atlantic, rejecting the enervating, malarial environment of the tideless, effeminate Mediterranean.[5] When the sea-bathing fashion came to Spain, it took root on the Atlantic coast, especially along an arc which followed the Bay of Biscay from the French frontier to Santander. Its arrival in the late 1820s, at San Sebastián, came at one or two removes from the English origins of the previous century, mediated through the French aristocracy; and as a Spanish resort system developed hereabouts from the mid-19th century onwards, the visitors and those who catered for them had a limited awareness of the British origins of sea-bathing, taking French and Belgian resorts from Biarritz to Ostend as their reference group.[6] This engendered interesting cultural differences which had transatlantic consequences.

Beach tourism in the US emerged later than in England, although transatlantic cultural transfer was quick enough for Boston and Philadelphia to acquire their own sea-bathing resorts during the 18th century, and by the 1830s Newport, Rhode Island was catering for affluent visitors from both northern cities and southern plantations.[7] It was not until the second half of the 19th century that development really accelerated even in New England, however, with large-scale development on the New Jersey shore (from Atlantic City downwards) and a proliferation of little resorts catering for sharply-defined niche markets on islands and inlets.[8] Here at least claims that the American seaside was more democratic than the British were not borne out: they were challenged not only by Methodist resorts' efforts to keep out the ungodly, but more pertinently by hierarchies of snobbery which made the comfortably well-off aware of where on the resort ladder their holidays and second homes should be fixed. Anti-Semitism was present (also a common groundswell in English commentaries on resort life), and when blacks found themselves able to enjoy Atlantic City in the late 19th century, they were quickly corralled into their own part of town.[9] New York's Coney Island probably came closest to the ideal of democratic *bonhomie*, but England's Blackpool, whose visitor numbers marched in step with it in the late 19th and early 20th centuries, could make equal claims.[10] The geographical chronology of American settlement also meant that new areas of virgin coastline were opened out at later stages than in England: the emergence of seaside southern California in the late 19th century, and the development of Florida from the early 20th century, are the most spectacular examples.[11]

Developments in South America came later still, usually following Spanish rather than Anglo-Saxon models (despite the strength of British cultural influences in several capitals), and showed a marked concentration into the larger places. By the early 20th century, however, every Latin American country with a coastline had its sea-bathing resorts, many of which were marine suburbs of coastal cities. Montevideo was well to the fore by the 1870s, as its beaches catered for summer visitors from Argentina as well as Uruguay.[12] Valparaiso in Chile also had its marine suburbs by this time, and Rio de Janeiro's beach resort areas were developing by the turn of the century, although Copacabana's population of just under 18,000 in 1920 left it far short of the status it had attained by 1970 as one of the world's most heavily-populated urban areas, fueled by high-rise apartment construction since the 1940s.[13] Venezuela and Mexico were slower to acquire recognizable seaside resorts, and Acapulco, for example, was a product of the 1920s onwards.[14] Here, of course, the influence of the US soon made itself felt, as it did, for example, in Cuba, with Havana as transatlantic cultural melting-pot and enticing "other" for Americans in search of transgressive pleasures and money-making opportunities.

But the biggest and (for many years) most fashionable beach resort in Latin America was Mar del Plata, whose career began in earnest with the opening of the railway from Buenos Aires in 1886 and the concomitant development of the Hotel Bristol. It had a census population of 37,000 by 1924 and 120,000 by 1947, when "social tourism" was making the resort accessible to the working classes, and trade unions were opening special accommodation for their members. Here was one of the world's most well-frequented specialist beach resorts; by mid-century it was said to be attracting a million visitors per year. However, it developed significantly later than its peers in Europe and the older settlements of North America, and drew on Spanish rather than British, French or North American influences, although not all contemporaries were convinced of this.[15] Not only did Mar del Plata develop into one of the world's largest and most popular beach resorts, but it also provided an unusually free and easy bathing regime, which formed one of several bases for a critique of its allegedly demoralizing influence on Argentine society, as we shall see. But first we need a context for this critique.

As sea-bathing developed commercially, beaches became arenas of contention between "nature" and "culture," as the dictates of the developing medical specialism of "thalassotherapy" sought to specify the rhythm, nature and duration of the bathing experience and the ambience which should surround it. Private entrepreneurs and local governments modified shorelines for the comfort and convenience of the visitors, and rules were laid down to prevent bathers' behavior from giving offense. What these rules should be, where lines should be drawn and how enforced, raised a particularly vexed set of issues: the seashore was an intermediate space whose ownership was often itself problematic. Sea-bathing itself entailed undressing and personal exposure which ran against the grain of a self-conscious "civilizing process" which expected growing levels of self-restraint, urbanity, fashion-consciousness and the following of consensual codes of acceptable behavior. The beach environment, on the other hand, invited relaxation and the embrace of more "natural," less inhibited mores which might themselves be seen as healthy and worthwhile; and these contrasting perceptions, which were visible on both sides of the Atlantic, posed problems for those who needed to define what constituted proper behavior on this uncertain territory.[16]

These tensions were bound up with the marketing of the developing resorts, which needed to combine images of respectability and relaxation, formality and control in acceptable but varying mixtures of emphasis.[17] New fashions in both bathing dress and street clothing made the mixing of the sexes on the shore more generally acceptable, while the beach became a place for sociable gossip, picnics and children's play as well as—or instead of—the site for a controlled, limited therapeutic encounter with the waves. The rise of the cult of sun-bathing and the vogue for fresh air and outdoor exercise after World War I brought renewed conflict over the morality of laying bare and even showing off parts of the body which had hitherto been taboo, and religious influences (especially, where it was powerful, those of the Roman Catholic Church) became embroiled in controversy.[18]

European bathing regimes in general went through a phase of increasingly tight regulation, at least on paper, from the later 18th century to the end of the 19th, after which there followed a period of relaxation which coincided with the rise of sun-bathing and the development in many of the larger resorts of open-air sea-water baths with extensive accommodation for spectators. Furthermore, during the 1920s and 1930s, the "bathing beauty" became an appropriate icon of resort publicity. This evolution ran parallel with the rise and fall of the bathing-machine, a wooden box on wheels in which the bather was expected to change into a hired costume and then be drawn into the water by a horse. A "modesty-hood" could be lowered to give a completely enclosed space for therapeutic ablutions. Timid or uncertain bathers might be "dipped" by bathing attendants who were schooled in the medical requirements of the nature and duration of immersion. Bathing areas were segregated by sex, but even so, in many places bathing-costumes were required to cover most of the body. Such regulations were imposed with increasing elaboration by seaside municipalities from the mid-19th century onwards.[19]

This was a pattern common to 19th-century England and Spain, although with interesting variations in the detail, and across most of Northern and Western Europe. Some north German and other Baltic settings were much less restrictive, as the British communist Harry Pollitt found when he visited the new Soviet Union in 1921. Stopping off on the way at the Baltic port of Libau, he saw sun-bathing and naked bodies for the first time on the local beach, where he remembered "a man well over 6 feet in height, stark naked, swinging a cane and smoking a huge cigar as he strolled along the shore."[20] Such self-confidence could bring trouble when exported, as two German visitors to the Belgian resort of Knocke found in 1929 when they were imprisoned for three months for walking naked along the beach.[21] This illustrates the dangers of generalizing too readily about pan-European bathing cultures; but bathing was regulated in the interests of modesty and decorum, as well as safety, right across the continent's Atlantic coasts, although in France and Belgium, for example, mixed bathing from machines, cabins or tents was much more common. The regulations regarding costume and supervision at Ostend did not inhibit local artist James Ensor from producing a remarkable panoramic painting of the fashionable bathing beach at high tide, which featured an interesting cast of voyeurs and a wide range of alfresco sexual practices, both in the sea and in some of the bathing-machines.[22]

As regards Britain, however, John Travis has argued convincingly that although strict regulations might exist on paper, they were in practice honored more in the breach than in the observance even at the height of official Victorian prudery, so long as a modicum of discretion was observed. Municipalities needed to be seen to have bathing regulations in place, and it was in the economic interests of bathing-machine proprietors to secure a measure of enforcement; but in practice the significant number of middle-class Victorian men who wanted to bathe unencumbered were able to bathe in the early morning, or at low tide, and braved the stares (censorious or prurient) of watching ladies as they emerged unrepentant from the waves. As families began to enjoy the beach for picnics, shrimping and sandcastle-building in the later 19th century, the relaxation of bathing mores became increasingly widely tolerated. Such changes in official attitudes ran in step with a move away a narrowly therapeutic, medically-policed view of bathing to a broader acceptance of enjoying the sea as a pleasurable environment.[23] In the inter-war years bathing-machines gave way to cabins, while "mackintosh bathing" (covering a bathing costume with a raincoat for the short walk to the beach), and even changing on the beach itself while protecting modesty with a towel, tended to go unmolested. In many of the larger and more popular resorts, open-air sea-water bathing-pools or "lidos" opened during the early 20th century, and public bathing became an acceptable spectacle. Watchers who had paid for admission outnumbered the bathers in their municipally-approved costumes, and expert swimmers showed themselves off on the new diving boards, while officially-appointed lifeguards policed the pools. Some controversy continued when the rise of sun-bathing helped to encourage a trend to skimpier costumes, but general fashion trends were marching in the same direction. By the mid-1920s, according to Nigel Yates,

> the more adventurous female bathers were wearing costumes resembling a vest and shorts in cotton or wool, flexible enough to permit the serious swimming in which emancipated women were anxious to indulge[24]

It was not until the later 1930s, however, that it became generally acceptable for men to bare their chests, abandoning "their full costumes for the shorts or trunks worn by Hollywood film stars." Women, meanwhile, were moving on to new "stretch swimsuits made from elasticized fabric and the first two piece costumes had been introduced." The bathing beauty's journey from dubious postcard to municipal advertising might stand as symbol of the wider transformation in attitudes to the representation of the female body. The bathing-machine disappeared into oblivion, and parliamentary campaigners for the maintenance of restrictions received short shrift from ministers and civil servants who preferred to extend free trade principles to popular pleasures.[25]

The Spanish case was broadly similar in outline, but interestingly different in detail. This does not just apply to the oxen which drew the bathing-machines at San Sebastián or the closed chairs like wickerwork sentry-boxes (an idea borrowed, it seems, from Belgium or the Netherlands) in which bathers at Santander sheltered from the sunshine as they acclimatized themselves to the marine environment The social life of the more developed beaches came to center on the *balneario*, a wooden and later more permanent building which provided changing cubicles, hot and cold showers and baths, drying facilities, a covered promenading, relaxing and viewing space, and in its more sophisticated incarnations, a bar, restaurant and dance-floor. Developments of this kind sprang up along the Atlantic coast of northern Spain from the late 1860s onwards, with regular rebuildings and upgradings in the larger places. Just as the bathing beach more generally was sectioned into male and female areas, so the *balneario* was similarly divided, and the wearing of bathing dress was frowned upon in the more formal eating and entertainment areas. Quite strict rules governing the segregation of the sexes and the protection of modesty were brought in as soon as the San Sebastián bathing season began: a municipal code of 1839 laid out the details and the penalties, after an earlier code of 1826 had said nothing about the issue. These were reinforced and modified by regular edicts from the mayor, as was the case at Santander, where the first surviving code was issued in 1846. Special municipal police forces were allocated to the beaches to keep order, protect property and uphold a vision of public decency which prescribed sexual segregation and modest bathing dress.[26]

In practice, however, as in Britain, the Spanish bathing beach was a more relaxed area than these requirements would seem to indicate, at least for those who could afford to enjoy its amenities in comfort. In the middle decades of the 19th century, in San Sebastián at least, restrictions were only enforced during the fashionable bathing period in mid-morning. This was itself a distinctive feature of Spanish as compared to British practice, and it remained important even as the bathing hour eased back towards lunchtime over the years. Moreover, the bathing-machines were rarely trundled all the way to the sea, and this meant that women in bathing-dress, which often clung to the contours of the body after immersion, became the objects of a devouring male gaze from the promenade and along the beach. This was reinforced by the transition to bathing-cabins in the 1920s, but even before this move took place, a cartoon of 1916 from Santander shows the demarcation between the bathing areas reduced to an imaginary and permeable line across which men and women exchanged looks and conversation. By this time the beach had become more a sociable gathering-point for families in their street clothes, with picnics, children's games, sporting activities and flirtations, than a place whose identity was based on bathing as such. Social status was becoming as important as gender in reading the beach, and San Sebastián's La Concha, was described in 1913 in terms of a steadily ascending gradient from plump, comfortable bourgeois families at the town end to fashionable gilded youth around the *balneario* of La Perla del Océano, culminating in the splendors of the royal bathing-machine, a turreted construction in the Moorish style which ran on rails. All who were unable to keep up appearances were frozen out, and working-class bathers were banished to the perils of the river estuary and the unfashionable eastern beach of Gros, with its dangerous currents.

At San Sebastián as at Santander, segregation between the sexes went almost unenforced by this time, although an area was set aside for women who wanted to avoid masculine eyes. The main discordant element arose from the fashion for sun-bathing, and the related tendency for bathing dress to become fashion-led and expose more of the body. This was much more controversial than in Britain, and began earlier, with a male fashion for tanning and displaying the body causing comment by 1918, and skimpy female bathing-suits generating outraged comment from Catholic moralists soon afterwards, culminating in ferocious attacks on the immoralities of the beach in religious publications of the mid-1930s. Sun-bathing was confined to certain areas, but the protests made little headway otherwise, although they were part of a general disaffection among the religious Right. Such aspects of the leisure revolution of the 1920s and 1930s, and as such formed an important if neglected part of the background to the outbreak of the Spanish Civil War in 1936.[27]

The European politics of the beach and of bathing lack serious parallels in the US. Here, the beach was a much more relaxed pleasure environment from an early stage, with much frolicking and little regulation. Mixed bathing was the norm rather than the exception, and the bathing-machine failed to impose its regime on American beaches. Many visitors merely left their belongings on the sand, even where changing-rooms were available for hire, and informality extended to the promiscuous mixing of excursionists and longer-stay visitors, wage-earners and the wealthy, on the same democratic stretches of shore. To escape such contact, the snobbish had to escape to elite resorts which sought to exclude the inferior by cutting off their means of transport. Accounts of beach life at resorts such as Atlantic City in the later 19th century feature mixed parties gamboling and performing elaborate dance steps in the surf. Single people of both sexes found the atmosphere conducive to holiday romance, and kissing in public was entirely acceptable, in complete contrast to the situation in most of Europe. Applegate's Pier even had a "Lover's Pavilion." Similarly, beach society at Coney Island was marked by informality of dress, horseplay, dramatic poses for the camera, and exhibitionism. As befitted this free-and-easy sociability between the sexes, the fashion cycle in beachwear became important much earlier here than in Europe, for men as well as women. Not for nothing was Hollywood the model for the belated appearance of bathing trunks at the English seaside.[28]

To judge from two early-20th century critiques of its bathing mores, however, Argentina's Mar del Plata went even further as an example of the New World celebrating shoreline liminality and casting aside the inhibitions of the old. The journalist José Zorrilla's general commentary on the Mar del Plata season in 1913 emphasized the resort's unusual mixed bathing arrangements, whereby families would subscribe to a *balneario*, on the Spanish model, and organize the beach aspect of their holiday around it. Some ladies and young girls did completely cover their bodies and feet (which were clearly perceived as highly-charged erotic objects), but at least as many wore short bathing-dresses and went barefoot, exposing themselves to the concupiscent gaze of lustful men. There was no need for the binoculars which were often deployed at European bathing resorts, and to make matters worse, ladies from Buenos Aires high society were featured, recognizably, in beach undress on postcards showing *"grupos de bañistas."* Zorrilla complained that exhibitions of the female body, which would be prohibited in theaters and concert-rooms, were tolerated on the beach; and he quoted from a musical comedy song (a *zarzuela*): "Don't display your calves on the beach, because there are many sharks near the shore." But he recognized that most women were prepared to take, or even enjoy, this risk, and that it was widely believed that segregating the sexes would reduce the popularity of bathing and of the resort.[29]

Much more outspoken, ten years later, was Jaime Alfonso de Guzmán y Clarafuente. As part of a wholesale moral critique of the Mar del Plata season, he inveighed against *"desnudismo"* on the beach, which was much more dangerous for women than for men, as "no woman who undresses does so innocently." The bathing system encouraged lust, undermined female virtue, and threatened marriage and the Argentine way of life:

> The new woman which the bathing resort has given us, is a hybrid and unmanageable creature with an anarchic idea of freedom, professing feminism as a liberation rather than a way of integrating herself into society. She does not resolve to be, within her sphere, a public and private collaborator with a husband. She wants equality with men... By this route, little by little, she comes to hate men.[30]

This apocalyptic denunciation was part of a much wider critique, whose virulence perhaps owed more to the initial assumptions and expectations of the commentator than to a genuinely more sexualized and liminal beach culture at Mar del Plata as compared with, say, Atlantic City. Bathing itself was anyway becoming less important to the recreational life of developed seaside resorts in all four countries by this time. Guzmán y Clarafuente complained that modern civilization had invented the "bathing resort in which bathing itself is not the first essential": if visitors danced, drank and played roulette with appropriate panache, it did not matter if they did not bathe, so long as they showed themselves off in a bathing costume for two hours a day.[31] Already in 1865 the Santander newspaper *El Verano* commented satirically,

> To take a sea-bathing cure, it is sufficient just to visit a resort, stay there for twenty, thirty or more days, promenade, find entertainment, inhale the fresh breeze and think about the marvellous effects of bathing. But actually to bathe? To get even slightly damp? Not a thought of it...[32]

Such trends were universal as "artificial" attractions proliferated in all the larger resorts towards the turn of the century, especially in England and the US, causing euphoria in some quarters at this evidence of rising material living standards, but dismay in others. The growing obsession with pleasure-seeking and conspicuous consumption at the seaside was part of a wider perceived problem of the seaside resort, as vector for the importation of dangerous foreign ideas, corrupter of morals and underminer of virtuous national and provincial cultures, which were being articulated in several settings in the early 20th century. Guzmán y Clarafuente's critique of Mar del Plata was a particularly telling example.

For Guzmán y Clarafuente, Mar del Plata as it had evolved by the early 1920s threatened to destabilize the whole of Argentine society. He provides a flawed but sophisticated analysis of the nature of resort society and the problems to which it gave rise:

> Sociologists assert that frontiers are places of diminished morals. This is due to natural causes, like the hatred which the inhabitants of different regions bear towards each other and their discrepancies in feelings and ideas, and to artificial ones like the customs regulations which are the origin of smuggling and piracy. The fact is that no frontier city can ever have the dignity and moral worth of a city situated in the middle of a nation.... The resort can be considered similar to the frontier city. In the resort, too, different kinds of people are gathered and mixed together and it is not always possible to differentiate between the adventurer who plays dangerously at roulette and the respectable man who lives moderately and goes to the seaside to bathe... It is on the seashore that the roles of morality are weakened and relaxed to the point where they resemble those which govern men in frontier cities.[33]

Having thus anticipated (albeit with a different moral agenda) arguments which were to be advanced by academics in sociology and cultural studies 60 and 70 years later (the seaside resort as "place on the margin," liminal space where rules are relaxed and the carnivalesque can run riot, and anonymous setting in which visitors are free to posture, display themselves and try out new identities), Guzmán y Clarafuente proceeded to attack the influence of Mar del Plata on Argentine virtue and identity. The hectic pleasures of Mar del Plata undermined morals, the due subordination of the woman within the family, the physical health of the visitors (through over-excitement and over-indulgence), and the future of the race, because they undermined the capacity of women to bear "useful children," instead of which they would produce "seaside resort children," physically and morally enfeebled. And here there was a strong transatlantic agenda, fuelled by his own direct experience of European resorts, which seems to have been widely shared among Latin American elites.[34] Mar del Plata was an exotic implant from Europe, "another invention of the disreputable Europeanism" which had filled Buenos Aires with vile buildings and threatened to undermine the agrarian virtues of Argentina as a new country which needed to carve out its own civilization, ridding itself of European snobbery and decadence. It raised the specter of Anglo-Saxon or Russian immorality and social collapse: the Russian revolution, after all, had been caused by the aristocracy's addiction to casino gambling in European beach resorts. The Ocean Club, with its casino and tango dancing, involving an immoral level of bodily contact between the sexes, was particularly disreputable, a focus of Anglo-Saxon corruption with its drink and dancing and jazz bands. Here the target broadened to include the US: "We are not *yanquis*, and we must live the way we are." But the main focus was on Europe: "Mar del Plata, as a bathing resort, is not an Argentine city. It is a beach resort of decadent Europe." Montevideo showed similar symptoms. The only way forward was to turn Mar del Plata into a truly Argentine resort reflecting the national virtues rather than imported European vices. How this was to be achieved was left unclear.[35]

A similar critique in San Sebastián, aiming at the defense of "traditional" Basque virtues and Christian values from the worldliness of summer visitors from Madrid and European high society, shared such views of the beach resort as a damaging site for social change, bringing external fashions to corrupt the innocent locals—the other side of the coin from those who saw the diffusion of new fashions and "civilized" habits as healthy signs of progress.[36] Such critiques focused particularly fiercely on casino gambling and all the vices that were held to accompany it, from prostitution to suicide and bankruptcy; and this was a strong theme across Europe, although roulette and related activities were unthinkable at the English seaside until the late 20th century. In Belgium, for example, there was furious debate over the legitimacy of casino gambling in Ostend and Spa, which took up a considerable amount of parliamentary time.[37] But here the arguments developed within European societies, without the overt agenda of transatlantic corruption that we see in Mar del Plata. The same applies to the bootlegging, vice, gaming and racetrack frauds which came to be associated with the American seaside (as well as other locations) from Florida to Coney Island at various points in the 20th century.[38]

There was, however, an important flow of debate in the reverse direction: the alleged Americanization of the British seaside, and especially the popular northern resort of Blackpool, from the 1930s onwards. But this was at the level of popular culture and reflected a suspicion of imported commercial entertainment that Guzmán y Clarafuente might have recognized. In a British context, this meant the elite suspicion of the subversion of healthy, earthy, participative popular culture by an alien leisure capitalism. This was, for example, the core of J. B. Priestley's 1934 critique of Blackpool's amusements, despite his own status as radical "middlebrow." The traffic in fairground innovations between Coney Island and Blackpool's Pleasure Beach was part of this story, as Lancashire working-class holidaymakers were regaled with the "Monitor and Merrimac" American Civil War naval battle show. But other commentators stressed the continuing autonomous vitality of indigenous popular entertainment at the British seaside, and a more plausible (though still oversimplified) rendition of inter-war Blackpool presents it as a pole of northern English popular culture, set against the metropolis, the "south" and all the pejorative assumptions that might be attached to those "other" identities.[39]

And thus to conclude. As befits a speculative first venture into transatlantic comparison, this chapter raises more questions than it can hope to answer. Yet what it does do is provide a series of case studies that get beyond the local. Attempts to generalize across continents have to take account of a variety of experiences within a very broad common framework, and in this case approaches to transatlantic comparison are cross-cut by cultural similarities which link the Anglophone societies on either side of the water together, and by others which are shared by the Spanish-speaking nations. This makes for richer but more complex analysis where transatlantic crossings and pairings are embraced, rebuffed, and incorporated in ways that were not, perhaps, at first apparent.

[1] The author would like to thank Fran Dawbarn for making him aware of Mar del Plata. He takes responsibility for all translations from Spanish in the chapter.

[2] J. Towner, *An Historical Geography of Recreation and Tourism in the Western World, 1540-1940* (Chichester: Wiley, 1996), Chapter 7; L. Lencek and G. Bosker, *The Beach: the History of Paradise on Earth* (Harmondsworth: Penguin, 1999).

[3] R. Shields, *Places on the margin* (London: Routledge, 1991); Tony Bennett, "Hegemony, Ideology, Pleasure: Blackpool," in T. Bennett et al. (eds.), *Popular Culture and Social Relations* (Milton Keynes: Open University Press, 1986); J. Fiske, *Reading the Popular* (London: Routledge, 1989), Chapter 3.

[4] R. Lewis, "Seaside Holiday Resorts in the United States and Britain," in *Urban History Yearbook* (1980), 44-52; J. V. N. Soane, *Fashionable Resort Regions* (Wallingford: CAB, 1993); J. K. Walton, "The Seaside Resorts of Western Europe, 1750-1939," in *Recreation and the Sea*, ed S. Fisher (Exeter: Exeter University Press, 1997), 36-56; J. K. Walton, "Seaside Resorts and Maritime History," *International Journal of Maritime History* 9 (1997): 125-47; J. K. Walton, "Leisure Towns in Wartime: the Impact of the First World War in Blackpool and San Sebastián," *Journal of Contemporary History* 31 (1996): 603-18; J. K. Walton, "Consuming the Beach: Seaside Resorts and Cultures of Tourism in England and Spain," in *Tourism and Consumption in Modern Europe*, eds. E. Furlough and S. Baranowski (University of Michigan Press, forthcoming); H. Meller, "Nizza e Blackpool: due città balneari agli inizi del Novecento," *Contemporanea* 4 (1998): 651-80.

[5] J. K. Walton, "Seaside resorts of Western Europe."

[6] J. K. Walton and J. Smith, "The First Century of Beach Tourism in Spain: San Sebastián and the 'playas del norte' from the 1830s to the 1930s," in *Tourism in Spain: Critical Perspectives*, ed. M Barke et al (Wallingford: CAB, 1996), 35-61.

[7] Towner, 192.

[8] Charles E. Funnell, *By the Beautiful Sea: the Life and High Times of That Great American Resort, Atlantic City* (New York, 1975); Rev. Frederick Denison, *Narragansett Sea and Shore* (Providence, R.I.: J. A. and R. A. Reid, 1879).

[9] Donna Brown, *Inventing New England* (Washington: Smithsonian Institution Press, 1995); Funnell, 30-31.

[10] J. F. Kasson, *Amusing the Millions: Coney Island at the Turn of the Century* (New York: Hill and Wang, 1978); Kathy Peiss, *Cheap Amusements* (Philadelphia: Temple University Press, 1986); J K. Walton, *Blackpool* (Edinburgh: Edinburgh University Press, 1998).

[11] J. Valerie Fifer, *American Progress: the Growth of the Transport, Tourist and Information Industries in the Nineteenth-Century West* (Chester, Conn.: The Globe Patriot Press, 1988); Ann Armbruster, *The Life and Times of Miami Beach* (New York: Alfred A. Knopf, 1995); Southern California

Railway, *Summer homes at San Diego and Coronado Beach* (1896: British Library 10412.aa.26).

[12] Orestes Araujo, *Guía pintoresca de Montevideo* (Montevideo: Imprenta Artística, de Dornaleche y Reyes, 1907), 121; Julio Cesar Gascon, *Orígenes históricos de Mar del Plata* (La Plata: Taller de Impresiones Oficiales, 1942), 115.

[13] Charles Domville-Fife, *The Real South America* (London: George Routledge, 1922), 33; Gilberto Velho, *A utopia urbana: un estudio de antropologia social* (Rio de Janeiro: Zahar Editores, 2nd ed., 1975), 21-28.

[14] Tomás Otieza Iriarte, *Acapulco: la ciudad de las Naos de Oriente y de las sirenas modernas* (Mexico City: Editorial Diana, 1973), 387-400; Domville-Fife, 26.

[15] Gascon, 86-132; Ente Municipal de Turismo, *Mar del Plata: Historia, Geografia, Economía y Turismo* (Mar del Plata, undated pamphlet, unpaginated, *c*.1995); E. Pastoriza, *Los trabajadores de Mar del Plata en visperas del peronismo* (Buenos Aires: Centro Editor de America Latina, 1993), 28; José M. Zorrilla, *Veraneo en Mar del Plata* (Buenos Aires, 1913), 146.

[16] Lencek and Bosker, 113-71, 196-222.

[17] Morgan and Pritchard, *Power and Politics at the Seaside* (Exeter: Exeter University Press, 1999), Chapter 5. John Beckerson of the University of East Anglia is currently working on these themes.

[18] Walton, "Consuming the beach"; P. Florizoone, *James Ensor: les bains à Ostende* (Brussels: Snoeck-Ducajou et Zoon, 1996), 105.

[19] Lencek and Bosker, 113-38.

[20] Harry Pollitt, *Serving my Time* (London: Lawrence and Wishart, 1941), 134.

[21] *La Saison d'Ostende et du Littoral*, 8 June 1930.

[22] Florizoone, passim.

[23] J. Travis, "Continuity and change in English sea-bathing, 1730-1900," in *Recreation and the Sea*, ed. S. Fisher, 8-35.

[24] F. Stafford and N. Yates, *The Later Kentish Seaside* (Gloucester: Alan Sutton, 1985), 181-83.

[25] Walton, *British seaside*, Chapter 5; F. Stafford and N. Yates, 181-83.

[26] Walton, "Consuming the beach."

[27] Gil de Arriba, 73.

[28] Lencek and Bosker, 146-71; Kasson, 44-47; Funnell, 37-39.

[29] Zorrilla, 64-77.

[30] J. Guzmán y Clarafuente, *Mar del Plata: veneno de Buenos Aires* (Buenos Aires, 1923), 67-74.

[31] Ibid., 14.

[32] Gil de Arriba, 50.

[33] Guzmán y Clarafuente, 11-14.

[34] Florizoone, 145.

[35] Guzmán y Clarafuente, 17-18, 24-32, 53-54, 79.

[36] J. K. Walton, "Tradition and Tourism: Representing Basque Identities in Guipuzcoa and San Sebastián, 1848-1936," in *Northern identities*, ed. N. Kirk (Aldershot: Ashgate, 2000), 87-108.

[37] A. Gielen, *Ostende et Spa* (Brussels, 1912); *La Saison d'Ostende et du Littoral*, 28 April 1921, 18 September 1921.

[38] G. Sternlieb and J W. Hughes, *The Atlantic City Gamble* (Harvard University Press, 1983); Armbruster, *Miami Beach.*

[39] J. B. Priestley, *English Journey* (London: Heinemann, 1934), 267; Cross, *Worktowners at Blackpool* (London: Routledge, 1990); Walton, *Blackpool*, 173; Bennett, "Hegemony."

Chapter 11

Transatlantic Literary Tourism and Travel

Heidi Slettedahl Macpherson and Will Kaufman

In examining transatlantic narratives, clear patterns emerge whereby the characters reconstruct the transatlantic encounter either as a rejection of or continuation of "home." These literary tourists and travelers seek or resist identification with the new cultures they encounter. While gender and race inflect these experiences, the phenomenon is more complex than a simple mapping of masculinity and femininity, ethnicity or nationality allow. Consider two transatlantic tourist figures from 20th century American fiction. Macon Leary of Anne Tyler's *The Accidental Tourist* wraps his Americanness about him like a security blanket, shutting out the foreign as much as possible. Avey Johnson in Paule Marshall's *Praisesong for the Widow* is hailed—but refuses to recognize—similarity between herself and the Caribbean islanders who greet her as one of them. In both cases, these characters begin their narratives as witnesses of the foreign in everything but themselves. To some theorists, this is a fundamental aspect of literary tourism.

Tourists, theoretically, pursue a consumerist, non-transformative experience, but there are also characters of another breed, sometimes dubbed "travelers," regardless of the length of their sojourn. Travelers may well begin as tourists who, often in spite of themselves, undergo a more significant transformation than the expectations of casual tourism would allow. "Travel," it is true, suggests a more transient state than "exile" or "expatriation," but, like other literatures, the literature of transatlantic encounters tends to construct even exile or expatriation as an unfinished journey, reflecting back upon one's own origins as well as upon the newly adopted environment. Thus, as we shall discuss, David, the narrator of James Baldwin's *Giovanni's Room*, can only conceptualize the nature of home from the vantage point of "away"— namely, exile in Paris. In similar fashion, Helga Crane of Nella Larsen's *Quicksand* (originally published in 1928) goes to Denmark to embrace her Danish side, not realizing that she will be unable to "leave the Negroes behind" because her blackness is pronounced against the Danes—even as it is misrecognized:

> Here it was that one day an old countrywoman asked her to what manner of mankind she belonged and at Helga's replying: "I'm a Negro," had become indignant, retorting angrily that, just because she was old and a countrywoman she could not be so easily fooled, for she knew as well as everyone else that Negroes were black and had woolly hair.[1]

These examples suggest at least three things: the attempt to establish "home" and "not home"—especially through writing—will first entail the mythological re-creation of both through some conception of "the foreign." Secondly, however much fictional characters attempt to define themselves with a stable identity based on location, a host of perceptions will combine to undermine that stability. Finally, the theoretical distinction between tourist and traveler is fluid, at best.

Given the fact of literary fabrication, it is especially fitting for a self-aware fictional character to marvel at the audacity of any novelist's attempt to create a stable national identity through fiction—as does one of Carlos Fuentes' many transatlantic narrators in *Terra Nostra*: "Idiot," he exclaims: "you have been thinking like a white-wigged Encyclopedist. How can one be a Persian? How, in truth, is it possible to be a Mexican, a Chilean, an Argentinian, or a Peruvian?"[2] Given the shape-shifting nature of national identity in fiction, the answer may well be: only with practice. But it is not just fictional characters who experience the transatlantic as a *terra incognita* waiting to be filled up with mythic identities. As Langston Hughes recounts in his autobiography, *I Wonder as I Wander*, the transatlantic (initially at least) promises it for all—including the anonymous woman he encountered in Paris, who said she was from Java, part Dutch and part Javanese, but who spoke hesitant English and broken French with a Georgia drawl. John Davis whispered to me over the champagne he had bought that he was sure she was colored, from somewhere in Dixie, passing for Javanese in Paris, which amused him greatly. The girl was so exotic-looking that I doubted she was American, and disputed his insistence on it. I was wrong. Later I ran into the girl in New York talking perfectly good Harlemese, and not passing for anything on Lenox Avenue where she was quite at home.[3]

It is almost a commonplace to say that, for travel writers since the earliest voyages of transatlantic exploration, mythologizing has been a defining, self-conscious process. Writing of Cabeza de Vaca's sixteenth-century narrative, Haniel Long notes that this repentant conquistador knowingly "ceases to be a historical personage and becomes a symbol"—of rebirth, compassion, and cultural sensitivity.[4] Three hundred years later, Mark Twain famously became a (shrewdly crafted) symbol of American innocence abroad, while a fellowship of European writers (de Tocqueville, Dickens, Frances Trollope and others) wrote themselves into symbols of Old World-weary sophistication to plot against the myth of pervasive, monolithic American naivety. For 20th century travel writers operating in a global community, such generalizing about transatlantic innocence or sophistication is no longer an option; but when all else fails, there is always the time-honored device of exaggerated first-person discomfiture in an unfamiliar world—a hallmark of Bill Bryson as it was for Twain before him. As long as one can construct a "home" to compare with an equally constructed "away," and fabricate a textual self to pit against a textual other, the transatlantic is an eternally open bridge.

The black travel writers represented in Alasdair Pettinger's seminal anthology, *Always Elsewhere: Travels of the Black Atlantic*, are, it is true, in a special category. As Pettinger writes:

For many authors ... it is not always clear where "home" is. And for that reason it is the subject of a much wider range of emotions—nostalgia, indifference, exasperation, perplexity, embarrassment. In any case, the expected contrast between the familiarity of home and the strangeness of abroad that underpins so much travel literature is often absent.[5]

But diasporic writers share with all travel writers the necessity to re-create a shifting sense of identity on the basis of where they come from and where they are going. It is the degree of that shift that provokes the first questions about the theoretical distinction between tourism and travel, in literature as in life.

For pleasure, comedy or "instruction," countless authors have depicted the transatlantic journey and its subsequent consequences for narrators—and readers—alike. They have created a body of fictional and non-fictional narratives that conspire to illuminate and mythologize aspects of national character, as well as to problematize the politics of tourism and travel. The texts we have chosen to discuss project and define a highly unstable cultural geography, as they place their narrators in the position of tourists and travelers encountering the familiar in the "foreign," and vice versa. As Paul Fussell suggests, "to speak of 'literary traveling' is almost a tautology, so intimately are literature and travel implicated with each other."[6] It is no surprise that travel texts perform the dual role of illumination and fictionalization, given that tourists and travelers themselves participate in a similar process of construction—of identity and nationality, self and other. As Zenga Longmore suggests:

> The English become laughably cockney or Bertie Woosterish when American tourists are anywhere around, thinking that that is what the Americans like, and the sad fact is that it actually *is* what they like. In Zimbabwe, the false "African Villages" that are built for the tourists are chock-a-block with clucking Europeans and clicking cameras, whereas the *real* African villages are totally ignored as if they didn't exist. This practice of the locals establishing the sham to please the tourists is upheld all over the globe.[7]

But it is through travel texts, both fictional and non-fictional (perhaps more than through the experience of travel itself) that we see the tendency to establish a qualitative difference between tourism and travel—even as the texts themselves problematize this tendency. For example, Jamaica Kincaid's *A Small Place* is a blistering exposé of the Antiguan tourist industry, which positions local people as commodities in a brutal market of transatlantic exotica. From a local viewpoint, Kincaid constructs the tourist as "an ugly human being" who turns the "banality and boredom [of the indigenous population] into a source of pleasure" for him or herself.[8] In this she mirrors the approach of some theorists who posit tourists as narcissistic parasites using the encountered world only to reflect back upon themselves:

> If travelling implies a journey of metamorphosis and transformation, in which the self is changed by the experience of alterity

encountered in a dialectic of difference, then tourism implies a circular confirmation of self-identity.[9]

While the distinction between traveler and tourist depends entirely on one's critical perspective, these constructions pervade transatlantic literature—and often interact.

The transatlantic tourist, whether fictional or real, populates beaches and beachside reading with equal measures. And of all tourists, it is perhaps Anne Tyler's Macon Leary who is the most exaggerated, most enclosed and most afraid of the "foreign." He is the archetypal American traveler who wonders why everywhere else is different from the US. *The Accidental Tourist* is both the name of Tyler's novel, and the name of the series of guidebooks that Macon Leary reluctantly writes. His hatred of travel propels him anxiously through various European cities, only comfortable (and then, never quite) when he is eating in restaurants named Yankee Delight, U.S. Open, or New America. His guidebook doesn't rate restaurants by traditional stars, but through whether "genuine" American food can be found there: "Did Mexico have a Taco Bell? Did any place in Rome serve Chef Boyardee ravioli?"[10] If Disney could create Europe, it would be so much tidier, so much less authentic, and therefore so much more comfortable. Macon would be the ultimate consumer of Baudrillard's hyperreality—if only he attempted to engage with any sort of "real" at all. It is no coincidence that the Leary family's favorite—and inscrutable—game is a home-made card game they call Vaccination or that Macon's only foreign language is Latin. Macon desires most to be untouched, and his tourism is stereotypically American:

> *I am happy to say that it's now possible to buy Kentucky Fried Chicken in Stockholm. Pita bread, too,* he added as an afterthought. He wasn't sure how it had happened, but lately pita had grown to seem as American as hot dogs.[11]

Macon's guidebooks only cover cities, since the businessmen for whom he writes never visit the countryside and mostly wish they hadn't left home at all. *The Accidental Tourist* is the logical extension of Roland Barthes' analysis of *The Blue Guide*, a travel guide that, by picking out only what there is to "see," conveniently manages to become "through an operation common to all mystifications, the very opposite of what it advertises, an agent of blindness."[12] Similarly, Barry Curtis and Claire Pajaczkowska note that "[a]ll guidebooks and tourist literature offer advice on what to 'look out for', which implies the more interesting question of 'what is to be overlooked.'"[13]

That Macon's guide "sees" something different from the traditional tourist guide—reminders of home rather than stunning (foreign) beauty—is irrelevant. Or, perhaps more accurately, it is a comment on the nature of the tourist: selective, unbending, less willing to encounter a myriad of sites or experiences than anyone might admit. As Heather Henderson writes of factual travel literature, "the genre that by rights seems most likely to take both writer and reader out of their usual surroundings, is actually most at home with itself when it reveals how neither has ever really left the armchair."[14] Macon, in looking for home, only ever encounters pale imitations, which lead to inevitable homesickness. His refusal to encounter the foreign is a comment on American tourism, and on the "safety" of modern travel which cocoons the tourist from the "foreign" as much as possible.

Of course, Tyler isn't the only American writer to critique the (non)experience of tourism. Paule Marshall uses Avey Johnson much as Tyler uses Macon—as a representative of the enclosed American whose travel never moves very far from home. It is not coincidental that *Praisesong for the Widow* opens on a cruiseship, that symbol of cocooned travel which Paul Fussell calls "tourism with a vengeance."[15] As an African-American woman, Avey Johnson may appear to be miles away from Macon Leary, yet both are infected with the same distrust of foreignness which leads them to start for home as quickly as possible. Avey abandons her cruise—not in order to engage more with the islands that the boat circumscribes, but in order to keep at bay any possible feelings of "foreignness." It is ironically appropriate, therefore, that she finds herself surrounded—and hailed—by the Caribbean islanders she is trying so hard to avoid:

> The problem was, she decided, none of them seemed aware of the fact that she was a stranger, a visitor, a tourist, although this should have been obvious from the way she was dressed and the set of matching luggage at her side. But from the way they were acting she could have been simply one of them there on the wharf.[16]

Avey shrinks from their touch and almost hysterically imagines her fate as an unwilling hostage. The experience is "unintelligible," "puzzling," and "irritating": "For the first time ... she experienced the special panic of the traveler who finds himself sealed-off, stranded in a sea of incomprehensible sound. *When would a taxi come?*"[17] Comfortable only with tourist transport—cruiseships and taxis—Avey manages to make her way to a tourist hotel which keeps her safe from the "real" experience of the island. Indeed, the beach, at a safe distance of eight stories, is described as a set: "a vast stage that curved inward, with the sky its proscenium arch and the sun a single huge spot that illuminated it from end to end."[18]

As its noteworthy exchange of the two terms indicates, *Praisesong for the Widow* reveals in particular the difficulties of attempting to establish a clear demarcation between "tourist" and "traveler," precisely because of the unstable concept of "the foreign" upon which both designations implicitly depend. Certainly, Avey's experience is more transformative than mere tourism would seem to allow—at least according to the criteria proposed by Curtis and Pajaczkowska. Hers is both "a journey of metamorphosis and transformation" *and* "a circular confirmation of self-identity." Like Macon, Avey eventually learns to embrace the foreign and through this, find familiarity that is more genuine and less manufactured.

Her initial discomfort relates to her own foreignness even on the cruise ship. It is only in recognizing that she's become a foreigner to herself that Avey can embrace ways of being that are "different." Madan Sarup argues that "the foreigner is a 'symptom': psychologically, s/he signifies the difficulty we have of living as an other and with others"[19] Julia Kristeva goes further to argue that (in the 20th century at least) "[a] person ... can exist honestly only as a foreigner."[20] But Marshall's novel suggests that in spite of such a universalizing intent, there is a particular difficulty in considering "the foreign" in a diasporic context like that of the Black Atlantic, in which one's foreignness is as pervasive at "home" as it is "away"—a foreignness not willingly shared by a dominant majority (*pace* Kristeva). Moreover, if tourism suggests the more casual commodification of the foreign, as opposed to the deeper, transformative nature of travel, then (one might think) the realities of Black Atlantic history would ensure that all its writers would be permanent travelers, with the cheap thrills of tourism out of their reach even if actively sought. As Pettinger writes: "If the Black Atlantic began with the trauma of the enforced movement of people, it has become a domain in which even the most mundane forms of travel can become exceedingly difficult."[21] If tourists are, by definition, "ugly human beings," such a difficulty might be a blessing; but, as Pettinger continues, it carries its own racist assumptions:

> In a recent anthology, one writer suggests that the very *idea* that Black people might actually travel for the sake of it is hard for some to accept: "Are you visiting relatives?" "Do you work here?" But then, as a contributor to the same collection half-answers, "former sharecroppers do not teach their children to travel for pleasure." And even if they learn some other way, their options still appear to be

restricted, as a third author discovered when her travel piece was
turned down by her editor. "With pity in his voice he blurted, 'Black
people don't go to Iceland.'"[22]

The most disturbing implication here, of course, is that writers of
the Black Atlantic will have conceptions of "foreignness" thrust upon
them wherever they go, including the domain of the casual tourist.
Tourism is not their territory. The privilege of conferring foreignness
upon others, the right of objectification, is not theirs—that one-way
commodification of the sort practiced (for example) by Edith Wharton
in her mythologizing of the "dark, fierce and fanatical" *souks* of North
Africa:

> Fanatics in sheepskins glowering from the guarded thresholds of the
> mosques,... mad Negroes standing stark naked in niches of the walls
> and pouring down Soudanese incantations upon the fascinated
> crowd, consumptive Jews with pathos and cunning in their large
> eyes and smiling lips,...—from all these hundreds of unknown and
> unknowable people, bound together by secret affinities, or intriguing
> against each other with secret hate, there emanated an atmosphere of
> mystery and menace more stifling than the smell of camels and
> spices and black bodies and smoking fry which hangs like a fog
> under the close roofing of the *souks*.[23]

Clearly, then, foreignness is not only an unstable construct, but one
that implies a struggle for power. As Toni Morrison writes,
"definitions"—of foreignness or anything else—belong "to the definers
and not to the defined,"[24] and the transatlantic exchange, if nothing
else, imposes constant role reversals on the "definers" and the
"defined." A clear example of this is the outright construction of
African-American Helga Crane by her Danish relatives in Nella
Larsen's *Quicksand*. This early 20th century novella sets the
transatlantic up as an alienating space that can neither be bridged nor
avoided. Larsen's heroine feels set apart in Harlem as well as the rest of
the US through her mixed race parentage, and she flees to Denmark in
order, naively, to leave questions of race and race allegiance behind. It
is, however, her very "foreignness" (read ethnicity rather than
nationality here) which Helga's Danish relatives value:

> Her aunt's words came back to her. "You're young and a foreigner
> and—different." Just what did that mean, she wondered. Did it mean
> that the difference was to be stressed, accented? Helga wasn't so
> sure that she liked that. Hitherto all her efforts had been toward
> similarity to those about her.[25]

Eventually, she embraces this otherness, and even helps to construct it: "Intentionally she kept to the slow, faltering Danish. It was, she decided, more attractive than a nearer perfection."[26]

Helga is no tourist, living two years in Copenhagen and even contemplating marriage to a Dane. Yet her transatlantic experiences are hardly more "authentic" than those of the tourists above. Indeed, the narrative focuses on what Curtis and Pajaczkowska call the "three paradigmatic moments of tourism: eating, shopping and sightseeing."[27] What makes Helga different is her willingness to become a tourist exhibition herself: she is the gazed upon, not the gazer, an experience echoed by other black travelers. As Tété-Michel Kpomassie notes in *An African in Greenland*, "I had started on a voyage of discovery, only to find that it was I who was being discovered."[28]

Yet Helga considers herself an immigrant, and for most of her sojourn, she has no intention of crossing the Atlantic again. Ann E. Hostetler argues that "Helga's constant shifting from one place to the next emphasized the narrowness of place defined by race in the United States of the 1920s."[29] Yet she cannot escape race by traversing the Atlantic, by becoming an immigrant, and in fact the transatlantic experience, rather than rooting Helga, divides her in two:

> two parts in two lands, into physical freedom in Europe and spiritual freedom in America .... mentally she caricatured herself moving shuttle-like from continent to continent. From the prejudiced restrictions of the New World to the easy formality of the Old, from the pale calm of Copenhagen to the colorful lure of Harlem.[30]

Clearly, the transatlantic narrative is, in some important ways, defined by the textual recreations of encounters between people, and the power struggles that ensue in the attempt to impose or resist conceptions of foreignness. Often, as all the texts demonstrate, it is the engagement with the power struggle—the transformative experience of it—that may well convert tourists into travelers. James Baldwin's narrator in *Giovanni's Room* describes just such a power struggle between himself and his Italian lover, both of them self-exiled in Paris:

> When Giovanni wanted me to know that he was displeased with me, he said I was a "*vrai americain*"; and conversely, when delighted, he said that I was not an American at all; and on both occasions he was striking, deep in me, a nerve which did not throb in him. And I resented this: resented being called an American (and resented resenting it) because it seemed to make me nothing more than that,

whatever that was; and I resented being called *not* an American because it seemed to make me nothing.[31]

David hits upon the chimerical nature of the foreignness imposed upon him by Giovanni: he realizes that without his national identity, he is in danger of being reduced to "nothing," but a national identity ("whatever that was") is indefinable even to him. Thus when he encounters a group of American tourists, he is none the wiser as to why he or they should be so defined: "I was aware that they all had in common something that made them Americans but I could never put my finger on what it was. I knew that whatever this common quality was, I shared it."[32] Yet in a moment of extreme alienation, the foreignness imposed upon him not only through his expatriation but also through his sexuality *vis-à-vis* conservative America leads him to fabricate the common identity of these American tourists when he constructs *them* as the "others":

> [W]alking into the American Express Office one harshly bright, midsummer afternoon, I was forced to admit that this active, so disquietingly cheerful horde struck the eye, at once, as a unit. At home, I could have distinguished patterns, habits, accents of speech—with no effort whatever; now everybody sounded, unless I listened hard, as though they had just arrived from Nebraska.[33]

David here imposes upon his fellow Americans a fabricated strangeness, wholly unsolicited and similar to that imposed upon the ordinary, workaday people in the Marrakesh *souks* by Edith Wharton, who with the stroke of her pen, transforms them into something sinister and uncanny. As Karen Lawrence notes, "[t]he uncanny terrifies because it collapses the distance between the familiar and the foreign" in an unexpected manner.[34] If David is not as terrified by his "others" as Wharton is by hers, he is no less responsible for the construction of the uncanny as she is. Baldwin's choice of a blonde, Anglo-Saxon narrator speaks volumes here: he is the constructor, as well as the constructed, and his Caucasian ancestry is put in relief by his dark, Italian lover; ethnicity here is a subtext, which hides the more dangerous message of racial blurring which could not be accommodated in 1950s' America. Homosexuality, "otherness," and the foreign remain *out there*; but the transatlantic expanse allows them to be mapped onto *here* (wherever *here* is).

All the texts we have discussed suggest that, ultimately, foreignness is *not* a given: it is a human invention. As Mark Twain wrote in his globe-spanning travel account, *Following the Equator*: "It is your human environment that makes climate."[35] The climate of the transatlantic is one of crisscrossing fortunes and positions, where travel—and tourism—blend. Paul White suggests that "dislocation and ensuing marginality are some of the most important influences subverting long-standing beliefs in the linearity of progress and the stability of cultural identity."[36] Nowhere is this more apparent, it seems, than in the transatlantic desire for home and foreignness, tourism and travel. These disparate, sometimes conflicting desires are in evidence in all narratives of the transatlantic encounter. We have focused only on a few noteworthy textual recreations of this encounter, not to privilege them above all the others, but in order to further the dialogue about the transatlantic in literature, and to place literature firmly at the core of transatlantic studies. Geography, migration, economics, law and education set the larger scene of the transatlantic, but the arts, too, have something to say—and it is sometimes through examining the fictional side of the transatlantic that its factual nature is the most clearly illuminated.

---

[1] Nella Larsen, *Quicksand and Passing* (London: Serpent's Press, 1995), 76.

[2] Carlos Fuentes, *Terra Nostra*, trans. Margaret Sayers Peden (London: Secker and Warburg, 1977), 771.

[3] Langston Hughes, *I Wander as I Wonder* (1956), in *Always Elsewhere: Travels of the Black Atlantic*, ed. Alasdair Pettinger (London and New York: Cassell, 1998), 252.

[4] Haniel Long, *The Power Within Us: Cabeza de Vaca's Relation of His Journey from Florida to the Pacific, 1528-1536* (Nevada City: Harold Berliner, 1975), 12.

[5] Alasdair Pettinger, introduction, *Always Elsewhere: Travels of the Black Atlantic* (London and New York: Cassell, 1998), xvii.

[6] Paul Fussell, *Abroad: British Literary Traveling Between the Wars* (Oxford: Oxford University Press, 1982), 212.

[7] Zenga Longmore, *Tap-Taps to Trinidad* (1989), in Pettinger, 265.

[8] Jamaica Kincaid, *A Small Place* (London: Vintage, 1997), 14, 19.

[9] Barry Curtis and Claire Pajaczkowska, "'Getting There': Travel, Time and Narrative," in *Travellers' Tales: Narratives of Home and Displacement*, ed. George Robertson et al. (London: Routledge, 1994), 206.

[10] Anne Tyler, *The Accidental Tourist* (New York: Berkeley, 1986), 11.

[11] Tyler, 11, emphasis in original.

[12] Roland Barthes, "The Blue Guide," in *Mythologies*, trans. Annette Lavers (London: Cape, 1972), 76.

[13] Curtis and Pajaczkowska, 209.

[14] Heather Henderson, "The Travel Writer and the Text: 'My Giant Goes with Me Wherever I Go,'" in *Temperamental Journeys: Essays on the Modern*

Literature of Travel, ed. Michael Kowaleski (Athens, GA: University of Georgia Press, 1992), 247.

[15] Fussell, 41.

[16] Paule Marshall, *Praisesong for the Widow* (London: Virago, 1993), 69.

[17] Marshall, 70, emphasis in original.

[18] Marshall, 79.

[19] Madan Sarup, "Home and Identity," in Robertson et al., 100.

[20] Julia Kristeva, in *The Kristeva Reader*, ed. Toril Moi (New York: Columbia University Press, 1986), 286.

[21] Pettinger, xiii.

[22] Ibid.

[23] Edith Wharton, *In Morocco* (1920), in *Travellers' Tales*, ed. Eric Newby (London: Picador, 1986), 85.

[24] Toni Morrison, *Beloved* (London: Picador, 1988), 190.

[25] Larsen, 72.

[26] Larsen, 74.

[27] Curtis and Pajaczkowska, 207.

[28] Tété-Michel Kpomassie, *An African in Greenland* (1983), in Pettinger, 138-39.

[29] Ann E. Hostetler, "The Aesthetics of Race and Gender in Nella Larsen's *Quicksand*," *PMLA* 105, no. 1 (1990): 38.

[30] Larsen, 96.

[31] James Baldwin, *Giovanni's Room* (London: Penguin, 1990), 85-86.

[32] Baldwin, 85.

[33] Baldwin, 86.

[34] Karen R. Lawrence, *Penelope Voyages: Women and Travel in the British Literary Tradition* (Itatha: Cornell University Press, 1994), 4.

[35] Mark Twain, *Following the Equator* (Mineola: Dover, 1989), 109.

[36] Paul White, "Geography, Literature and Migration" in *Writing Across Worlds: Literature and Migration*, eds. Russell King et al. (London: Routledge, 1995), 6.

Chapter 12

Dialogic Encounters and Hybrid Routes in the Fiction, Travel Writing, and Translations of Paul Bowles

Neil Campbell

> It takes two to tango. Morocco is there, and I'm here, and we got together.[1] (Paul Bowles)

This chapter examines the ways in which Paul Bowles's writings trace varieties of transatlantic experience that begin to map out a sensibility of exchange and dialogue across cultures, ranging from destructive collisions and romantic desires, to hybrid co-presence and collaboration. This mapping is never final, but tentative and fluid in the spirit defined by Paul Gilroy as "stereophonic, bilingual, or bifocal ... dispersed ... rooted in and routed through ... the effort involved in trying to face (at least) two ways at once."[2] Out of his own unease with his homeland of America, Bowles charted a journey of an alternative, "transcultural, international formation" that examined the notion of "(at least) two ways" through a range of writings: fiction, travel and translation.[3]

Paul Bowles's America was a Poe-like nightmare of restriction, surveillance and control, where individual lives were crushed and molded by the relentless pressures of a disposable consumerism built on conservative suburban values, where "civilization had turned and begun to devour its own body."[4] His determination to break away from a prescribed self and a place of restrictive rootedness—"I am here. I am here"—became the motivation for both his personal migrations and for his writings over the following 70 years.[5] Bowles tells of his rare delight in escaping his family's obsessive rules to enjoy the sensation of "letting myself float [upside down on a swing] in total awareness of the moment."[6] Home, however, was a place where regulation turned imagination into static dread, relieved only by his grandfather's boast to have "never slept twice in the same town," something the young Bowles felt was "[t]he perfect life."[7] Movement, traveling and contact with people who lived different, unmanaged lives, with alternative ways of seeing the world, connoted steps outside his enclosed American suburban family. Writing years later from his adopted "home" of Morocco, Bowles commented that "each day lived through on this side of the Atlantic was one more day spent outside prison."[8] Yet it was the tension of this "transatlantic" world—of moving between the two—which appealed to Bowles, who would explore its ambivalent dimensions throughout his career as a writer.

Bowles's writings "travel" to places and spaces where norms and structures of thought come into contact with alien cultures and traditions that stand outside the apparently coherent, rational, and orderly world of American modernity. His work is only "decadent" when interpreted by people "who take it for granted that the US has the highest moral standard in the world, and that the 'outlook' of its inhabitants is automatically 'healthier' than elsewhere."[9] Bowles loved Dada and Surrealism because of their dislocative, destructive challenge to social and psychological norms, and their transnational composition which asserted difference over narrow nationalism. Bowles, too, wanted to jar the reader out of the normalized sphere of thought with a "temporary smearing of the lens of consciousness" causing "a certain amount of questioning of values" and a realization that there are other ways of seeing the world.[10]

These early excursions show Bowles's determination to find ways of confronting American national identity by a process of defamiliarization, of "making strange," as one culture encounters another. This is the beginning of transatlantic sensibility in Bowles's work by creating a space of estrangement between worlds, referring to both and yet confined by neither. As Bakhtin writes:

outsideness is a most powerful factor in understanding ... [for] in the eyes of another culture ... foreign culture reveals itself fully and profoundly.... A meaning only reveals its depths once it has encountered and come into contact with another, foreign meaning: they engage in a kind of dialogue, which surmounts the closedness and one-sidedness.... Such a dialogic encounter of two cultures does not result in merging or mixing. Each retains its own unity and open totality, but they are mutually enriched.[11]

Bowles's writings created dialogical encounters to challenge the homogenized and centralized official discourse which spoke of a nation's imagined community and its values whilst viewing "the polyglossia of the barbarian world with contempt."[12] This meant that alternative forms—marginal and "folk" voices—were held at bay by "centripetal" forces, or "norms" insisting upon unitary structures. For Bowles, this was a vision of colonial, global power manifested through language and cultural control by the dominant regime of representation whose "monoglossia" denied and silenced other voices of difference and heterogeneity. The "zone of contact" for Bakhtin was a space in which many voices operated, exchanged, and negotiated with one another in the production of discourse. Similarly, Mary Louise Pratt defines a contact zone as a place where "disparate cultures meet, clash, and grapple with each other, often in highly asymmetrical relations of domination and subordination—like colonialism, slavery, or their aftermaths"; however, what emerges is a "co-presence of subjects previously separated by geographic and historical disjunctures ... whose trajectories now intersect" with the possibility of dialogical encounters.[13]

Bowles's works, in different modes, testify to a migratory sensibility defined not by the exclusive attachment to one place, but to an identity constructed precisely by complex dialogical contacts and mobilities. Bakhtin saw dialogues in everything, but recognized that "embedded in them [was] one as yet unfolded,"[14] that is, an emergent "third" voice coming from within the dialogical encounter. Bowles's experience was of moving between cultures, languages, sexualities, always in the "fold" from where might emerge a new "unfolding," a hybrid form and identity that partakes of and enriches both. As Bakhtin notes, such a process of collision cannot exist with any "naive absence of conflict," for what emerges is often a painful rejection of myth and tradition which "will occur only when a national culture loses its sealed-off and self-sufficient character, when it becomes conscious of itself as only one among other cultures and languages."[15] From these ideas of contact, dialogical encounter, and conflict comes a version of Bowles's transatlantic sensibility that will be worked out in his subsequent writings.

Fictions of Travel/Traveling Fictions

In the 1920s American modernists crossed the Atlantic "from a world they felt was overly secure" to engage in "voluntary homelessness," a "tourism" looking voyeuristically "elsewhere" for "markers of reality and authenticity" whilst perpetuating an "exoticization of the past ... another gender, race, or culture."[16] For Caren Kaplan, this is "an act in consonance with imperialist nostalgia" and not one about "fuller understanding of the histories and particularities of the places they have travelled through."[17] Although Bowles was engaged by many aspects of this same modernist process when he left the US for Paris in 1929, "a year of Modernist monuments," he quickly tired of "the binary model of modernity, oscillating between past and present, home and away, center and periphery" and sought a different form of experience.[18] Bowles's work interrogates the "escape fantasies" of expatriates like Port Moresby in *The Sheltering Sky*, who "did not think of himself as a tourist" hurrying "back home," but as a traveler who, "belonging no more to one place than to the next, moves slowly, over a period of years, from one part of the earth to another."[19] The novel dissects Moresby's exile and his desire for "singularity, solitude, estrangement, alienation" as a part of his individual salvation in the Sahara.[20] The assumptions of romantic exile are, to borrow a term from Kaplan, "recoded" in this novel, as in most of Bowles's other works, so that what is undergone is not a binary retrieval of some lost, essential being, or an awakening to a purer world, but a complex, contradictory contact wherein assumptions are dissolved in the often destructive collision of differences. Moresby, like many of the modernists, believed that travel enabled him to "reject ... those elements ... not to his liking," such as "war" and the "mechanized age," and to lose himself in some far away place detached from his previous existence. However, ultimately the journey is without any responsibility because "they could always cross over if it failed to work out" and return to the secure, if dull, world of "home."[21] Increasingly, Bowles dramatized the impossibility of a simplistic shift from one identity to another, suggesting instead that one is always *between*, mixing identities and constructing subjectivity in the process of traveling.

When asked "perhaps you would never have been a writer if you had stayed in the States," Bowles answered, "Quite possibly not," acknowledging the connection between exile, travel and writing in his mind.[22] Thus, travel became a site of contradictions in his work, signifying an escape from America, and at the same time a problematization of the reasons for that travel and the relations it created *en route*. In "Windows on the Past," Bowles states that "[t]he trend of the century is being set by America for the entire world," a trend defined by "technique," technology, and reason. However, Americans were still "looking across the Atlantic for guidance," with "deeper reasons why Europe still holds something for us."[23] Like Kaplan, Bowles believed that Americans were searching for "something more all-embracing" to "bring back": "I should call it childhood ... we seem to have forgotten this true past, lost contact with the psychic soil of tradition in which the roots of culture must be anchored."[24] In the rush to "technique" and reason, Americans lost their imagination to a "gadget civilization" lacking any "connection with the past" or to "the other part of the mind, the part that actually determines preferences rather than explaining them." Consequently, "[w]here we could learn why, we try to teach them (the African tribes) our all-important how, so that they may become as rootless and futile and materialistic as we are."[25] Bowles later explained in an interview,

> If a Westerner encounters an archaic culture with the idea of learning from it, I think he can succeed. He wants to absorb the alien for his own benefit. But to lose oneself in it is not a normal desire. A romantic desire, yes, but actually to try and do it is disastrous.[26]

The painful realization of the futility of the "romantic desire" to "lose oneself" is played out in *The Sheltering Sky, Let It Come Down*, and *The Spider's House* where displaced characters are typically made uneasy and uncertain, with their value systems scrutinized and tested; for it is "[t]he transportation of characters ... [that] acts as a catalyst or a detonator, without which there'd be no action."[27] Port Moresby, for example, journeys deep into the Sahara because "the very silences and emptinesses ... touched his soul ... [with] solitude and the proximity to infinite things."[28] However, as he moves on, the reader realizes what Moresby cannot, that his quest is a romantic dream: "The landscape was there, and more than ever he felt he could not reach it. The rocks and the sky were everywhere, ready to absolve him, but as always he carried the obstacle within him."[29] Moresby's need to control his world—as his obsession with maps and his use of prostitutes show—are clues to his inability to get beyond his old selfish identity and to learn from Africa. Instead, his "existence [is] unmodifiable" and ironically fixed, "pinned ... to the earth ... impaled ... the endless black wall rising ahead of him."[30] Similarly, Stenham in *The Spider's House* hated those Muslims who had "forsaken the concept of a static world to embrace a dynamic one," preferring to hold on to a predefined notion of the East as "natural" and "eternal," derived from "the point of view of an outsider, a tourist who puts picturesqueness above everything else."[31]

In *Let It Come Down*, cultures collide in Tangiers' International Zone, a petri-dish of treachery, corruption and game-playing where everyone uses the next person in a pyramid of power. The possibility of transatlantic exchange and cooperation in this meeting place of different nationalities is disintegrated by Bowles's depiction of a place where "you could get anything you wanted if you paid for it. Do anything too, for that matter—there were no incorruptibles. It was only a question of price."[32] Relations in this system are of predator to prey, without any sense of reconciliation between groups or across cultural divides. The Zone is a dark vision of "transatlantic" colonial contact in which the common denominator is greed, the ultimate aim is power and control, and all relations are ruthlessly self-serving. Within this apparently dynamic atmosphere, Nelson Dyar believes he can transform his life: "to discover the way out of the fly-trap, to strike the chord inside himself which would liberate those qualities capable of transforming him from a victim to a winner."[33] Dyar, like Moresby and Stenham, thinks that he can jettison one life—his "New York self"— and be magically transformed from "victim" to "winner" just because he wills it. However, his contact reveals that life is not linear and made of cohesive "parts" that add up to a total sum, or to a final, integrated notion of self, but a multiple, contradictory and fragmented identity constantly adjusted and transformed by the contacts it has with the world in which it exists and through which it moves. This mobile, migratory self is not what Bowles's characters desire, for they long for transformative certainties and absolute locations: "connection," "freedom," "infinite things," "love" and control. Dyar's desired freedom is as impossible as the notion of a coherent, single self, for Tangiers and New York are too "alike," revolving "around making money ... [where] everyone is dishonest ... each man's waiting to suck the blood of the next."[34] This vampiric system shows how colonialism's International Zone simulates America as a "model of corruption": "no country ... a counterfeit, a waiting-room between connections, a transition from one way of being to another, which for the moment was neither way, no way."[35]

In these transatlantic contacts, Moresby and Dyar are destroyed and their values revealed and analyzed as part of the system of global "monoglossia"[36] referred to in Bowles's travel writings, where "[h]uman behaviour is becoming everywhere less differentiated"[37] because of its "unquestioning ... acceptance of ... Judaeo-Christian civilization," leaving "only the one direction in which they can go."[38] This "one direction" could only be countered by further movement and the possibility of its dynamic instability:

> writing about any part of Africa is a little like trying to draw a picture of a roller coaster in motion. You can say: it *was* thus and so, or, it is *becoming* this or that, but you risk making a misstatement if you say categorically that anything *is*....[39]

This sense of "becoming" is akin to Bowles's interest in Berber music, an "improvised," "hybrid product" born from "many elements of Arab music" and the music of Negro slaves.[40] This mixing of tradition, improvisation, and the qualities of hybridity appealed to Bowles as a more healthy meeting of cultures than those of Moresby and Dyar, a dialogical encounter of forms and styles to counter the "one direction" of globalization.

Morocco epitomized this contradictory space, being both a timeless world of magic and tradition and a dynamic, ever-changing place, a cultural crossroads, an Inter[contact]zone mixing strict Muslim culture with the experimentalism of the Euro-American avant-garde, in a geographical space where Europe and Africa met and a complex web of histories intersected.[41] One of the attractions of Tangiers for Bowles was its mixture of cultures, where you might "run into a Polish refugee ... an American construction worker ... a tailor from Rome" and where "the past and the present exist simultaneously in proportionate degree, where a very much alive today is given an added depth of reality by the presence of an equally alive yesterday."[42] This meeting place of simultaneity was a "contact zone," as Bakhtin and Pratt termed it, where multiple identities, cultures and traditions bled into each other, producing unstable but exciting new conditions. Thus, when Bowles claimed that Tangiers was "an enormous market" where goods, information, and people were "bought and sold ... unloaded and reloaded ... without valid documents to identify them," he echoed Pratt's "contact zone" as a dynamic space of appropriation, exchange and reciprocity, or what James Clifford terms "intercultural import-export."[43] In this uneasy dialogue, identities are formed and old assumptions and values are modified. In Bowles's later work these dialogic encounters become central as the cultures hybridize through his translations and stories.

From Collision to Collusion: Translated Lives

Unable to continue his travels due to the illness of his wife, Bowles employed translation as a new mode of "travel" precisely because it enabled one to "learn a lot about peoples, cultures, and histories different from your own."[44] Living in Tangiers full time, Bowles developed a greater awareness of its cultural differences and in particular its secret world of magic, which, like Surrealism, proposed an alternative mode of being that challenged the very basis of Euro-American thinking in science and reason. He wrote that "a widespread system of practical magic is an important phenomena [sic]; it keeps the minds of its participants in a healthy state of personalised anarchy."[45] This anarchic potential appealed to Bowles because it questioned and intruded into the apparently smooth-running, logical world of technique and systemized patterns of thought. The fantastic, magical, metamorphic stories he began to translate opened "a whole new dimension to my writing experience," permitting, like the folk music he was collecting, a chance to preserve aspects of a disappearing culture and bring him into contact with unfamiliar cultural practices.[46] The translations form a significant element in Bowles's transatlantic sensibility, bringing together in a new hybrid form the mind of the American traveler-writer and the stories of an alien land. In an interview, the point is made that in Spanish "*translador*" means one who "transports things from one place to another, from one country to another," to which Bowles added, "I want to carry it over the border intact."[47]

Creating various cross-cultural dialogues, Bowles maintained his traveling via words and through a process of creative reinvention, acting as an intermediary, a carrier transporting stories across borders and between cultures. These are not authentic, purely Moroccan works, but "co-authored" out of the contact between voices and traditions. In Bowles's story, "A Distant Episode," the linguistics professor is told that he cannot be "there and here"—in the comfort of his hotel *and* in the dangerous world of the tribes he studies; however, in the act of translation Bowles comes closest to this position of "co-presence."[48] As editor/translator, he produces a text which is *simultaneously* a version of the oral story and an original, hybrid work in itself, bringing another world-view into the increasingly standardized Euro-American community. Culturally, translations

> cut across and intersect natural frontiers that are composed of people who have been *dispersed* forever from their homeland … [and] obliged to come to terms with the new cultures they inhabit, without simply assimilating to them and losing their identities completely …

they are irrevocably the product of several interlocking histories and cultures.[49]

Bowles, an outsider in an alien land, and the Moroccan tellers, moving in and out of their native cultures, are part of this process of "dispersal," no longer rooted in a single vision of culture as pure or absolute, but hybrids, "translated" between cultures, existing within both at the same time. Out of such a mix, new hybrid or syncretic forms emerge, reflecting upon both cultures from positions of difference and creating a "movement of meaning ... that ... 'puts the original in motion to decanonise it, giving it the movement of fragmentation, a wandering errance, a kind of permanent exile'"[50] Just as Bowles's earlier dislocative works were marked by an urge to destabilize established systems, the translations "desacralize ... the transparent assumptions of cultural supremacy."[51] They achieve this by dissolving or blurring the boundaries of the "real" and the "imaginary" through magic and metamorphosis with the purpose of questioning patterns of assumption and identity. In the act of translation and in the different stories he wrote as a consequence, Bowles shifts his direction towards an articulation of the uneasy alliances and intersections across cultures, creating new forms through which to express this tense, ambiguous perspective.

Bowles's developing transatlantic sensibility relates to a diasporic identity possessed by those who "make some kind of difficult 'settlement' with the new, often oppressive, cultures with which they were forced into contact."[52] Out of this contact, whether forced or chosen, there might be a "fashioning [of] new kinds of cultural identity, by consciously or unconsciously, drawing on more than one cultural *repertoire*" by people

> who belong to more than one world, speak more than one language (literally and metaphorically), inhabit more than one identity, have more than one home; who have learned to negotiate and translate between cultures, and who, because they are irrevocably the product of several interlocking histories and cultures, have learned to live with, and indeed speak from, *difference*.[53]

Bowles's own "diasporic" route from America was to find a "root" as an exile in Morocco, an unstable, contradictory place of magic and censorship, rigid religious orthodoxy and surprising social freedom, where his multi-lingual, multiple identities found a space "between" cultures. This allowed Bowles to write from "in-between," "always unsettling the assumptions of one culture from the perspective of another, and thus finding ways of being both *the same as* and at the same time *different from* the others amongst whom they live."[54] Salman Rushdie labels this a "translated" identity in which some things are "lost" but where "something can also be gained,"[55] suggesting Bowles's position working across and between "Atlantic" cultures, fixed by neither, but able to engage his readers in the relationships and differences in both.

Bowles once commented that he loved "folk music all over, in every part of the world, *completely dispersed*, which is a different thing," suggesting that rather than a "loss" of tradition, he was acknowledging, however reluctantly, the process of dispersal by which "roots" travel and engage with difference along cultural "routes."[56] In this respect, Bowles's hybrid translations and new stories were creating what his friends William Burroughs and Brion Gysin called a "third mind": "the complete fusion in a praxis of two subjectivities ... that metamorphose into a third; it is from this collusion that a new author emerges, an absent third person, invisible and beyond grasp, decoding the silence."[57] Homi Bhabha would later explore a similar idea in relation to the process of cultural translation and hybridity—"third space"— which "displaces the histories that constitute it, and sets up new structures of authority ... which are inadequately understood by received wisdom."[58] This is particularly evident as Bowles moved to writing his own Moroccan stories born out of the experience, knowledge and uneasiness of the translations.

In referring to his later stories as "synthetic," as in "putting together" or building up separate elements into a connected whole, Bowles related them to the translations, for they brought together his American outsider's identity and his increasing knowledge of Moroccan cultural forms in a dynamic, transnational creativity. Bowles made no pretence of being an "insider" or of being able to speak for the "Other," for as he has said, "I am a foreigner. It makes no difference that I've lived here 59 years. You can live your whole life and still be a foreigner.... [I]f you're not a Muslim, they don't accept you."[59] So even his later stories maintain thematic threads of alienation and disjunction, but often with the emphasis upon Moroccan lives. Rather than depicting journeys from the point of view of occidentals like Moresby or Dyar, these works "translate" to show how Moroccans engage with a changing world.

This can be seen in his collection *Midnight Mass*, unified around tensions between the old ways and the new, between the varieties of folklore and the pressure to conform to modern medicine and patterns of thought. Tourist developments crowd out the old "anarchy" that

Bowles had once admired in Morocco: "new villas covered the countryside.... The country club, nestling in an oasis of greenery. Behind the club-house ... the golf course." Increasingly, gardens are precious spaces of ease and timelessness, but not those of the Europeans who want only artifice and "each plant ... in the right place." In gestures of on-going tension against the new order, a Moroccan gardener "severed their roots or tubers ... and carefully replanted them exactly where they had been."[60]

In the novella *Here to Learn*, Bowles adopts a familiar structure— that of the traveler—but reverses the roles, so that the central character is a young Moroccan girl, Malika, moving out from the traditional Moroccan home in a version of diasporic flight in search of a dream of freedom and new identity. Malika's life is examined from outside, and in so doing, Bowles brings together the two cultures, that of Morocco and Euro-America, as the girl herself is routed through both. Initially it is her traditional "roots" that are described, not as an idealized, romantic view of the old ways, but a desperately isolated life bereft of contact. Her father tells the beautiful girl that "Allah has sent us here to learn"[61] and so encourages his daughter's education, whereas her mother disapproves of the Spanish nuns' influence on her. Looking at the town and her grandmother's face, Malika is struck by the ravages of age, time and change and desires something beyond the boundaries of her own traditions. She meets Tim, an American, who both takes her photograph, which, according to the local beliefs, "steals her soul," and promises her a new life. As she shifts between worlds, Malika learns from glamor magazines the "perfect pose," moves men, learns English, becomes rich, but feels that "she had gone much too far away—so far that now she was nowhere. Outside the world...."[62] The price of "learning" for Malika has reversed Moresby's journey, for in swapping identities she has embraced American values just as he had sought to shed them, arriving in Los Angeles, a city with "no pattern to it," feeling like "someone shipwrecked on an unknown shore peopled by creatures whose intentions were unfathomable," having "left behind everything that was comprehensible."[63] Her travel is unproductive, a shipwreck, because it is becalmed in one culture, America; she has failed to learn from her experience of both worlds. The Americanized Malika returns to her old home, now a pile of rubble in "a new landscape of emptiness," to find that she cannot go back; it is "too far for the possibility of return"[64] and the price she pays is alienation, like the plants severed from their roots, belonging nowhere.

It is precisely the failure to "learn" from different cultural contacts that haunts Bowles's work. When travel becomes an alienating, self-contained activity, dialogue is replaced by the imposition of a single viewpoint or the need to assert a dominant idea at the expense of others. Whether those of Moresby or Malika, cultures must learn from each other and not become entrenched in nationalist ideologies or singular identities, for in both lie the seeds of totalitarianism that Bowles could not tolerate. To challenge such static, standardized norms, Bowles evolved a transatlantic sensibility born of "interliterary dynamics ... contact, relations, transfer and appropriation,"[65] valuing restlessness and questioning, and championing productive travel in all its literal and metaphoric forms. Iain Chambers describes this sensibility:

> Movement and multiplicity frustrate any logic that seeks to reduce everything to the same, to the apparently transparent discourse of "history" or "knowledge".... [They] provide the thresholds for new encounters, new openings, unrehearsed possibilities, that "alienate the holism of history."[66]

Such is the "state of hybridity" where "no single narrative or authority—nation, race, the West—can claim to represent the truth or exhaust meaning."[67] Thus, it is natural that Bowles, who had always mistrusted fixity and sought opportunities to undo social categorization and closure through surrealist technique, existential disintegration of the ego, or personal mobility, would be interested in intense dialogic encounters and hybridity. Of course, in Bowles's work such encounters are often uncomfortable and dark as well as "mutually enrich[ing],"[68] but it is in the bringing together of cultures that all possibility remains, for it is in contact that energy is created.

Bowles embodied a particular transatlantic sensibility through "interfac[ing] with other world cultures,"[69] destabilizing national identity, and "chang[ing] the meaning by changing the context."[70] His works enact various transatlantic "sites of exchange," creating "interferences" that counteract established modes of thought through cultural interaction, displacing notions of absolute rootedness whilst generating vibrant, new, hybrid critiques and raising complex cultural tensions. In this "traveling writing," Bowles shares much with other radical thinkers, "constantly ... shift[ing] out of habitual formations," progressing

> from convergent thinking [and] analytical reasoning that tends to use rationality to move toward a single goal (a Western mode), to

divergent thinking, characterized by movement away from set
patterns and goals and towards a more whole perspective, one that
includes rather than excludes.[71]

Without settling for any single point of view or any easy reconciliation
of difference, Bowles's work offers a complex map for Transatlantic
Studies to examine, for he is fascinated by movement, by people
"routed" and "rooted" in cultures, sometimes connecting, sometimes
destroying, but always intermeshed in each others' lives. Bowles's
work may never show the final destination, but it will always offer
valuable, if dangerous, routes to follow, for, ultimately, as he has said,
"One belongs to the whole world, not just one part of it."[72]

---

[1] Paul Bowles in *Conversations with Paul Bowles*, ed. G. Dagel Caponi
(Jackson: University Press of Mississippi, 1993), 215.

[2] Paul Gilroy, *The Black Atlantic: Modernity and Double Consciousness*
(London: Verso, 1996), 4.

[3] Ibid.

[4] Paul Bowles, *Without Stopping* (London: Peter Owen, 1972), 341.

[5] Ibid.

[6] Ibid, 10.

[7] Ibid., 19.

[8] Ibid., 164.

[9] In Caponi, 4.

[10] In Caponi, 96-97.

[11] Mikhail Bakhtin, *Speech Genres and Other Late Essays* (Austin: University
of Texas Press, 1990), 7.

[12] Ibid., 67.

[13] Mary Louise Pratt, *Imperial Eyes: Travel Writing and Transculturation*
(London: Routledge, 1995), 4, 6-7.

[14] Mikhail Bakhtin, *The Dialogic Imagination* (Austin: University of Texas
Press, 1990), 324.

[15] Ibid., 368, 370.

[16] Caren Kaplan, *Questions of Travel: Postmodern Discourses of Displacement* (Durham: Duke University Press, 1996), 44.

[17] Ibid., 47, 34, 45, 49.

[18] Malcolm Bradbury, *Dangerous Pilgrimages: Trans-Atlantic Mythologies
and the Novel* (London: Secker and Warburg, 1995), 351.

[19] Paul Bowles, *The Sheltering Sky* (New York: Ecco Press, 1978 [1947]), 14.

[20] Kaplan, 28.

[21] Bowles, *The Sheltering Sky*, 14.

[22] In Caponi, 115.

[23] Paul Bowles, "Windows on the Past," *Holiday* 17 (January 1955): 32-34,
109-13.

[24] Ibid.

[25] Paul Bowles and Peter Haeberlin, *Yallah* (New York: MacDowell, 1956), 17.

[26] In Caponi, 77.

[27] Ibid., 123.

[28] Bowles, *The Sheltering Sky*, 100.

[29] Ibid., 168.

[30] Ibid., 223, 232.

[31] Paul Bowles, *The Spider's House* (London: Macdonald, 1957), 209, 182.

[32] Paul Bowles, *Let it Come Down* (London: John Lehmann, 1957), 21.

[33] Ibid.,176.

[34] Ibid., 126-27.

[35] Ibid.,151.

[36] The term "monoglossia" is derived from Bakhtin, where it is used to describe a "one-voiced," centralized and standardized system where different, alternative "voices" are marginalized or excluded.

[37] Paul Bowles, *Their Heads Are Green* (London: Peter Owen, 1963), 8.

[38] Paul Bowles, "Kif—Prologue and Compendium of Terms," in *The Book of Grass: An Anthology on Indian Hemp*, ed. G. Andrews and S. Vinkenoog (London: Peter Owen, 1967), 108.

[39] Bowles, *Their Heads Are Green*, 70.

[40] Ibid., 96.

[41] Bowles's friend William Burroughs called Tangiers the "Interzone" in his novel *Naked Lunch*, and Beat writers like Jack Kerouac and Allen Ginsberg visited in the 1960s.

[42] Paul Bowles, "The Worlds of Tangiers," *Holiday* 23 (March 1958): 68.

[43] James Clifford, *Routes: Travel and Translation in the Late Twentieth Century* (Cambridge: Harvard University Press, 1997), 230.

[44] Ibid., 39.

[45] Paul Bowles, "The Point of View," *View* 5 (May 1945): 5.

[46] Bowles, *Without Stopping*, 348.

[47] In Caponi, 199.

[48] Paul Bowles, *Collected Stories* (Santa Barbara: Black Sparrow, 1979), 41. The term "co-presence" refers back to Mary Louise Pratt, *Imperial Eyes*, above.

[49] Stuart Hall, *Modernity and Its Futures*, ed. S. Hall, D. Held and T. McGrew (Cambridge: Polity Press, 1992), 310.

[50] Homi Bhabha, *The Location of Culture* (London: Routledge, 1994), 228.

[51] Ibid.

[52] Stuart Hall, "New Cultures for Old," in *A Place in the World?*, ed. D. Massey and P. Jess (Oxford: Oxford University Press, 1995), 206.

[53] Ibid.

[54] Ibid.

[55] Salman Rushdie, *Imaginary Homelands* (London: Granta, 1991) 17. Rushdie explains that the word "translation" comes from the Latin "bearing across," and links it to the idea of "Having been borne across the world, we are translated men."

[56] In Caponi, 23. Emphasis mine.

[57] William Burroughs and Brion Gysin, *The Third Mind* (London: John Calder, 1979), 18.

[58] Homi Bhabha, "The Third Space," in *Identity, Community, Culture, Difference*, ed. J. Rutherford (London: Lawrence and Wishart, 1990), 211.

[59] In Caponi, 239-40.

[60] Paul Bowles, *Midnight Mass* (Santa Barbara: Black Sparrow Press, 1981), 39, 99,102.

[61] Ibid., 43.

[62] Ibid., 53, 76.

[63] Ibid., 79, 84, 77.

[64] Ibid., 84.

[65] Armin Paul Frank, "Transatlantic Responses: Strategies in the Making of a New World Literature," *Comparative Criticism* 15 (1993): 57-79 (75).

[66] Iain Chambers, *Migrancy, Culture, Identity* (London: Routledge, 1994), 27.

[67] Ibid.

[68] Bakhtin, 7.

[69] Paul Giles, "Virtual Americas: The Internationalization of American Studies and the Ideology of Exchange," *American Quarterly* 50, no. 3 (1998): 523-47 (545).

[70] Paul Giles, "Reconstructing American Studies: Transnational Paradoxes, Comparative Perspectives," *Journal of American Studies* 28, no 3 (1994): 335-58 (352).

[71] Gloria Anzaldua, *Borderlands/La Frontera: The New Mestiza* (San Francisco: Aunt Lute, 1987), 79.

[72] In Caponi, 90.

Chapter 13

Transatlantic Influences on Contemporary Visual Arts

Kathleen Kadon Desmond

Thinking about Flemish, Netherlandish, or Germanic art conjures up images by Van Eyck, Rembrandt, Vermeer, and Dürer—or maybe Rene Magritte, Piet Mondrian and Kathe Kollwitz. American art brings to mind romantic landscapes by Asher Brown Durand and social landscapes by Thomas Hart Benton. Later works by Georgia O'Keeffe and Andy Warhol are remembered as uniquely American. But what images or ideas are evoked when "contemporary" is the prefix to visual art in Central Europe and the US? What transatlantic influences are at work in contemporary visual art and how can they be explained? Contemporary aesthetics and art theory, contemporary artists and the art they make have all changed the very nature of art collecting and preservation. They have also changed the role of art museums and their curators, along with the strategies that viewers employ in order to understand and appreciate contemporary visual art.

Radical changes in visual art ideas, artists, art works, the role of art museums, curators, collectors and viewers can be explained through examples of transatlantic influences on contemporary art collections in museums such as the Museum of Modern Art Brussels, the Ludwig Forum in Aachen, Germany, the Stedelijk Museum in Amsterdam, and

Dundee Contemporary Arts in Scotland. The philosophical underpinnings of the contemporary art collection at the Bonnefantenmuseum in Maastricht, the Netherlands, provides a case study for thinking about the transatlantic influences on contemporary visual art. Its seminal collection is rooted in the work of German artist Joseph Beuys, includes the Belgian French-speaking traditions with the work of Marcel Broodthaers, and develops a direct transatlantic connection between Italian *arte povera* and American Minimalism.

Contemporary art has had an impact on the museum as a cultural institution, the role of the museum curator as presenter and preservationist, and the role of the contemporary art viewer. Since the radical shifts within the contemporary art world during the mid-1960s, curators have been required to think about the preservation, presentation and development of their collections in new ways, and viewers have had to develop new ways of thinking about and viewing visual art.

Contemporary Art Ideas

From a transatlantic perspective, contemporary visual art ideas that come immediately to mind, because they have been so influential to the art of the later part of the 20th century, are those that were born in Fluxus and live on in the work and legacy of German artist, Joseph Beuys. When Fluxus activities began in the late 1950s,

> a lot of artists and composers and other people who wanted to do beautiful things began to look at the world around them in a new way (for them). They said: Hey!—coffee cups can be more beautiful than fancy sculptures. A kiss in the morning can be more dramatic than a drama by Mr. Fancypants. The sloshing of my foot in my wet boot sounds more beautiful than fancy organ music.[1]

Artists began to question, "Why does everything that's beautiful like cups and kisses and sloshing feet have to be made into a part of something fancier and bigger? Why can't I just use [these elements] for their own sake?"[2]

In the early 1960s Fluxus was a ground-breaking and idiosyncratically imaginative *avant garde* movement with a prehistory in experimental music and the concrete poetry of the 1950s and a posthistory in minimalism and the conceptual and performance art of the 1960s, 1970s and 1980s. Although Fluxus began with a series of concerts organized in New York City, it grew into a sort of improvisational clearinghouse for artistic events and activities in

Western Europe, especially in Paris, Copenhagen, and Dusseldorf. The German-American connection was crucial to early Fluxus.[3]

Fluxus was a vital tradition with significant influences on the aesthetic practices of many subsequent visual art movements and individual artists. It never came close to being a "school" or an art movement in the traditional sense. Perhaps best defined as Neo-Dada, Fluxus activities paved the way for contemporary artists to take new, international directions and adopt transatlantic attitudes.

With a shift in the center of the art world from Paris to New York in the mid-20th century and the domination of American art in Europe, the art world developed several transatlantic contextual strands. American artists strove for independence from the past, particularly from European traditions, and argued for a more theoretical and impersonal attitude. Artists had operated on a more explicitly international level within various groups and collaborative contexts since the mid-20th century and had responded to various past abstract-expressionist and figurative tendencies by seeking new meaning for their work. Contemporary artistic attitudes are resistant to the idea that art works should provide access to a world of beauty, peace and harmony or that an art work can provide direct insight with respect to the artist's subconscious.

Later 20th-century American and European artists took a stance and adopted an attitude that was in direct opposition to the personal and emotional art of the past. These new artistic attitudes changed aesthetics and were more or less synchronous with new ideas whose influences were felt in social and intellectual arenas. These new beliefs were interpreted and carried out in a direct, radical way and reached audiences quickly by means of simple and inexpensive dissemination through publication or performance.[4] These attitudes led both to a fairly direct form of political art and to criticism of the traditional means and classification of art, which came to be seen as offshoots of a now discredited society. In a radical departure from the heroic projects of previous artists, a new pragmatism was adopted, which preferred to launch its critical assault from within the prevailing order. Those like Fluxus artists who sought a different approach risked being marginalized—seen and heard only to a very limited extent.[5]

In Europe, artists were casting fragments of mass consumption in a repetitive aesthetic model or concealing progressively larger parts of the world, while Americans were tinkering with the fundamental principles of a work of art, attempting to liberate art from all prejudice in the way of aesthetic perception. In order to evade the tyranny of the historically charged view, artists on both sides of the Atlantic did not consider their objects to be sculptures, or part of the history of sculpture. They attempted to free their work from the traditional interpretive model that sought to project a narrative into the representation (so, for example, they did not title their work). This required the viewer to consider the aesthetic merits of this art in terms of its mass, volume, surface and proportions, thus making the environment a major criterion for designating the object a work of art and defining its special status.[6]

Another late 20th-century transatlantic change was the abandonment of traditional easel painting and pedestal sculpture in favor of a freer manner of presenting art work. No longer hindered by or struggling against previously set norms with regard to the material construction, size and function, artists were experimenting on a large scale. Artists employed new and advanced technical aids or materials such as fast drying acrylic paint, polyester or neon lighting—the idea being that it was an advantage that these elements were not burdened with art historical connotations.[7]

Contemporary Artists and Their Art

Joseph Beuys brought these new positions from the German-American connection of Fluxus to a prominent place in Germanic history and art. Beuys perhaps even foretold the *arte povera* movement and certainly laid the foundation for the work in the prestigious Whitney Biennial 2000, in terms of medium, materials and meaning. The art instructor who became a political activist, founded political parties, used a wide variety of materials and processes to create mysterious and compelling artifacts and performances, and functioned as a poetic social critic and teacher of humanity, appealed greatly to artistic imagination and aesthetic sensibilities.[8] Beuys expressed the beatific suffering found in Medieval religious paintings, the transcendent expressions in Dürer's engravings, recreated myths, spiritual beliefs and tormented angst of German Expressionism. His art extends beyond historic sources to create a compelling and disturbing contemporary social and aesthetic dynamic.[9] In Beuys, the art world found a leader whose activities and ideas were admired and imitated. His ideas not only crossed the Atlantic, but they continue to influence the work of artists around the world today.

Belgian artist Marcel Broodthaers provides another thread in the transatlantic perspective. With his roots in Surrealism, Broodthaers focused on the relationship between text as image and text as text. He focused on issues with works in which the text was rendered in individual handwriting, giving it pictorial value.[10] Literary in his orientation, Broodthaers used the relationship that exists between language and image as his instrument for artistic innovation and far-reaching social changes. He raised the issue of the context of cultural institutions. In Broodthaers's world, the interested viewer discovers countless ambiguities behind which the artist seems to take refuge as a poet, a collector, or even as a museum curator. Whereas the works of Beuys bring one into a world full of personal history and passion, with mystical and magical rituals, those of Broodthaers expose mystifications.[11]

The relationship to the environment, which has acquired importance in contemporary art, extends not only to the exhibition context but to the wider social one as well. Marcel Broodthaers combined his preoccupation with the social function of an art work with spatial installations. For instance, in his installation, *L'Entree de l'Esposition,* visitors are welcomed into elegant surroundings where they can rest for a moment among exotic palms and handsomely framed photographs and screen prints before actually entering the museum to become acquainted with the visual cultures of the centuries. The sophisticated viewer will approach the rest of the collection with a certain sense of uneasiness, however, because the elegant palms partly block the view of the art works, and the photographs and prints actually contain hidden warnings. In *Museum/Museum,* screen prints are part of the installation, and the institution of the museum is linked with imitations, falsifications and a gold standard. The photographs that provide a summary of his previous work as a visual artist show that this warning does not exclude Broodthaers himself.[12]

The work of Beuys and Broodthaers can be seen as the continuation of two important visual cultures: the Northern and Central European culture, in which the personal myth is a binding element, and the French-speaking culture, which is especially influenced by language and literature.[13] And while we still expect artists such as these to present us with the ethical and aesthetic refinement of their cultures, their art ideas engender a critical-mindedness on the part of both the artist and the viewer towards everything that appears to confirm the existing world. Artists do not produce their work in a vacuum, but they, too, are subject to political and economic power structures and linguistic codes.[14]

The art works and ideas of Joseph Beuys, Marcel Broodthaers, the Italian Luciano Fabro and the American Robert Ryman give evidence of another way of thinking about contemporary art issues as they fit within a contextual framework that establishes transatlantic perspectives on contemporary artistic and aesthetic trends. This framework was expanded when the Italian a*rte povera* movement met a thoroughly different type of art from the US in the mid-1970s— minimal art. *Arte povera* brought a third visual culture to contemporary art: the Southern European and Byzantine cultures, individual and radical, poetic and classical. A fourth visual culture of American minimalism was in direct opposition to the poetic writings of the *arte povera* movement with its impersonal attitude and promotion of the recurrent principal: maximal content through minimal form.

Arte povera was a term first used in exhibitions in Italy in the late 1960s and refers to the materials used in the art work, not to the content. Coal, steel plates, rubber, pieces of burlap and other anti-aesthetic and easily obtained primitive or raw materials are used to make works of art. These materials, free of art historical reference, function as a medium for metaphors. Through the consistent use of a variety of materials in one work, a contrast between nature and culture can be expressed in many *arte povera* works.

A thoroughly individual, radical, and poetic art movement, *arte povera* can be clearly exemplified in the work of Luciano Fabro. In two of Fabro's sculptures, *Prometeo* and *La nascita di Venere,* classical references abound. The title of the works provide interpretive clues. For instance, *Prometeo,* or Prometheus, the Greek Titan, created the first human being out of clay and stolen fire from the gods. The sculpture was made in 1986, the year of the disaster at the Chernobyl nuclear power plant. Nuclear energy, a natural force comparable to the stolen fire of Prometheus, is an uncontrollable force. By way of this sculpture, Fabro suggests that, in comparison to nature, human activities are chaotic, despite attempts at order, and that humans have forces at their disposal that can destroy nature.

Prometeo has a rigid base of eight upright marble pillars from which upside-down surveying markers protrude vertically. Several measuring sticks rest on top of the grayish white marble. The pillars are arranged in an organized fashion, not immediately recognizable as triangular and pentagonal. Despite the materials from which the sculpture is made, sturdy marble pillars and scientific measuring devices, its general appearance is one of instability and disorder: the measuring sticks seem to be lying pointlessly on top of the pillars. Even when the basic geometric forms that make up the piece are recognized, the construction remains an enigma. In the style and materials there are symbolic references that provide an iconographic interpretation.

La nascita di Venere alludes to classical mythology with its title and material, like *Prometeo.* The birth of Venus was often portrayed in classical Greek sculpture. Venus, the goddess of love and fertility, born from the sea and cast onto land by the waves, bends over on the beach as she wrings the sea-water from her long hair. Created of a pillar of marble and installed in sand, Fabro's work refers to myths that designate primal forces surrounded by mystery and uncertainty. Through titles, materials and the work itself, Fabro evokes the dark and mysterious side of classical mythology to explain the relationships between humans and nature.

Although American minimal art developed at the same time as European neo-constructivism, its influence was far greater and more sustained. The theoretical basis of minimal art, translated by artists trained in art history, was independence from European traditions, an impersonal attitude very different from the *arte povera* writings of the same time. Minimal artists sought to produce non-emotional and non-expressive works of art—art that was pure and consistent. They sought to create maximum content using minimal form. Minimalists had a preference for geometric structures and modular principles. Each component within the work of art was equal in terms of form and value. Industrial techniques and materials, and consequently industrial execution, were favored. Many works were made specifically for galleries and museums, such as wall paintings or light sculptures. Sometimes the work existed only for the length of the exhibition, a precursor of conceptual art. The concepts and design sketches needed for the execution of minimalist works became significant because of the transient nature of the actual work. Works of art were as concrete and as objective as possible. Sculptors Richard Serra and Sol LeWitt are considered, along with painters Robert Mangold and Robert Ryman, to be among the major figures in minimal art.

Robert Ryman's paintings make an interesting example of minimal art and it is represented in the seminal collection of contemporary art at Maastricht's Bonnefantenmuseum. Ryman does not make use of elaborate preliminary studies and models in creating his paintings. As his finished works demonstrate, preliminary studies and models would scarcely be able to portray their most striking quality, which is the relationship of the painting to its immediate environment. Ryman's paintings make use of subtle visual means that only become evident when the installation is carried out properly. In the painting *Journal*, for instance, the reflection of light on the wall behind the painting is an intended result of the way it is made and attached to the wall. Without the utmost precision in installing such works, a great deal of the content and quality of the work would not emerge. The system by which the work is attached to the wall is meant to be obvious. Normally not visible, the metal spacers have been transformed by Ryman into a compositional element. *Journal* exemplifies Ryman's minimalist desire to create a painting that would both be shallow and lean against the wall, without the painted surface being directly attached to the wall.

Even within the new tendencies that *arte povera* and minimalism brought about, fundamental changes and boundaries are found. Contemporary art history defined this period of "image breaking" so quickly that areas soon became delineated, making new traditions discernible. Robert Ryman's white paintings and Luciano Fabro's marble sculptures became acknowledged as points of reference comparable to such historically-influential works as Pablo Picasso's cubist canvases or Piet Mondrian's neo-plastic paintings.[15]

The Role of Contemporary Art Museums, Curators, Collectors and Viewers

Traditionally art history has internalized the ideologies of the dominant cultural centers that have contested authority over the canon of "great" art. This has changed in the last 25 years. The discourses of gender and race have been prominent in the displacement of a canon, as have the reappraisal of art's social origins and a revised view of "peripheral traditions" within Europe itself. The task of contemporary art museums now includes a responsibility to the viewers exercised through looking, living with and criticizing art and the conditions of its making and reception. Curators attempt to create an openness and continuity of dialogue so that museum viewers can freely contribute rather than passively accept the single voice of the authoritarian lecture: "That which is done for itself, which imagines being to the fullest, which requires no *illiminati* but is open to any inquiring and engaged intelligence, is the space of an unbounded meeting."[16] Thus, museums with contemporary art collections are no longer "chambers of aesthetics."[17] They are not, like historical art museums, institutions of cultural elitism or sanctums of an aesthetic removed from daily, lived experiences. Contemporary art museums attempt to collect and preserve objects, organize experiences, clarify looking, make visual ideas understood, sharpen vision and "by the demands which the work makes upon the looking, induce the viewer *to see*."[18]

Since the late 19th century, art has oscillated between reliance on the museum and the impetus to establish its social meaningfulness beyond the museum's walls. As formalism faded, in the post-colonial period, the plurality of cultures was asserted, even within the "old cultures" of Europe, and the bonds between artistic practice and the historical circumstances of traditions and existing conditions of production became more apparent.[19] One result is that contemporary museums are a mass of contradictions. Originally, museums were intended to make available to the public, through exhibitions, the collection of artifacts and curiosities belonging to royalty, the aristocracy or the societies of cultured citizens. It is this public access to collections, which are often not public property today, that is a distinguishing feature of a museum. At the same time, museums are obligated to preserve their collections. These two most important duties of a museum, the preservation of a legacy for future generations and the displaying of artifacts to the general public, validate each other, yet are also in direct conflict with each other. From the preservationist point of view, the collection would best be stored in the dark or at least out of the public's reach. In practice, however, within certain acceptable boundaries, museum objects are exposed to dangers that shorten or directly threaten their survival. Thus, the museum is continually faced with the task of making compromises between its two main functions.[20] The curator of contemporary art is confronted with the task of enabling the public to share in the experiences of looking at art works that have not yet been bestowed with historical interpretation while also ensuring that future generations will be able to partake of these works.[21] Further, contemporary art collections include works of a temporal nature like documentation of Beuys's performance pieces or Broodthaers's text and image pieces, or work made with impermanent materials or specific installation requirements like Fabro's *arte povera* pieces and Ryman's minimalist paintings. Contemporary art collections redefine the role of the museum as a cultural institution, the work of the curator as preservationist, and the viewer as a passive participant in the art viewing experience.

In keeping with the new roles of a contemporary art museum, in 1975 the Bonnefantenmuseum invited Joseph Beuys to explain his ideas about his position as an artist and teacher, as well as his views on the purpose of an art work within what he called the *"Erweiterter Kunstbegriff"* (extended idea of art), by means of an exhibition, a lecture and a discussion. After the installation of the exhibition, Beuys donated all of the displayed documents to the museum. The value of this collection lies not only in its completeness—almost all of the documents from the period 1960 to 1975 are represented—but also in the rareness of many of the publications. By signing the documents Beuys gave them a place in his oeuvre. Their significance as a source of his art work is all the greater due to the disintegration of many autonomous works of art by Beuys. The disappearance of these autonomous works is a consequence of Beuys's disregard for the preservation of materials. *"Akitonen"* (performances) and installations have, due to their ephemeral nature and material, a limited life span. The consciousness that the works represented, not the archival nature of the materials he used, was of prime importance to Beuys. In the museum's vast collection of documentary works, posters, books and prints by Beuys, one can see how drastically the world of contemporary art has changed.[22]

The Bonnefantenmuseum also owns a group of about 400 black and white photographs by Broodthaers and a large number of manuscripts concerning South Limburg[23] dating from 1960-1970. While these photographs are important for the study of Broodthaers's *oeuvre*, the majority of them were produced when he was working as a journalist and poet and not yet as a visual artist. At that time he had not yet found the right form for his largely language-oriented intellectual play on images and words. Broodthaers published curious articles about the landscape and history of Limburg in Brussels magazines and newspapers. Like the documentation of Joseph Beuys, these are not intended to be works of art, but rather as a chronicle of an artist's developing attitude toward the art world.[24]

Museum curators must necessarily think beyond the preservation of art works and also think in terms of encountering the visual. They think about the psychological and expressive effects of the art work as much as the techniques and materials of the works. They imagine transitions between the works in an exhibition as they create an experience to affect a variety of perceptual, affective and cognitive senses. They work "through visual metaphors, echoes and homologies, between representations, abstractions and traces, in relations of simplicity and complexity between three-and two-dimensions, static and time-based media, and through relationships of content and theme."[25] Transitions may create a flow from one work to another or they may be disjunctive and dramatic. These transitions may require the viewer to make imaginative leaps from one work to another as "works assert themselves and define the domain of their power."[26]

In this light we may see how the Bonnefantenmuseum set out to collect works that played a historically significant role and which represented a later phase of the transatlantic artist's development. Thus, the works in the Bonnefantenmuseum show a synthesis of a given artist's personal traits and the elements that point to new transatlantic developments.[27] The central and influential location of the Bonnefantenmuseum—Maastricht, the Netherlands—demands consideration in its impact on contemporary art collection policies adopted by museums in the neighboring areas of Germany and Belgium and enables this museum to serve particularly well as a case study of transatlantic influences on contemporary art. Other museums within its sphere of influence include the Museum of Modern Art Brussels, one of the Royal Museums of Fine Arts in Belgium, which houses both historical, modern and contemporary art, the Stedelijk Museum, and the Rijksmuseum in Amsterdam. Two nearby German museums, the Ludwig Forum in Aachen and the Ludwig Museum in Cologne, focus specifically on contemporary art which also demonstrates the transatlantic nature of their collections, not only with their American Pop Art collections but also with their contemporary photographs and video collections. In addition, the Dundee (Scotland) Contemporary Arts opened on March 19, 1999, with works by a host of contemporary performance and installation artists hearkening to Fluxus, Beuys and Broodthaers and to the more contemporary visual ideas brought about by *arte povera*, American pop art, minimalism and conceptual art.

All of these collections demonstrate that one of the most radical changes in the contemporary art world is the acknowledged responsibility of the museum in mediating the relationship between artists and viewers. A significant consequence of formal innovations like the relinquishment of the frame of the painting and the removal of the pedestal beneath a sculpture is that the viewer must take on a more active relationship with the work of art. The desire to involve the viewer more intensively with the art work has led to artists creating art forms such as installations and environments in which the viewer is completely surrounded by the physical presentation.[28] The ideas and art works of contemporary visual artists have led to new works of art and to new ways of thinking about the role of the art museum, the museum curator and the viewer of contemporary art. As I have demonstrated, these developments are rooted in several important perspectives of a transatlantic nature.

---

[1] Janet Jenkins, ed., *In the Spirit of Fluxus* (New York: Distributed Art Publishers, 1993), covers.

[2] Ibid.

[3] Andreas Huyssen, "Back to the Future: Fluxus in Context," in Jenkins, 142-50.

[4] Aloys Van Den Berk, "Contemporary Art," in *Bonnefantenmuseum, Maastricht* (Maastricht: Bonnefantenmuseum, 1995), 292.

[5] Ibid.

[6] Frederik Leen, "Contemporary Tendencies," in *The Museum of Modern Art Brussels* (Ludion-Ghent: Credit Communal, 1996), 113-20.

[7] Ibid., 291-93.

[8] Van Den Berk, *passim.*

[9] Howard J. Smagula, *Currents: Contemporary Directions in the Visual Arts* (Englewood Cliffs, New Jersey: Prentice-Hall, 1989), 217.

[10] Leen, 118-19.

[11] Ibid.

[12] Ibid.

[13] Van Den Berk, 291-316.

[14] Leen, 113-20.

[15] Van Den Berk, 291-316.

[16] Euan McArthur, "Seeing Ourselves as Other," in *Dundee Contemporary Arts* (Dundee: Dundee Contemporary Arts, 1999), 15-19.

[17] Ibid., 18.

[18] Ibid., 15.

[19] Ibid., 18-19.

[20] D. H. Van Wegen, "The Position of the Curator of Contemporary Art: Between Fetish and Score," unpublished manuscript for *Modern Art: Who Cares? The Book.* (Amsterdam: Netherlands Institute for Cultural Heritage, 1999).

[21] Ibid.

[22] Van Den Berk, 291-93.

[23] Maastricht is in the Province of Limburg.

[24] Van den Berk, 296.

[25] McArthur, 15.

[26] Ibid.

[27] Van den Berk, *passim.*

[28] Ibid., 292.

Part Four:
Power, Politics and Legislation

Chapter 14

Transatlantic Perspectives on Religious Rights in English Law

Peter W. Edge

Until recently, it was a commonplace that the United Kingdom's methods of protecting fundamental human rights relied upon negative liberty and a medley of individual mechanisms, rather than an overarching set of positive rights backed by judicial enforcement. With the Human Rights Act 1998 (HRA) incorporating the European Convention on Human Rights (ECHR) during 2000, however, the United Kingdom has now moved closer towards such a positive system, making the approaches of other jurisdictions of more immediate relevance to the development and critique of English law. Lord McCluskey has suggested that the HRA sets high targets for the analyst, practitioner, and citizen:

> In future no lawyer will be able to advise a client on any matter which might involve a public authority without studying not just the European jurisprudence—as [sic] he will read the Strasbourg report [sic] as I have done—but also American case-law, Canadian case-law and even Indian case-law and New Zealand and Australian case law.[1]

This chapter contrasts the religious liberty guarantees under the US Constitution with those under the HRA/ECHR, and explores the value of a transatlantic perspective on the development of religious rights in the English jurisdiction.

Religious Rights Under the US Constitution

The US Constitution adopted in 1787 was the result of a number of compromises between the different States and groups within them.[2] Although the Constitution contained some guarantees which in effect provided for the protection of individual rights, there was no Bill of Rights "of the sort which had already become a well-known feature of most, though not all, state constitutions."[3] This deficiency was rectified very quickly, with the ratification by the States of the first ten amendments to the US Constitution, commonly referred to as the Bill of Rights, in 1791.[4] Originally interpreted as limiting the power of the Federal government only, these rights have since been applied to limit the actions of the individual States.[5]

The First Amendment to the US Constitution provides that "Congress shall make no law respecting an establishment of religion, or prohibiting the free exercise thereof." This provision contains two distinct, albeit related, guarantees. Firstly, there is the prohibition on the "establishment of religion." Secondly, there is the guarantee of "free exercise" of religion. The two clauses probably share a common definition of religion as a group which constituted a religion for free exercise purposes, but not for establishment purposes, and which would be able to claim the protection offered by the free exercise clause without being subject to the restrictions on state linkage contained in the establishment clause.[6] Identifying this shared definition, however, is extremely problematic. In *Davis vs. Beason* (1890), the Supreme Court stated that "religion has reference to one's views of his relations to his Creator, and to the obligations they impose of reverence for his being and character, and of obedience to his will."[7] The Supreme Court has since rejected any requirement for a Supreme Being,[8] but has been reluctant to develop a comprehensive definition in its jurisprudence, perhaps because "the content of the term is found in the history of the human race and is incapable of compression into a few words."[9] The closest comes from *United States vs. Seeger* (1965), where the Court defined religion as :

> A sincere and meaningful belief which occupies in the life of its possessor a place parallel to that filled by the God of those admittedly qualifying for the exemption.... This construction avoids

imputing ... an intent to classify different religious beliefs, exempting some and excluding others.[10]

It is not necessary to belong to an organized church, sect, or denomination in order to be able to claim rights under the First Amendment.[11] Single-faceted ideologies, however, such as vegetarianism or Social Darwinism, may not be protected.[12] Nor, it seems, will choices which are "merely philosophical and personal rather than religious."[13] Additionally, claims which are considered to be insincere may fail. In *United States vs. Kuch* (1968), Kuch failed to show that the Neo-American Church was a religion, as the Court gained "the inescapable impression that the membership is mocking established institutions, playing with words and totally irreverent in any sense of the term."[14]

There is a considerable body of academic commentary seeking to draw out a more coherent, and comprehensive, definition of religion, but nothing approaching any academic consensus as to what the term means.[15] It should be noted, however, that the term is clearly capable of encompassing some form of beliefs which do not involve positive statements as to metaphysical reality. This may be a consequence of the wording of the First Amendment which in contrast with, for instance, the European Convention on Human Rights does not provide any express protection for conviction or belief.

Turning to the establishment clause, the First Amendment, originally intended to restrict the power of the Federal government, was aimed at preventing the establishment of a national Church. It has developed into a prohibition on establishment at both Federal and State level. Establishment is a complex concept, but the Supreme Court has stated that:

> Neither [federal nor state governments] can pass laws which aid one religion, aid all religions, or prefer one religion over another. Neither can force or influence a person to go to or to remain away from church against his will or force him to profess a belief or disbelief in any religion. No person can be punished for entertaining or professing religious beliefs or disbeliefs, for church attendance or non-attendance. No tax in any amount, large or small, can be levied to support any religious activities or institutions, whatever they may be called, or whatever form they may adopt to teach or practice religion. Neither a state nor the Federal Government can, openly or secretly, participate in the affairs of any religious organizations or groups and vice versa.[16]

This constitutional separation leaves considerable areas of uncertainty in the relationship between religious organizations and the State. For instance, some State involvement in supporting religious education is permitted, but it is easy to go too far. Additionally, while the State may not endorse particular religious tenets, it may date official documents "in the year of our Lord" or call upon God during legislative and judicial ceremonies.[17] Nonetheless, although the details of the separation of religious organization and State can be difficult to determine, the general philosophy is clear. The State should not become too closely entangled with any religious organization, nor should religious organizations become too closely entangled with the State.

Turning to the free exercise clause, the key debate here is the extent to which the free exercise clause places an additional limit on the State.[18] In a pair of polygamy cases, the Supreme Court considered that the First Amendment prohibited any law against mere opinion, but did not protect "actions which were in violation of social duties or subversive of good order."[19] In *Cantwell vs. Connecticut* (1940), the Supreme Court accepted that acts could be entitled to the protection of the First Amendment, as free exercise "embraces two concepts— freedom to believe and freedom to act. The first is absolute, but in the nature of things the second cannot be."[20] In *Sherbert vs. Verner* (1963), the Supreme Court endorsed this acceptance of actions and indicated that a burden on religion can be justified only by a compelling state interest.[21]

This approach aims to deal with substantive neutrality—that is, the impact of laws on the religious adherent, even when those laws are, on their face, neutral and applicable to everyone within the jurisdiction. An alternative, and now dominant, theme in the Supreme Court jurisprudence concentrates on formal neutrality.[22] In *Employment Division vs. Smith* (1990), the Supreme Court were required, albeit indirectly, to consider whether a free exercise argument could protect the ingestion of peyote, a hallucinogen controlled by the relevant Criminal Code. The Court found that "generally applicable, religion-neutral laws that have the effect of burdening a particular religious practice need not be justified by a compelling governmental interest."[23] This decision was extensively criticized, and in 1993 Congress enacted the Religious Freedom Restoration Act in order to revive the test developed by *Sherbert vs. Verner*. The Constitution strictly divides the exercise of judicial, legislative, and executive powers, however, and this legislation was later found to be an infringement of the separation of legislative and judicial powers, and hence invalid.[24] Following the survival of *Smith*, commentators have begun seriously to consider whether the religion clauses of the US Constitution, as interpreted by the Supreme Court, need revision.[25]

Even in the light of *Smith*, however, free exercise retains some meaning. In *Church of the Lukumi Babalu Aye, Inc. vs. City of Hialeah* (1993), a unanimous Supreme Court upheld a free exercise claim against a criminal law. In that case members of the Santeria religion wished to build a church in Hialeah, Florida. Santeria practices include animal sacrifice. In an attempt to stop the sect from building a church, the city passed an ordinance criminalizing the ritual sacrifice of animals, but not slaughtering simpliciter. The law punishing animal cruelty, including animal sacrifice which was not intended primarily for consumption as food, was rejected on the basis that it had both the purpose and effect of restricting religious conduct, and did not address non-religious conduct causing similar harms.[26]

The Human Rights Act and the ECHR

The ECHR is a regional human rights instrument, requiring a broad range of States to meet minimum standards in

> those rights and essential freedoms which are practiced after long usage and experience in all the democratic countries. While they are the first triumph of democratic regimes, they are also the necessary conditions under which they operate.[27]

These rights include freedom of religion, belief, and conscience, primarily contained in Article 9 of the Convention :

> 9(1). Everyone has the right to freedom of thought, conscience, and religion; this right includes freedom to change his religion or belief and freedom, either alone or in community with others and in public or private, to manifest his religion or belief, in worship, teaching, practice, and observance.
> 9(2). Freedom to manifest one's religion or beliefs shall be subject only to such limitations as are prescribed by law and are necessary in a democratic society in the interests of public safety, for the protection of public order, health or morals, or for the protection of the rights and freedoms of others.[28]

As with the model discussed above, the bare text has been developed by its application to particular cases.[29] In the case of the ECHR, a strong enforcement mechanism has allowed individuals to bring member States, including their own, before Convention organs to rule whether there has been a violation. This has produced a rich body of

Convention jurisprudence on many articles, although the volume and quality of the jurisprudence under Article 9 has been the subject of strong criticism.[30] The article consists of two rights—an absolute right to freedom of thought, conscience, and religion; and a qualified right to manifest religion or belief, restrictions on which can be justified by reference to Article 9(2). As with the First Amendment, it seems probable that a single definition of religion applies to both elements.[31] Similarly, the European Court of Human Rights has been reluctant to provide a clear definition of religion, although examples of protected belief systems can be extracted from the cases. Religious belief, in a non-theistic sense including atheism and agnosticism, is protected by the article.[32] A metaphysical element is not required, however, as ethical or philosophical convictions such as opposition to abortion, pacifism, and veganism are also protected.[33] There is also a suggestion in the jurisprudence that the beliefs must be distinguishable from mere opinion, and attain a certain level of cogency, seriousness, cohesion and importance.

The absolute right under Article 9 requires the State to respect the beliefs of the individual. In particular, it "affords protection against indoctrination of religion by the State,"[34] and can also require the State to protect the individual against such improper influence to change their beliefs.[35] Although interference with this right cannot be justified by reference to Article 9(2), this is not as startling as may appear, as the right is basically internal: the right of the individual to be free of attempts to change their beliefs or indoctrinate them. Actions other than simple holding of belief are manifestations of that belief.

Manifestation of belief can take a number of forms.[36] Most obviously, this includes religious worship, educating oneself or others in the belief, proselytizing, proclaiming belief publicly, or observing dietary or similar prohibitions.[37] However, not every action motivated by religious belief is a manifestation of that belief. In *Arrowsmith vs. United Kingdom* (1978), the applicant had been convicted for distributing leaflets intended to discourage soldiers from serving in Northern Ireland. Not every part of the leaflet endorsed pacifist philosophy, and it did not constitute a general call for persons to give up all violence. Arrowsmith claimed a violation of her right to manifest pacifism under Article 9. The Commission noted:

> The Commission considers that the term "practice" as employed in Article 9(1) does not cover every act which is motivated or influenced by a religion or belief.... [W]hen the actions of individuals do not actually express the belief concerned they cannot

be considered to be as such protected by Article 9(1), even when motivated or influenced by it.[38]

Later cases support the view that religious motivation is insufficient to bring Article 9 into effect—there must be some characteristic about the activity itself which is of a religious or conscientious nature. Thus, participating in an action designed to provoke a strike in public civil service, refusing to perform administrative functions following from a position in a state religion, or refusing to pay taxes towards state revenue used to fund objectionable purposes do not fall within Article 9.[39] Rather, the behavior must be "the direct expression of a religious or philosophical conviction."[40]

As well as being subject to a restrictive interpretation, manifestations may be restricted by reference to the competing interests in Article 9(2). These restrictions are similar to those found elsewhere in the Convention, and have been applied in a similar way. In particular, the Court has recognized that its role is not to second-guess the domestic authorities, but rather to act as a Court of review, ensuring the decisions of local bodies act within the national margin of appreciation.[41] The exact extent of this margin of appreciation in relation to religious rights remains uncertain.[42]

Although the United Kingdom took an important role in the drafting of the Convention, and was one of the first States to ratify it, there was no obligation for the United Kingdom to incorporate it into English law. So long as the rights under the ECHR were adequately guaranteed, the Convention did not lay down a form in which this was to be achieved. Accordingly, for a considerable period the United Kingdom was bound to observe guarantees which were not actually part of domestic law.[43] In 1996 the new Labour government noted that the current arrangement had considerable practical and rhetorical disadvantages, and began to plan for the incorporation of the ECHR into English law through a Human Rights Act.[44]

The Human Rights Act 1998 seems set to have a massive impact upon rights protection in the English jurisdiction. In particular, all public bodies will be required to act in accordance with the ECHR if it is lawful for them to do so (Section 6); all legislation is to be interpreted as complying with the ECHR "so far as it is possible to do so" (Section 3(1)); and a special mechanism has been created to allow speedy alteration of Acts of Parliament found incompatible with the Convention (sections 4 and 10). The HRA incorporates Convention texts and continuing jurisprudence of Convention organs, but includes a number of additional provisions, including the opaque section 13(1):

If a court's determination of any question arising under this Act might affect the exercise by a religious organisation (itself or its members collectively) of the Convention right to freedom of thought, conscience and religion, it must have particular regard to the importance of that right.[45]

Transatlantic perspectives

The full implications of the HRA remain to be played out. A recurring theme in commentary and debates is the need for a working in period, during which key issues of interpretation and application will be tested before the courts. Lord Donaldson of Lyminster suggested, "We will have to start with a deluge of claims of breach of the Convention. If the Canadian experience is anything to go by, it will range from the arguable through the just arguable to the plain preposterous."[46] This section considers the extent to which US materials and perspectives can assist in this development.

The first point to make is that the HRA is primarily an English statute; secondarily, a document incorporating the ECHR; and only residually a member of the family of domestic human rights guarantees which includes the US Bill of Rights. This has important implications, contra Lord McCluskey's suggestion earlier, for the way in which English lawyers and judges approach these areas of uncertainty. The HRA, in marked contrast to the US Bill of Rights, has no greater authority than any other Act of Parliament, and has been carefully drafted to accommodate the current United Kingdom constitution. It falls to be interpreted as an Act of Parliament, under the guidelines for construction developed by the English legal system. Thus, there is limited scope for transatlantic perspectives. The HRA is, however, an act intended to incorporate the ECHR into English law. In particular, it is intended to provide domestic remedies for the bulk of Convention violations within the jurisdiction. When faced with acts intended to meet the international obligations of the State, the courts will have regard to this purpose. This indicates that the HRA will be interpreted to cover liability under the ECHR, as interpreted and developed by Convention organs, but may not be taken any further. So, if the ECHR allows a particular State action, the HRA may well be interpreted so as to allow that State action, regardless of insights from other jurisdictions.

The incorporation of the ECHR may not, then, result in the English jurisdiction directly joining in the process by which national constitutional guarantees are developed in a transnational context, whereby perspectives and theoretical underpinnings are shared across jurisdictions. Nonetheless, the HRA gives some scope for judicial creativity. The courts will be required to apply Convention jurisprudence to particular legal situations. For instance, the courts may be required to consider whether a particular planning decision infringes rights under Article 9. Where the scope of the ECHR guarantee is clear, this might fairly be seen as primarily involving creativity and development of English planning law, rather than fundamental religious rights. Where the Convention organs have not given clear guidance, however, the English courts will be required to develop their own interpretation of the ECHR. In particular, the concept of the margin of appreciation may allow the English courts sufficient room to develop their own body of jurisprudence.

Even if the English courts do not develop their own reading of the fundamental rights under the ECHR, they will be concerned to ensure that their application of the HRA does not cause the United Kingdom to violate the ECHR. The courts will, then, attempt to predict the interpretation that the European Court of Human Rights would give to the Convention were the case to come before them. As the HRA does not exclude the operation of the Convention's own enforcement mechanism, we can expect a sizable proportion of the more contentious predictions to be tested out at the European level. Thus, transatlantic perspectives on religious rights are important to the development of religious rights under the Human Rights Act insofar as they provide a sound foundation for predicting European Court of Human Rights developments of the ECHR.

This chapter has identified a number of areas of uncertainty where neither the US constitutional guarantees, nor the jurisprudence under the ECHR, has provided a clear statement of the law. In these areas, it is likely that jurisprudence and commentary in all jurisdictions will be taken account of in seeking further clarity. Thus, for instance, it seems probable that an English court seeking to interpret Article 9 would have recourse to US materials when seeking to develop the meaning of religion, and those factors which make a particular exercise of religious rights more or less fundamental. The range and importance of these areas of shared uncertainty should not be underestimated. Nor should the extent to which political, legal, and philosophical traditions are shared by the two systems be ignored. Common arguments can be seen in both US and ECHR jurisprudence on religious rights, and there are good reasons why lawyers and judges in both systems should have some familiarity with the arguments being developed in the other.

Even within these areas of uncertainty, however, it is important that the differences between the two systems be properly recognized. The First Amendment to the US Constitution is an elderly document compared with Article 9 of the ECHR. Although Article 9 is more explicit in its protection, in particular with the grounds allowing restriction on manifestation in Article 9(2), the longevity of the First Amendment has led to a rich body of commentary and precedent. There are more substantive differences between the two. The First Amendment deals with "religion," while Article 9 deals with "thought, conscience, and religion" and "religion and belief," thus clearly encompassing at least some philosophical as opposed to metaphysical stances. The First Amendment enshrines a particular vision of the separation of Church and State which is not only not central to Article 9, but contrary to the practice of many European countries. Many signatories to the ECHR have a quite different model of Church/State relations—one which allows an intimate connection between the State and religious organizations, so long as others are not thereby discriminated against. The First Amendment, whatever its origins, is now a constitutional guarantee for an entire nation, rather than a federation of sovereign States. The ECHR, on the other hand, although at least partly drafted as a Bill of Rights for a United Europe, remains a regional human rights guarantee for an increasingly diverse group of sovereign states. Finally, Feldman sees a profound distinction between the individualistic philosophy of the US Constitution and the more communitarian approach of the Convention, so that "[g]reat caution should be exercised before cases from the US are used."[47]

In conclusion, there is room for a fruitful exchange between the two systems of protecting religious rights. Use of materials from the two systems must take account of the particular legal, and ideally social, context of the two systems. Even a sensitive use of US materials is likely to be uncommon in the development of the Human Rights Act. The HRA is primarily a statute for incorporating the ECHR, and US materials are relevant insofar as they can assist English courts in predicting the decisions of the European Court of Human Rights on religious rights.

---

[1] 582, House of Lords Debates, 1268.

[2] R. Hodder-Williams, "The Constitution (1787) and Modern American Government," in *Constitutions in Democratic Politics*, ed. V. Bogdanor (Aldershot: Gower Publishing, 1988), 72-104.

[3] D. Fellman, "The Nationalization of American Civil Liberties," in *Essays on the Constitution of the United States*, ed. H. J. Abraham et al. (London : National University Press, 1978), 51.

[4] D. McKay, *American Politics and Society* (Oxford: Blackwell Press, 1993), 39-50.

[5] R. C. Cortner, *The Supreme Court and the Second Bill of Rights* (Madison: University of Wisconsin Press, 1981), 279-301.

[6] V. D. Ricks, "To God God's, To Caesar Caesar's, and to Both the Defining of Religion," *Creighton Law Review* 26 (1993): 1056-60 (1053).

[7] *Davis vs. Beason*, 133 US 333 (1890), at 342.

[8] *Welsh vs. United States*, 398 US 333 (1970).

[9] *United States vs. Kauten*, 133 F.2d. 703 (1943).

[10] *United States vs. Seeger*, 380 US 163 (1965), at 176.

[11] *Frazee vs. Illinois Dept. of Employment Security*, 489 US 829 (1989); *United States vs. Ballard*, 322 US 78 (1944).

[12] *Africa vs. Pennsylvania*, 662 F.2d. 1025.

[13] *Wisconsin vs. Yoder,* 406 US 205 (1972).

[14] *United States vs. Kuch*, 288 F. Supp. 439 (1968).

[15] For an introduction see Ricks; also W. P. Marshall, "Truth and the Religion Clauses," *DePaul Law Review* 43 (1994): 243.

[16] *Everson vs. Board of Education*, 330 US 1, 15-16 (1947). See also P. W. Edge, "Reorienting the Establishment Debate: From the Illusory Norm to Equality of Respect," *Anglo-American Law Review* (1998): 265-84.

[17] S. B. Epstein, "Rethinking the Constitutionality of Ceremonial Deism," *Columbia Law Review* 96 (1996): 2083.

[18] S. L. Carter, "Comment: The Resurrection of Religious Freedom," *Harvard Law Review* 107 (1993): 118.

[19] *Reynolds vs. United States,* 98 US 145 (1878) at 164; see also *Davis vs. Beason*, 133 US 333 (1890).

[20] *Cantwell vs. Connecticut*, 310 US 296 (1940), at 303-4.

[21] *Sherbert vs. Verner*, 374 US 398 (1963).

[22] S. E. Williams, "Religious Exemptions and the Limits of Neutrality," *Texas Law Review* (1995): 119.

[23] *Employment Division vs. Smith,* 494 US 872 (1990), at 886.

[24] M. S. Sheffer, "God Versus Caesar: Free Exercise, the Religious Freedom Restoration Act, and Conscience," *Oklahoma City University Law Review* 23 (1998): 929.

[25] K. Greenawalt, "Should the Religion Clauses of the Constitution be Amended?," *Loyola of Los Angeles Law Review* 32 (1998): 9; R. P. George, "Protecting Religious Liberty in the Next Millennium: Should We Amend the Religion Clauses of the Constitution?," *Loyola of Los Angeles Law Review* 32 (1998): 27.

[26] *Church of the Lukumi Babalu Aye, Inc. vs. City of Hialeah*, 113 S.Ct. 2217, 2227 (1993).

[27] Consultative Assembly of the Council of Europe, *Official Report*, 7 September 1949, at 127.

[28] Ibid.

[29] P. Mahoney, "Principles of Judicial Review as Developed by the European Court of Human Rights: the Relevance in a National Context," in *The Human*

Rights Act: What It Means, ed. L. Betten (London: Martinus Nijhoff Publishers, 1999), 65, 73-78.

[30] See, for instance, T. J. Gunn, "Adjudicating Rights of Conscience Under the European Convention on Human Rights," in *Religious Human Rights in Global Perspectives: Legal Perspectives,* ed. J. D. van Vyver and J. Witte (Amsterdam: Kluwer, 1996).

[31] P. W. Edge, "Current Problems in Article 9 of the European Convention on Human Rights," *Juridical Review* (1996): 42.

[32] *Kokkinakis vs. Greece* (1994), 17 EHRR 397.

[33] Respectively *Knudsen vs. Norway* (1986), 8 EHRR 45; *Le Cour Grandmaison and Fritz vs. France* (1989), 11 EHRR 46; *H. vs. United Kingdom* (1993), 16 EHRR CD44.

[34] *Angelini vs. Sweden* (1988), 10 EHRR 123.

[35] *Kokkinakis vs. Greece* (1994), 17 EHRR 397; *Dubowski and Skup vs. Poland* (1997), HUDOC 18 April.

[36] H. Cullen, "The Emerging Scope of Freedom of Conscience," *European Law Review Checklist* 22 (1997), HRC32 at HRC33-36.

[37] Respectively *Holy Monasteries vs. Greece* (1994), 20 EHRR 1; *Kjeldsen, Busk Madsen and Pedersen vs. Denmark* (1976), 1 EHRR 711; *Kokkinakis vs. Greece*; *App. 9820/82 vs. Sweden* (1982), 5 EHRR 297; *Stedman vs. United Kingdom* (1997), HUDOC 7 April.

[38] *Arrowsmith vs. United Kingdom* (1978), 3 EHRR 218, paragraph 71.

[39] Respectively *App. 10365/83 vs. Germany* (1985), 7 EHRR 409; *Knudsen vs. Norway* (1986), 8 EHRR 45; *Bouessel de Bourg vs. France* (1993), 16 EHRR CD49.

[40] *Faclini vs. Switzerland* (1993), 16 EHRR CD13.

[41] N. Lavender, "The Problem of the Margin of Appreciation," *European Human Rights Law Review* 4 (1997): 380.

[42] P. W. Edge, "The European Court of Human Rights and Religious Rights," *International and Comparative Law Quarterly* 47 (1998): 680.

[43] A. Lester, "Fundamental Rights: The United Kingdom Isolated," *Public Law* (1984): 46.

[44] J. Straw and P. Boateng, "Bringing Rights Home: Labour's Plans to Incorporate the European Convention on Human Rights into United Kingdom Law," *European Human Rights Law Review* (1997): 71.

[45] Human Rights Act 1998.

[46] (532, House of Lords Debates, 1292).

[47] D. Feldman, "The Human Rights Act 1998 and Constitutional Principles," *Legal Studies* 19 (1999): 204.

Chapter 15

The International Dimensions of Conflict and the International Criminal Tribunal for the Former Yugoslavia

Lesley Hodgson, Andrew Thompson, and Donald H. Wallace

Those who pushed for the creation of the International Criminal Tribunal for the Former Yugoslavia (ICTFY) argued that properly conducted international criminal trials could legitimately accomplish several goals—among them, deterrence, atonement, relief for victims and families, and reaffirmation of the rule of law.[1] This chapter examines the efforts put forward to gain political legitimacy for the ICTFY at the international level on both sides of the Atlantic. Our position is that the international community failed to successfully address issues early on within the former Yugoslavia on the basis of ethical principles that could transcend state-centered expediency. Subsequently, the ICTFY itself has evolved into an unfortunate admixture of approaches; ethical principles have been balanced against expedience, and the result is a compromise of legal systems that represent the differing positions of the states involved in its development. Consequently, the architects of the ICTFY and the tribunal have not maintained a consistent focus on creating a perception of international legitimacy.

The International Dimension to the Break-up of Yugoslavia

The break up of Yugoslavia, while influenced to a degree by enmities that have existed since the birth of the country in 1918, was to a greater extent propelled by more immediate events. A deteriorating economic environment and ensuing struggles for control of resources, combined with political leaders who mobilized opposition against fellow republics within the federation, produced a situation that was riven by internal tensions. The speed at which this climate took a turn for the worse and the manner in which it disintegrated cannot, however, be viewed solely in terms of domestic factors: the international dimension is also of pivotal importance.

The roles played by international organizations and foreign governments were crucial in various aspects of the break up of Yugoslavia. The absence of a consensus on what strategies to adopt contributed to the deteriorating situation. In the course of the deliberations on the part of international bodies, the questions of whether or not to intervene—and if so, how—often differed from country to country. In the case of key international organizations such as NATO, the UN, the European Community (EC),[2] or the Conference on Security and Cooperation in Europe (CSCE), there were sharp differences of opinion. These were exemplified by the various strategies pursued by the different international actors with regard to the recognition of those republics seeking independence from the federal structure. In 1991 both Slovenia and Croatia had declared their intentions to secede from Yugoslavia. Prior to this, however, the leaderships of these republics had been engaged in seeking to mobilize international support for their respective causes.

The initial response from CSCE and NATO was negative; both rejected the idea of direct intervention in the internal affairs of Yugoslavia. The strategies pursued by the Croatian and Slovenian delegations did, nevertheless, bear significant fruit in mid-1991 when, before the Croatian and Slovenian parliaments had made official their secessionist intentions, the European Parliament—with considerable internal division—supported the principle of self-determination with respect to the republics and provinces of Yugoslavia.[3] However, the position of the EC was also to recognize the continued territorial integrity of Yugoslavia, a position shared by the governments of the US and USSR, as well as the CSCE, NATO, and the UN. For each of these parties, however, this position was to change as fighting intensified in Croatia and as the possibility of a peaceful confederal solution appeared less likely. The spiral of violence and the increasingly warlike relations between the Croatian and Yugoslav leaderships galvanized opinion in favor of greater international involvement in the crisis.

In August 1991, the EC established the Badinter Commission to arbitrate between the various domestic parties in Yugoslavia.[4] Meanwhile, the Austrian, German, and Italian governments announced preparations to recognize Croatian and Slovenian independence by the end of 1991, against the EC requirement for the unanimous agreement of its Member States. Their position, too, ran contrary to that of the UN chief negotiators, Cyrus Vance (US) and Lord Carrington (UK), who held that recognition of Croatia and Slovenia would herald the end of the Hague Conference that had been seeking, since September 1991, to find a peaceful solution to the conflict. After negotiations between EC ministers in December 1991, at which it was agreed that the republics could apply for international recognition, Germany broke rank and made public its recognition on December 23, 1991. The EC itself followed this, recognizing Croatia and Slovenia in January 1992. Recognition therefore progressed in spite of warnings from a number of international participants that such measures could well exacerbate problems, rather than create solutions.[5] Moreover, recognition also progressed in spite of the clear evidence that the requisite criteria set out by the Badinter Commission were not met in the case of Croatia, specifically the entrenchment of principles of human rights and protection of minority rights. In short, then, recognition did not address the central problem that underpinned the different wars: the treatment of national minorities. The question of recognition had even more profound implications with respect to Bosnia-Herzegovina, where the existence of three different national groups, in the context of the expansionist military strategies of the Croatian and Serbian governments, would create additional problems. This was all too evident when, after a referendum on independence in February 1992 that the Bosnian Serbs boycotted, the EC and the US recognized Bosnia-Herzegovina. It became the arena for an even more devastating war than had been experienced in Croatia.

The multifarious process concerning the question of recognition leads to the second main facet of the international dimension: the issue of direct intervention, which had been subject to debate since the conflict first erupted in Slovenia in 1991. As we have already noted, NATO and the CSCE initially rejected the idea of direct intervention. The increasing violence, however, served to provoke a more engaged response from international actors. Whereas these organizations had previously held that the territorial integrity of Yugoslavia should be preserved, the hostilities between the Yugoslav National Army (JNA) and paramilitary units acting on behalf of the Slovenes and the Croats—as well as hostilities between the Krajina Serbs and Croat militias—led some international actors to declare that the integrity of Yugoslavia could not be preserved by force. A crucial factor emerging from these changes of opinion was the increasing agreement among international actors, particularly in the latter half of 1991, that the principle of territorial integrity should be applied to the republics themselves, a process that gave them *de facto* recognition. In the discussions that centered on bringing about a peaceful solution to the conflicts, the chief difficulty was the unwillingness and/or inability to commit ground forces to keep the peace (once, of course, peace accords had been reached). The US made it clear that it was unwilling to commit ground forces to Yugoslavia, a situation that lasted until President Clinton sanctioned the participation of 20,000 US troops as part of the NATO Implementation Force (IFOR) that followed the 1995 Dayton Peace Accord.[6] The CSCE and the EC were both unable to provide a multinational peacekeeping force and continued to pursue economic sanctions and diplomacy. In the case of the conflicts involving Slovenia, Croatia, Serbia, and the JNA, conventional diplomacy did produce ceasefires, such as that negotiated by Cyrus Vance in late 1991 (only to be broken by Croatia in mid-1992).

In the end, direct international involvement emerged in 1992 in the form of a UN Protection Force (UNPROFOR) designed, in the case of Croatia, to monitor the ceasefire with the Krajina Serbs, and, in the case of Bosnia-Herzegovina, to support the UN High Commissioner for Refugees in providing humanitarian relief. Despite the unprecedented extent of UN commitment in the former Yugoslavia through UNPROFOR, its role has been hampered in a series of ways. First, UNPROFOR had the responsibility of addressing a situation that had been exacerbated by earlier international involvement, notably as a consequence of the recognition policies. In the case of Croatia, for example, there was no commitment on the part of the Croatian government to address the political status of Serbs residing in Croatia. The Vance-negotiated ceasefire in Croatia, therefore, was unlikely to be anything but temporary, given the likelihood of resumed fighting, and there was, then, a lack of clarity concerning what exactly the role of UNPROFOR should be. Second, even where there is a peace to keep, the role of UNPROFOR is limited due to the absence of political settlements that have the potential to bring long-term peace.[7] Third, UN intervention depends greatly on the willingness of its members to provide the necessary resources to support the campaigns in which it is engaged, and the history of recent international involvement in Yugoslavia in the early 1990s is marked by considerable ambiguity in this respect. In short, the situation in Croatia, and later in Bosnia-Herzegovina, exposed the problems of introducing international peacekeeping troops without first establishing a clear set of international objectives. Even when there is a peace accord and a set of working objectives for peacekeeping troops, as in the case of IFOR since 1995, the task of securing these objectives is taking considerably longer than first anticipated.

The difficulties facing international actors in providing a tailored solution to the problems in Bosnia-Herzegovina are both example and consequence of the third main facet of the international dimension to the break up of Yugoslavia: the failure to work towards a common solution to the crisis. There had been no universal recognition of the republics, in spite of just such a measure being entrenched in the EC negotiations in late 1991. For example, despite Macedonia meeting the criteria on minority rights and the specified democratic standards laid down by the Badinter Commission, it was refused recognition by the EC as part of a deal to secure the support of the Greek government for the Maastricht Treaty. International actors also failed to provide formal recognition not only of sovereign states, but also of the rights of the constituent nations of the former Yugoslavia. Thus, Croatia was accorded recognition without providing any firm political settlement for the Krajina Serbs, which ensured that the territorial war between Croatia and Serbia would continue. The recognition of Croatia and Slovenia, in absence of a clear policy as to how to proceed with respect to the remaining republics, illustrated the piecemeal approach to the Yugoslav crisis on the part of international actors, the EC in particular.

Establishing the Legitimacy of the ICTFY: the Legal Dimensions

Largely in response to the rising outcry of the media and public, the UN Security Council adopted Resolution 780 on October 6, 1992, establishing an investigative committee for the examination of violations of international humanitarian law in the former Yugoslavia. Upon the committee's recommendations, the Security Council decided that an international criminal tribunal should be created. Approving proposed Statute of the ICTFY, the Security Council adopted Resolution 827 on May 25, 1993, which established the tribunal. On November 17, 1993 the ICTFY first convened in The Hague.[8]

International factors have significantly influenced the direction in which the ICTFY has developed. On the negative side, the background of events surrounding the break up of Yugoslavia, especially the role of foreign governments and international organizations, has not helped establish a solid foundation of international political legitimacy for the ICTFY. More positively, the ICTFY is being watched closely as an example of how a future international criminal court might operate. Thus, the legitimacy established by the ICTFY will become the foundation for a permanent international court that will provide for future prosecutions against international criminal defendants.[9] The reputation of the ICTFY will depend on how evidence proving the guilt or innocence of the accused is presented and evaluated.[10] Substantively, the basis on which the law is applied and enforced in these trials must be viewed by observers of the ICTFY as being applicable to everyone universally.[11] Opponents of a permanent international criminal tribunal will certainly point to any perceived injustice stemming from the tribunal's procedures.[12] M. S. Ellis cites the ICTFY prosecutor's opening remarks in the *Tadic* trial to underscore the broader implications of the pursuit for justice: "The Tribunal has not been established to satisfy the victims only, but to bring justice to all, including the accused." Ultimately, the legitimacy of the ICTFY will be judged by the fairness of its proceedings and by the certainty that the accused are given a fair trial and proper defense.[13]

How, then, is the international legitimacy of the ITCFY to be established? The short answer is that the ICTFY must operate in accordance with internationally-recognized criminal procedural guarantees, as must any trial. Nevertheless, there are difficult political circumstances in which the ICTFY functions. Internationally-accepted legal procedures that protect the rights of all parties are vital in establishing the ICTFY as a genuinely independent institution. In this respect, the ICTFY has learned much from the lessons of earlier war crimes tribunals, especially those of Nuremberg and Tokyo. The latter have both been subject to considerable criticism, generally on the grounds that their procedures favored the victors in World War II. For the ICTFY to function as a transnational legal institution, it is imperative that it transcends such partisan alignments.

Among the primary concerns raised about the legitimacy of its jurisdiction is whether the ICTFY is a legitimate body under international law. Historically, an international tribunal is created by a treaty drawn up by an international body, followed by a period of time for signature and ratification. This approach is, however, time-consuming, with no guarantee that the parties will ratify the treaty.

Thus, the UN Security Council elected to establish the ICTFY pursuant to Chapter VII of the UN Charter, the binding authority as confirmed in the *Tadic* appeal.[14]

A second concern for the legitimacy of the ICTFY is the right to be protected from *ex post facto* laws, which constitutes a fundamental right against unbridled abuse of power. A chief criticism of the Nuremberg precedent was its perceived application of such laws in holding persons responsible—for the first time in history—for the "crime of aggression," and by applying the concept of conspiracy which had never before been recognized in continental Europe. The UN Secretary General has stated that the ICTFY will *not* create new international humanitarian law but will only apply existing law. This is to ensure that the internationally-recognized prohibition against *ex post facto* laws is upheld. The ICTFY bases its decisions on law embodied in treaties, such as the Geneva Conventions, to which all of the parties involved in the Yugoslav wars are successors. One new interpretation, however, is that Article 3 of the ICTFY statute applies to war crimes even if they are committed in internal conflicts. The tribunal's Appeals Chamber has proclaimed that the distinction between interstate and civil wars is losing its value as far as human beings are concerned.[15]

A third concern for legitimacy is the right to be protected from double jeopardy, referred to in civil law countries as *non bis in idem*. This right is designed to prevent the state from repeatedly subjecting an accused to prosecution for offences arising out of the same event until the desired conviction is achieved. Within the framework of the ICTFY there is, however, potential for this right to itself be jeopardized by allowing the prosecutor the right to appeal. Article 25 of the ICTFY Statute provides that the Prosecutor may appeal an error on a question of law, or an error of fact that has occasioned a miscarriage, thus allowing the Appeals Chamber to reverse acquittals by the Trial Chamber. Additionally, Rule 119 allows the Prosecutor, within one year after the final judgment, to move a Trial Chamber for review where a new fact has been discovered which was not known to the Prosecutor at the time of the proceedings and could not have been discovered through the exercise of due diligence. Arguments of practicality support this authority for limiting a core procedural protection. Trials may be initiated prematurely due to political demands, while the ICTFY itself can, for various reasons, experience difficulty in controlling investigations; in these circumstances it may be necessary for a prosecutor to seek a review of an earlier acquittal. The effects of expediency may be responsible for limiting this core right. Thus, because of the lack of control of the ICTFY over the evidence, much of which may reside in the hands of those being sought for prosecution, a safeguard is allowed in permitting the prosecutor to obtain a review of an earlier acquittal. Cautionary concerns for justice are outweighed by the demands for prosecutions that may be initiated prematurely. The US Supreme Court, however, has declared that it is necessary to prohibit the possibility of a zealous prosecutor utilizing vast resources to continue to pursue a defendant. Moreover, the American Bar Association, in its 1993 report on the ICTFY, argued that the procedure of prosecutorial appeal that allows double jeopardy is difficult to justify.[16]

The right to equality of arms is a further concern of ICTFY legitimacy, as it is fundamental to modern criminal proceedings.[17] The right to equality of arms includes the right to adequate time and facilities for preparation of the defense and the right of confrontation and cross-examination. One important aspect of preparation is knowledge of the evidence that may be used against the litigant in the proceedings. The Nuremberg and Tokyo trials have been criticized on the grounds that there was an inequality of resources between the parties, and that the defense was denied access to relevant material and had inadequate time to prepare.[18] These concerns have been addressed by the historical development of the concept of "equality of arms" in human rights law. This concept has been applied by the ICTFY so that a procedure for discovery is in place and adequate time is allowed for preparation of the defense. The defendants before the ICTFY are thus entitled to discover any exculpatory evidence in the possession of the prosecutor.[19] Issues relating to discovery have, however, exposed the difficulties of international legal proceedings and highlight the manner in which national peculiarities can come into conflict with the conventions of another country. For example, in the *Tadic* litigation, the prosecutor wanted access to the written statements of defense witnesses. In the US the discovery of such statements would come within the "reciprocal discovery rule," but a basic principle of litigation in civil jurisdictions and common law systems outside the US is that the accused is under no duty to afford assistance to the prosecution. In *Tadic*, the Trial Chamber ruled 2-1 in favor of protecting the written statements of defense witnesses, with the judges from civil law countries voting against disclosure of defense witness statements while the judge from the US voted for disclosure.

The right to compulsory process, another issue of legitimacy, guarantees the assistance of a tribunal in obtaining the testimony of witnesses and the production of other evidence. Again, protecting this right can highlight the difficulties of ensuring cooperation between national governments and, as such, can hinder the effective development of international law. In the *Tadic* trial the defense argued that there was a serious inequality of arms stemming from a lack of access to key sites in the Prijedor region of Bosnia-Herzegovina, where the local Serbian authorities, in a bid to challenge the legitimacy of the ICTFY, had persisted in trying to derail the defense case.

Limitations on the right to confront and cross-examine have been maintained. The ICTFY has recognized the need to protect victims and witnesses without infringing the legal rights of defendants. Again, in the *Tadic* trial the Trial Chamber granted the prosecutor's motion requesting the anonymity of three witnesses. The absence of a long-term witness protection program, the nature of the witness experiences, and the understanding that these witnesses would not testify without anonymity, were the chief factors that led to the motion in favor of the prosecutor.[20] Some commentators have suggested that the protection of the victims of the war in the former Yugoslavia is crucial to the wider international legitimacy of the ICTFY. A. C. Lakatos argues that whatever the achievements of the ICTFY, the lesson of promoting action to end crimes against humanity will be diminished should physical harm come to its witnesses.[21]

Clearly it is difficult for the ICTFY to entirely rise above the needs of expedience, specifically with respect to procedural rules. A number of the procedures highlight the difficulties of practicing transnational justice, wherein the parties involved are not in agreement on the actual procedures to be employed. Such differences may seriously weaken the international legitimacy of the ICTFY and highlight the distance yet to be traveled in developing instruments of transnational justice.

Establishing the Legitimacy of the ICTFY: the Psycho-social Dimensions

Disagreements between national legal systems do, then, raise the issue of how the ICTFY and its legitimacy are perceived by participants and observers. The refusal of summoned parties to accept the legitimacy of the ICTFY, such as local Serbian authorities in Bosnia-Herzegovina, can hinder its operation. Equally, it is crucial that those directly involved in the ICTFY, such as witnesses, victims, or accused, should accept the legality of the decisions made by the ICTFY if it is to act as a transnational legitimate institution.

The seminal work of J. Thibaut and L. Walker on the psychology of procedural and distributive justice holds that legal proceedings may enhance the sense of legitimacy on the part of participants and observers.[22] Here, distributive justice refers to the perception that the outcome of a dispute is fair and equitable, while procedural justice refers to the perception that the techniques used to resolve a dispute are fair and satisfying in themselves. Thus, with respect to the ICTFY, Scharf argues that "to achieve success [the ICTFY] must not only be fair, but be seen as fair."[23] According to Thibaut and Walker's thesis, the most effective way of attaining distributive justice is to ensure that process control is assigned to the disputants. Thus, proceedings will, among other things, involve the use of attorneys, the ability to discover, the presentation of one's own evidence, and the development of one's own strategy. Research has also shown that perceptions of procedural fairness are also foremost in informing perceptions of legitimacy among non-participant observers.[24]

Working with this thesis—that the greater the control by the parties over the process, the more likely a system will be viewed as legitimate—an adversarial system of justice appears best suited to producing this outcome. In adversarial systems, as opposed to inquisitorial systems, greater control is assigned to the disputants; in the latter a judge defines the issues and decides which witnesses to call at trial, and cross-examination by parties is minimal. Thus, we are of the opinion that the Anglo-American common law adversary system is more appropriate for the operation of the ICTFY than the continental European inquisitorial procedures, where people may speak only to the extent and in the form dictated by the judge. If the thesis is accurate regarding litigants' greater satisfaction with adversarial rather than inquisitorial methods of criminal procedure, then, as J. E. Alvarez contends, having greater control of the process is in itself a value for victims.[25] That is, the greater the view of procedural fairness held by participants and observers, the greater the enhancement of the legitimacy of the entire proceedings.

The ICTFY does give some degree of process control to the parties. There are, nevertheless, circumstances—such as where defendants may not be present during proceedings—in which extensive participation of the parties does not occur. The ICTFY Statute provides that defendants have the right to be present and participate in their own defense; thus, it prohibits trials *in absentia*, in contrast to the Nuremberg Tribunal. This conforms to the International Covenant on Civil and Political Rights (Art. 14(3)(d)), which requires the accused's presence in criminal prosecutions. It would seem that trials *in absentia* would be inherently vulnerable to abuse and would violate basic norms of due process.[26] The Nuremberg Tribunal's inattention to this basic due process concern stemmed from the absence of international human rights standards that have since evolved.[27] Unique to the ICTFY, however, is its authority under Rule 61 to allow the submission of evidence and witness testimony by the prosecution where the accused is not present in open court. It must nevertheless be demonstrated that there are substantial grounds for holding that the accused has committed all or any of the charges in the indictment, and that every reasonable measure has been taken to ensure the presence of the accused at the ICTFY. P. Akhavan argues that the purpose of this rule is to ensure that accused persons cannot leave their country and to eliminate the potential for future refuge in a third country.[28] Participation in a modified trial *in absentia*, under the Rule 61 proceedings, is, however, assured to the victims. This is justified on the grounds that Rule 61 proceedings facilitate a sense of reconciliation, and thus provide for a measure of distributive justice.

Of related concern is the matter of the privilege against self-incrimination, notably because of the differences between US and British case law in this respect. The ITCFY Statute enshrines this privilege, yet the Rules fail to clarify whether the tribunal may draw adverse inferences from a suspect or an accused who remains silent. In US Supreme Court case law it is not acceptable to draw such inferences. A recent law adopted by the British Parliament, however, allows the factfinder to draw incriminating inferences when suspects or defendants remain silent during police interrogations or at trial. G. W. O'Reilly argues that this is a move towards an inquisitorial system of justice, "jeopardizing many of the benefits protected by the accusatorial system of justice."[29] V. M. Creta specifically observes that cautioning suspects that their statements can be used against them and applying their resultant silence toward proof of guilt makes the fact-finding process of the ICTFY harshly incongruous.[30] Effectively, this undermines the defendant's control over evidence in the proceedings and diminishes this crucial aspect of procedural justice.

Differences between national legal systems, in the form of adversarial and inquisitorial systems, respectively, are also evident with regard to the inadmissibility of certain evidence. In the US, constitutional exclusionary rules, such as those that have been read into the US Bill of Rights protections, are rejected by inquisitorial systems in which there are few fixed evidentiary rules. The ICTFY employs elements of *both* adversarial and inquisitorial models. The presentation of evidence has followed the adversarial model; however, the rules governing the admissibility of evidence may be seen as more akin to the inquisitorial model and leave wide discretion to the judges.

Combining procedures from the two models of legal systems does not enhance justice when the procedures in one are inherently in conflict with the other. This is seen particularly with the limitations in the ICTFY on a defendant's right to confront and cross-examine witnesses. The ICTFY has interpreted the Statute's mandate that defendants have the right to examine witnesses to mean that the parties are entitled to carry out their own examinations and cross-examinations in an adversarial manner. In light of the witness protection rules, the ICTFY has preserved the large authority that is granted to inquisitorial judges, but only as related to defendants. The role that judges play in the traditional inquisitorial system does not necessarily hurt defendants, since prosecutors are subject to the same rules. However, under the tribunal's rules, the two parties are not treated equally, because the prosecutor's right to examine witnesses has not been similarly limited. Thus, although a defendant cannot cross-examine, likewise the State is similarly barred.[31] Support for this blending of models stems from the view that the sole purpose of the litigation is to seek the truth. This is a minimization of the goal of seeking the perception of justice underlying the adversary system, which ultimately serves to delegitimize the outcome and purpose of the ICTFY.

In summarizing the social dimensions of legitimacy, we argue that the procedural model utilized by the ICTFY does seek to ensure that the parties exercise a considerable degree of control over the process. As suggested by Thibaut and Walker, this is important for ensuring that the manner in which a trial is conducted is seen to be legitimate by participants and non-participants. Again, however, differences over the preferred procedural systems of particular countries or regions are apparent, whether with respect to the admission of evidence or in the right to cross-examine.

Throughout this chapter it has been our concern to highlight how international forces have impacted on events in the former Yugoslavia and on the developments linked to addressing the consequences of the war, especially the operation of the ICTFY. We have argued that the lack of a common position on how to address the process of fragmentation within the former Yugoslavia led to an *ad hoc* approach to the recognition of sovereignty, without ensuring the entrenchment of principles of human rights and the protection of minority groups. This piecemeal approach towards recognition meant that minority groups were left to suffer at the hands of the dominant national group. A deteriorating situation was therefore exacerbated by the absence of agreement on what strategies to adopt in relation to this situation. Moreover, when international peacekeeping troops were finally sent into the former Yugoslav states, there was no clearly defined set of international objectives that they should strive to attain. The slow progress in moving beyond a state-centered approach to international relations has, in our view, led to an inability to formulate universal ethical principles that could act as guides for a common response to problems occurring within sovereign states. In the case of the former Yugoslavia, this inability had devastating effects that ultimately necessitated the creation of the ICTFY.

The setting up of the ICTFY is a step forward in extending the scope of international responsibility for violations of human rights and in developing an emergent transnational legal forum for conflict resolution. The ICTFY has, nevertheless, faced considerable difficulties—political and legal—in transcending national conflicts of interest. This chapter has demonstrated the scope of the varied and complex legal requirements that need to be addressed in an effort to provide international legitimacy to the ICTFY. Legitimacy in this context is given primacy as any future international criminal court will be based on the foundation laid down by the ICTFY, and opponents of such an international mechanism will be quick to point to any perceived injustice rising from the ICTFY. Moreover, it is apparent that particular difficulties arise with an international approach that is largely dependent on the nation-state for implementation. This is forcefully brought to our attention in regard to the discussion of trials *in absentia*, and Rule 61. The tribunal has no legal right to remove individuals from a country without the cooperation of the state and, although Rule 61 provides a mechanism whereby an accused can be blacklisted and prevented from seeking refuge in a third state, it is still dependent on the nation-state to enforce such confinement. Finally, the ICTFY not only has to have legitimacy; it has to be *seen* as legitimate by the general public, observers, participants and the citizens of the nation-states to which it is applicable. The absence of a single paradigm approach emphasizing control by both parties over the process diminishes justice and therefore jeopardizes legitimacy, as does the reliance on expediency. If we are ever to see the development of an international approach to stem the rise of grave human rights abuses, these issues still need to be addressed.

---

[1] J. E. Alvarez, "Rush to Closure: Lessons of the *Tadic* Judgement," *Michigan Law Review* 96 (1998): 2031-112.

[2] Now the European Union, or EU.

[3] S. L. Woodward, *Balkan Tragedy: Chaos and Dissolution After the Cold War* (Washington: The Brookings Institution, 1995).

[4] M. Rady, "Self-Determination and the Dissolution of Yugoslavia," *Ethnic and Racial Studies* 19 (1996): 379-89.

[5] A. Roberts, "Communal Conflict as a Challenge to International Organization: The Case of the Former Yugoslavia," *Review of International Studies* 21 (1995): 389-410; see also Woodward.

[6] W. C. Banks and J. D. Straussman, "A New Imperial Presidency? Insights from US Involvement in Bosnia," *Political Science Quarterly* 114, no. 2 (1999): 195-217.

[7] See M. Goulding, "The Evolution of United Nations Peacekeeping," *International Affairs* 69 (1993): 451-64; also R. Higgins, "The New United Nations and Former Yugoslavia," *International Affairs* 69 (1993): 465-83.

[8] F. Newman and D. Weissbrodt, *International Human Rights: Law, Policy, and Process* (Cincinnati: Anderson Publishing, 1996).

[9] D. J. Brown, "The International Criminal Court and Trial *in absentia*," *Brooklyn Journal of International Law* 24 (1999): 763-96.

[10] R. Dixon, "Symposium: Developing International Rules of Evidence for the Yugoslav and Rwanda Tribunals," *Transnational Law and Contemporary Problems* 7 (1997): 81-102.

[11] E. J. Wallach, "The Procedural and Evidentiary Rules of the Post-World War II War Crimes Trials: Did They Provide an Outline for International Legal Procedure?" *Columbia Journal of Transnational Law* 37 (1999): 851-83.

[12] M. Momeni, "Balancing the Procedural Rights of the Accused Against a Mandate to Protect Victims and Witnesses: An Examination of the Anonymity Rules of the International Criminal Tribunal for the Former Yugoslavia," *Howard Law Journal* 41 (1997): 155-79.

[13] M. S. Ellis, "Symposium: Justice in Cataclysm: Criminal Trials in the Wake of Mass Violence—Comment: Achieving Justice Before the International War Crimes Tribunal: Challenges for the Defense Counsel," *Duke Journal of Comparative and International Law* 7 (1997): 519-37.

[14] A. Sherman, "Sympathy for the Devil: Examining a Defendant's Right to Confront Before the International War Crimes Tribunal," *Emory International Law Review* 10 (1996): 833-77.

[15] M. P. Scharf, "A Critique of the Yugoslavia War Crimes Tribunal," *Denver Journal of International Law and Policy* 25 (1997): 305-12.

[16] J. L. Falvey, "United Nations Justice or Military Justice: Which is the Oxymoron? An Analysis of the Rules of Procedure and Evidence of the International Tribunal for the Former Yugoslavia," *Fordham International Law Journal* 19 (1995): 475-528. The ABA's report is entitled the *Report on the International Tribunal to Adjudicate War Crimes in the Former Yugoslavia 43*.

[17] M. C. Bassiouni, "Human Rights in the Context of Criminal Justice: Identifying International Procedural Protections and Equivalent Protections in National Constitutions," *Duke Journal of Comparative and International Law* 3 (1993): 235-97.

[18] R. May and M. Wierda, "Trends in International Criminal Evidence: Nuremburg, Tokyo, The Hague, and Arusha," *Columbia Journal of Transnational Law* 37 (1999): 725-65.

[19] Scharf, 305-12.

[20] Momeni, 155-79.

[21] A. C. Lakatos, "Evaluating the Rules of Procedure and Evidence for the International Tribunal in the Former Yugoslavia: Balancing Witnesses' Needs Against Defendants' Rights," *Hastings Law Journal* 46 (1995): 909-40.

[22] J. Thibaut and L. Walker, *Procedural Justice: A Psychological Analysis* (Hillsdale, N.J.: Erlbaum, 1975); also J. Thibaut and L. Walker, "A Theory of Procedure," *California Law Review* 66 (1978): 541-66.

[23] Scharf, 305.

[24] E. A. Lind and T. Tyler, *The Social Psychology of Procedural Justice* (New York: Plenum, 1988).

[25] Alvarez, 2031-112.

[26] Falvey, 475-528.

[27] M. Thieroff and E. A. Amley, "Proceeding to Justice and Accountability in the Balkans: The International Criminal Tribunal for the Former Yugoslavia and Rule 61," *Yale Journal of International Law* 23 (1998): 231-274.

[28] P. Akhavan, "Enforcement of the Genocide Convention: A Challenge to Civilization," *Harvard Human Rights Journal* 8 (1995): 229-258.

[29] G. W. O'Reilly, "England Limits the Right to Silence and Moves Towards an Inquisitorial System of Justice," *Journal of Criminal Law and Criminology* 85 (1994): 402-452 (404).

[30] V. M. Creta, "The Search for Justice in the Former Yugoslavia and Beyond: Analyzing the Rights of the Accused Under the Statute and the Rules of Procedure and Evidence of the International Criminal Tribunal for the Former Yugoslavia," *Houston Journal of International Law* 20 (1998): 381-417.

[31] Sherman, 833-77.

Chapter 16

Republicanism and Constitutionalism: Transatlantic Connections

Javier Maestro

Republicanism and constitutionalism are distinct political trends attached to institutional modernity, and both have decisively framed contemporary and recent world history. Nonetheless, they are mainly European-American concepts, even if subject to polymorphous meanings and settings. Republicanism implies more than just a form of government opposed to monarchy and similar non-elective institutions. Republicanism, strictly speaking, is above all a regime embedded in a sovereign democratic civic society, governed by the rule of law, provided with all-embracing elective procedures and bequeathed with the consent of the governed. The same applies to constitutionalism: it implies more than just a written document of limited government, as it sets the rules for democratic sovereignty and thus the accountability of the ruling representative political institutions.

Needless to say, most conventional definitions of both terms are too neat. This is especially so in an age of sweeping technological change that goes hand in hand with globalization and the presumptive withering of the nation-state. Notwithstanding these preliminary remarks, it is clear that societies on both sides of the Atlantic have embraced constitutionalism either as a framework of limited government or as a spurious legitimacy of non-democratic regimes (with the exception of the long interlude of European absolutist monarchies). Republicanism, in turn, has had a more successful performance outside Western Europe, even if as a goal and movement, it is visible in the prospective political union of Europe. But the transatlantic connections between republicanism and constitutionalism are a matter of historical and practical fact: this chapter aims to free both ideas from a nation-bound perception, and emphasize their transnational nature and development in common.

The Great Tradition of Constitutionalism

Germanic law and feudalism, Roman concepts of Natural Law and Aristotelianism can rightly be considered as the three main doctrinal sources that have patterned modern constitutionalism.[1] Germanic law, as it developed in Northern and Central Europe during the early Middle Ages, bound the "law of the people" to a custom springing from inherited conceptions of Natural Law, and thus from complex Roman feudal systems. It countervailed the feudal subversion of public authority with the notion that the people make up a commonwealth as the repository of public interest. The English Common law system and the unwritten constitution belong to this Romano-Germanic tradition, as does the conception of commonwealth. Edmund Burke accordingly described the unwritten English constitution as a living document growing out of "the habitual conditions, relations and reciprocal claims" of the people of a country.[2]

The Roman law tradition itself was a written one, anchored in a commonwealth of reason duly disciplined by the rule of Natural Law as a trustee of moral justice and equity. This tradition became most firmly rooted in Central and South Europe, following the religious boundaries of Catholicism. Accordingly, society was considered natural and of a higher degree than a mere human design, but the concepts of law and government were underpinned with authoritarian Roman overtones of *imperium* and *auctoritas*.

The Aristotelian legacy established the rule of law as the basic principle of "good" political systems. It considered the "best practicable" political system to be one of "mixed constitutions," that is, moderate democracies composed of a widespread middle class, wherein democratic and oligarchic forces are appropriately balanced against each other. The underlying Aristotelian idea is that the many have more wisdom and virtue than the few, which means that a large free citizenship is more successful than oligarchic rule in imposing rightful laws and accommodating them to the majority will. But Aristotle also had in mind the tyranny of the majority and the corruptibility of human beings. He therefore staunchly supported the rule of law, because law is human reason "unaffected by desire," and the best medium of balancing quantity (democracy) with quality (elitism). Aristotle downgraded human nature even more, saying that "man, when perfected, is the best of animals, but, when separated from law and justice, he is the worst of all." The Aristotelian concept of law was a hybrid, a mixture of custom and political design and, as such, was conservatively tainted. He clearly preferred the "government of laws" to the "government of men." Here, as in so many other regards, Aristotelianism moved from Plato's idealism towards realism and empiricism based on remarkable fieldwork that provided him with deep insights concerning the practical workings of the numerous constitutions in the different Greek City-states of his time.[3] Aristotelianism became the guiding political philosophy in the late middle ages and throughout modern times, to the extent that even English and American Whig ideology was highly imbued with Aristotelian thinking in the form of aristocratic constitutionalism, although it soon faded away in the revolutionary battlegrounds.[4]

The concept of the separation of powers is another off-spring of Aristotelian political philosophy. Montesquieu later developed its practical mechanism, but he was mistaken in pinpointing the prevailing English constitution as a paradigm of the separation of powers. Notwithstanding all this, Aristotelian thinking always had an oligarchic bias, which is why early democratic political philosophy viewed it cautiously. But whatever the judgment one may have of Aristotelian political philosophy, it has undeniably influenced modern constitutionalism greatly. Machiavelli, Harrington and Sidney, the main modern supporters of Republican constitutionalism, were strongly influenced by the Aristotelian tradition. The philosophy of the Enlightenment and the subsequent cycle of Atlantic revolutions were no less tributaries of Aristotelianism at a time when European and American societies were beset with an increasingly self-reliant and rights-driven citizenry. The Madisonian American constitutional settlement was, in this spirit, wholly Aristotelian.

Natural Human Rights, Political Freedom and New Republicanism

New Republicanism sprang out of the enterprising commercial Italian Renaissance city-states that managed to dismantle the feudal order and create a civic society where virtue lay in successful, active individualism and the pursuit of enlightened self-interest. Rational calculation, experimentalism and secularized thinking went hand-in-hand with Republican regimes as the best suited to represent and serve collective individualism and the public spirit (*res publica*). And, of course, a mythologized Roman republicanism acted in Renaissance Italy as a legitimizing and fortifying factor more than as an actual mirror.[5] Republicanism became increasingly identified with a free, vigorous civic society. New Republicanism no longer relied on leisure and slavery, as in classical antiquity, but on a work ethic propounded by liberal republicanism.[6] This early transition towards modernity was best portrayed by Machiavelli's writings, so widely read and so strongly opposed by a dominant Christian world view that had long preached political obligation as ordained by God. However, Christianity soon gave in to the new spirit of the Renaissance that expanded throughout the most dynamic European commercial foci—the Netherlands, England and North Germany. Thereafter, the Enlightenment acted as the real universal driving force of the pre-industrial spirit inaugurated by the Renaissance. The spirit of Reformation paved the way towards religious freedom after protracted wars that eventually secured relative religious and political toleration. Without this spirit of toleration, the diffusion of printed ideas, and a receptive citizenry, later constitutional and social changes on both sides of the Atlantic would remain unthinkable.

Amidst religious and political turmoil, rebellion in the Netherlands and the Puritan Revolution appear as the spearheads of political change towards republicanism and constitutionalism. Spinoza, Althusius and Grotius symbolized an emerging political maturity in the Netherlands as much as Hobbes, Milton, Locke, and Harrington amongst others did in England. The changes that first took place in the Netherlands made this "confederation of provinces" a sanctuary of free thought and action. Not surprisingly, many of Europe's free-thinking intellectuals—John Locke, for example—found refuge there as exiles. The Natural Law theory, as developed from 1570 onwards by the Jesuit and Dominican Orders, was already entirely based on the law of Reason, but this same self-evident and universally accepted Natural Law was applied by Spinoza to morals in the form of geometrical demonstrations. Pufendorf and Grotius, in turn, propounded to establish a more systematic "general public law" (*allgemeines Staatsrecht*) that strengthened the philosophy of Natural Law in statecraft, international relations (*ius gentium*) and in all fields of human society. Grotius defined Natural Law in a manner that was later used to legitimate the "self-evident" right of North American independence:

> I have made it my concern to refer the proofs of things touching the law of nature to certain fundamental conceptions which are beyond question, so that no one can deny them without doing violence to himself. For the principles of that law, if only you pay strict heed to them, are in themselves manifest and clear, almost as evident as are those things which we perceive by the external senses.[7]

The anti-royalist Calvinism of Althusius also developed, according to principles of Natural Law, the first federalist theory to disrupt the prevailing assumptions that had conferred higher status to the social body as a whole than to its parts. He furnished the idea that the polity, as a natural relationship, is a combination of associative groups, each proceeding from simpler ones. Sovereignty originally lies, therefore, in the primary groups; but by mutual covenant they may transfer limited sovereignty to superior associations. Though Althusius was not thinking in terms of individuals but of voluntary corporations, there is no doubt that he significantly influenced the individualism of future American federalist thinking.

The scientific temper attached to what we now label the Newtonian-Cartesian paradigm unfolded in this changing scenario. Science and rational thought were becoming the primary sources of knowledge, seriously threatening the Church's previous monopoly. Humankind became the center of a world understood as a huge clockwork machinery that acted mechanically according to natural laws. Nature was thus provided with laws that only awaited human discover; by extension, human individual psychology and social relationships were determined by natural laws. Thomas Paine expressed this temper remarkably well in *Common Sense*: "[A]s the greater weight will always carry up the less, and as all the wheels of a machine are put in motion by one, it only remains to know which power in the constitution has the most weight; for that will govern."[8]

But while physical nature followed *harmonious* mechanical laws, such was not the case with human nature and society. As the European feudal order experienced serious setbacks, the new loci of freedom became the proper experimental fields for rational and scientific undertakings. Consequently, the Enlightenment condemned the greater past of humanity as a cumulus of errors and superstitions. This assumption lay at the core of republican and constitutional philosophy in revolutionary France: freedom, equality and fraternity would completely rewrite the future of humanity, following the prescriptions of Natural Law and Reason. But even earlier, in the rebellious Low Countries and in revolutionary England, the rediscovered Laws of Nature meant that human beings were born equal and free, that they were made different by society, and that society itself (as well as government) was a human construct designed to protect individual rights. If society and government were a freely agreed human artifact, it followed that they only existed with the tacit or expressed consent of all—or at least the majority of sovereign individuals.

In the immediate aftermath of the English civil war, a suspicious Hobbes, with a dim view of human nature, propounded in *Leviathan* a strong, absolutist state to protect natural human rights. But once the Glorious Revolution ended the bitter strife, a more optimistic Locke developed the theory of constitutional government resting on a never-ending contractualism and depicted human beings, as he imagined them, in a state of nature, naturally and essentially good, and rationally self-seeking. Locke developed liberal constitutionalism as it was thereafter understood, even if Hobbes could claim to be the real architect of liberalism. From then on, constitutionalism became a system basically aimed at protecting natural and self-evident individual rights, while the framework of government was only important inasmuch as it established the kind of system that best kept the covenant with the people and was least liable to misuse entrusted power on its own behalf. Such safeguards as divided power, checks and balances, and accountability through regular electoral procedures were the main provisions to be taken to "govern the government." Governmental powers were, on the whole, considered negatively, as mainly the power to control and punish. The less these powers were needed, the better. England soon provided the most advanced constitutionalist setting—even if less than one tenth of the population had voting rights.

Transatlantic Constitutionalism and Republicanism as *Novus ordo seculorum*

The fundamentals of American constitutionalism and republicanism were conveniently developed in Western European seedbeds. And, according to the "Founding Fathers" themselves, the American "project" was the culmination of Western civilization, a mix of idealized republican commonwealthism, liberal individualism and constitutional pragmatism.[9] Yet, contemporary scholars hold contradictory views concerning the temper of early American republicanism, a word which even then was attached to a host of meanings—anti-royalism, commonwealthism with Roman overtones and democracy, and American nativism itself.[10] Complex as it was, American revolutionary thought assembled the most advanced republican philosophy and experience of the time and applied it to the widest known geographical setting. As such, the US was envisioned as a site for the greatest political and social experimental endeavors of the era, as George Washington himself argued:

> The treasures of knowledge, acquired by the labours of Philosophers, Sages and Legislators, through a long succession of years, are laid open for our use, and their collected wisdom may be happily applied in the Establishment of our forms of Government.[11]

America had no fully feudal or semi-feudal order to dislodge from power, no established Church, and—amongst its citizens—no strict social stratification as was visible in the different European settings. The North American colonies had, on the contrary, promoted a free and egalitarian spirit as a compound of government; the individual and natural right to speak freely; dissent as the driving force to sustain freedom; and equality and the pursuit of happiness. All this was combined with a pioneer mentality that scorned scarcity through a pugnacious mobility in the search for new resources in the spirit of self-help and self-improvement. Government was originally envisioned as a rather invisible entity in America. As I. Kramnick notes,

> Like most revolutions, the American began as a repudiation of the state, of power, and of authority in the name of liberty. Like most revolutions, it ended with a stronger state, the revival of authority, and the taming of liberty's excesses.[12]

Like the Puritan Revolution in particular, the American Revolution was also strongly wrapped in a religious belief system.[13] And, like all millenarian or visionary revolutions, it was genuinely thought of in universal or at least continental terms as a manifest destiny. Accordingly, the new republican commonwealth was originally intended to permeate the American hemisphere. Hence the name of the First *Continental* Congress convened at Philadelphia in 1774, which was to have worldwide repercussions besides staging North American independence as a *novo ordo seculorum*. Most noteworthy was Simón Bolivar's "project" for an emancipated Spanish America that followed closely North American footsteps in the urge to create a Confederation of Central and South American Republics.

Lockean political philosophy underpinned the grand theory of American constitutionalism as it best invested individual rights and limited government with political legitimacy. This made American republicanism and constitutionalism almost synonymous with liberalism. But the American Constitution, as an unfolding instrument of government, was the outcome of protracted conflict—"a torrent of angry and malignant passions," as Hamilton predicted—between competing factions of Federalists and Anti-Federalists. Both operated with the "genius of republican liberty" that demanded a "strictly republican government"—understood as "a government which derives all its powers directly or indirectly from the great body of the people, and is administered by persons holding their offices during pleasure for a limited period, or during good behaviour."[14] This new republican democracy was so advanced that, as J. Nedelsky points out in a progressivist echo of Charles Beard's *Economic Interpretation of the Constitution*,

> the sense of vulnerability in a republic became the focus for the broader task of securing individual rights against the tyranny of the majority. This focus, in turn, led to the greatest weakness of our system: its failure to realize its democratic potential. The Framers' preoccupation with property generated a shallow conception of democracy and a system of institutions that allocates political power unequally and fails to foster political participation.[15]

The new Republic, as a "more perfect union," had to cope with a variety of problems. Nevertheless, democracy itself was the most pertinent issue in connection with the future of republicanism and constitutionalism—so suggested Alexis de Tocqueville when he set out to describe to his fellow-citizens in Europe how democracy actually worked in a socially unfettered political society. If the Madisonian settlement gave the Union a constitution that avoided democratic extremes through an indirectly elected executive and an appointed judiciary (in line with Montesquieu's aristocratic reservations), the first ten Amendments—in a Jeffersonian commitment to individual autonomy—aimed at securing an independent civic society.[16] Later Jacksonian democracy, as portrayed by Tocqueville, amounted to an enlargement of equal opportunities, and the subsequent introduction of universal white manhood suffrage was intended to *make* citizens participate in that juncture. But republicanism became all the more rhetorical as the common good was increasingly associated with the "opportunity society" and less with common-cause virtues and duties. Corrupt restrictive and blocking procedures jeopardized equal opportunities, and civic virtue meant taking care of oneself and not getting in the way of others—such was Tocqueville's depiction of the American democracy.

Tocqueville, of course, had the experience of his own country's revolution behind him. The French Revolution is commonly viewed as an outcome of the preceding American Revolution and the Enlightenment movement before it. It is also viewed as a *social* revolution triggered by a dissatisfied and powerful bourgeoisie, an oppressed and famine-driven peasantry and a state in bankruptcy. All in all, it suppressed feudal society domestically and rocked the feudal strongholds all across Western Europe. Republicanism and constitutionalism became thereafter synonymous with freedom, legal equality, limited government and democracy throughout 19th-century Europe, as it did across the Atlantic. Liberal revolutionary cosmopolitanism stretched from Spanish America deep into Europe's eastern hinterland, but the underlying structure was labile. Fraternal revolutionary universality was soon easily wrecked by Napoleon's imperial dressings and transformed into competing nationalisms all along continental Europe. European liberal constitutionalism thereby became increasingly subject to the designs of authoritarian interpreters.

Republican French constitutionalism also differed in another way from its American counterpart. It had no reverence towards private property rights if political and social stability were at stake. And, despite the fact that the *Declaration of the Rights of Man and the Citizen* put property rights in the forefront of Natural Rights, these could ultimately be overlooked at the convenience of the supremacy principle of popular sovereignty.[17] Parliamentary constitutionalism and a social rights philosophy, as Rousseau and French social thought had blueprinted it, made this possible.

In the wake of both the American and French revolutions, the European pendulum movement between liberal constitutionalism and Restored semi-absolutist monarchy was a drawn-out process attributable in part to a strongly polarized citizenry unable to sustain democracy and constitutionalism on a permanent basis. Universal male suffrage in Europe only became a generalized practice after the sweeping revolutionary democratic earthquake of 1848 that annihilated all vestiges of feudalism, serfdom, and all the dominant anti-constitutionalist revivals of the Old Regime, as sketched in 1815 by the Congress of Vienna. Most Western European countries adopted parliamentary government and became constitutional, but hardly democratic. Even in Great Britain, "democracy" was still a frightful word in 1850, frequently associated with a collectivist assault upon the stability of a wise and ancient social order.

Social Rights Versus Individual Rights: Constitutionalism, Democracy and "Survival of the Fittest"

The last decades of the 19th century and the early years of the 20th witnessed a widespread transatlantic democratization process fueled by both the ongoing industrialization that ushered in ideas of progress, scientism and order—very much in line with Comte's positivist gospel—and by Marxist revolutionary appeals against capitalism channeled by a growing European socialist movement in demand of radical democratic and social changes. The factually class-divided European society became *ideologically* divided on a rather permanent basis, but this new direction was uniquely European in the sense that the continent was beset by antinomies that the North American hemisphere for the most part lacked.

Indeed, America's faith in progress, science and freedom hardly slackened; in terms of industrial expansion, serious doubts were only raised against the unfair advantage of trusts such as Standard Oil and the collateral special interest groups that many thought were eroding constitutional democratic rules. In Europe, a scientism mostly based on biological rather than mechanical underpinnings became the most influential way of analyzing social phenomena. Herbert Spencer's widely read works promoted this new approach to liberal thought. Evolutionary liberalism thus depicted the selection of the fittest as a natural outcome, a sort of individual determinism that fostered a vigorous elitism. Likewise, dialectic materialism or "scientific" socialism led Marx to conclude that the future belonged to the proletariat. Nations were similarly portrayed as living organisms subject to selection according to their strength—hence the conspicuous emphasis placed upon a strenuous American expansion in the Pacific and the Caribbean at the turn of the century.

Scientism also found its way into European constitutionalist theory, specifying that constitutions are living, perfectible instruments of government that must live up to changing political conditions in a changing society. As living entities, constitutions were doomed to survive or perish. This way of thinking could ultimately lead to an outright suppression of constitutionalism as a defunct theory, an idea that totalitarian regimes eagerly embraced later in the 20th century. But it could also mean that constitutionalism ought to be reinforced, either by conferring wider powers upon the leading branch (the executive) or upon the pluralist branch (the legislative). Whether presidential or parliamentary, both forms of constitutionalism had to conform to a new, demanding, mass society, endowing it with equalized political rights and increased social rights as a means of guaranteeing the survival of society itself. On both sides of the Atlantic, this meant making governmental intrusions upon property rights, mainly introducing a mixed economy provided with direct taxation systems in a workable redistribution policy. The cornerstones of the contemporary welfare state were already set. But the inter-war years were undoubtedly the gloomiest for European republicanism, constitutionalism and democracy in particular. At the core of totalitarian ideology lay a spurious use of Hegelian philosophy, overemphasizing the "rational" superiority of the state over civil society and similarly diminishing individual rights and freedom to the status of "becoming."

To some extent, World War I also symbolized utter scientific destruction, but among its effects, as far as European constitutionalism and republicanism were concerned, was the breakdown of multinational autocratic empires, as most of the newly independent countries and defeated powers became—for however long or short a period—constitutional democratic republics. Similarly, the end of World War II transformed former totalitarian regimes into reinforced republican constitutional democracies, either by introducing federalist principles already put in practice across the Atlantic, or by instituting new electoral systems designed to avoid instability and political fragmentation. Most new European constitutions after 1945 referred to a "social state ruled by law," legitimizing increased individual and political rights (a woman's right to vote), increased social rights (signified by varying degrees of welfare), and safeguards to support a pluralistic democracy.

Contemporary Questions

From Latin America to Europe, crossing Africa and Asia, many authoritarian and dictatorial regimes have disappeared, and a majority of countries share common democratic values—whatever the overt or latent democratic shortcomings due to economic gaps between the First World and their own civic societies. Not only has the pre-1989 bipolar world ceased to exist, but forms of republicanism and constitutionalism have attained unprecedented worldwide momentum. In this sense we may speak of a truly global transformation. That complex, unstable word, "globalization," is usually more readily attached to new technologies, pervasive mass communication systems and a worldwide market system than to a republican constitutional commonwealth. Yet it indeed poses problems for our inherited structures of government and free institutions in general.

The process of globalization has included the establishment of supra-national organizations that continue to lay sovereignty claims over the member-states, as illustrated by the EU. How all their complex multi-jurisdictional issues are to be solved both constitutionally and democratically remains to be seen. Moreover, and paradoxically enough, one undesirable result of globalization has been accelerated national fragmentation and an ongoing nationalist patchwork process, especially in East Europe, resulting from inter-ethnic conflicts and an upsurge in nationalist movements. Furthermore, a visibly increasing process of atomization in transatlantic society and the ensuing political disengagement of the citizenry is becoming a dangerous trend that may foster more institutional and political bureaucratization, technocracy and a dislocation of the relationship between civic society and representative governmental institutions. Hence the increasingly visible proposals on educational agendas across the US and Europe to revive participatory democracy and a republican civic society, in the attempt to prevent further social fragmentation and a free-wheeling representative democracy.

And after all is said and done on a global scale, transatlantic republicanism and constitutionalism still confront their greatest traditional dilemma. On one hand, we are as constrained as ever to ask by what means self-seeking individualism is compatible with public spirit and participatory democracy, as neo-liberals have consistently maintained. And on the other, the same longstanding question from the Left: how are individual rights secured in a divided civic society, with the state itself ensnared in the machinery of inequality? The context may have become more global, but the questions are decidedly local.

---

[1] J-E. Lane, *Constitutions and Political Theory* (Manchester: Manchester University Press, 1996), 19-25.

[2] Edmund Burke, *Reflections on the French Revolution* (London: Dent, 1955), 281.

[3] F. Rodríguez Adrados, *Historia de la democracia. De Solón a nuestros días* (Madrid: Temas de Hoy, 1997), 26-32.

[4] M. P. Zuchert, *Natural Rights and the New Republicanism* (Princeton: Princeton University Press, 1994), 49ff.

[5] See especially Alfred von Martin's masterwork, *Sociologie der Renaissance* (Stuttgart: Ferdinand Enke Verlag, 1932).

[6] I. Kramnick, *Republicanism and Bourgeois Radicalis: Political Ideology in Late Eighteenth-Century England and America* (Ithaca: Cornell University Press, 1990), 1.

[7] Quoted in G. H. Sabine and T. L. Thorson, *A History of Political Thought* (Tokyo: Holt-Saunders International Editions, 1981), 395.

[8] Quoted in O. Gierke, *Natural Law and the Theory of Society, 1500 to 1800* (Cambridge: Cambridge University Press, 1950), 331.

[9] T. L. Pangle, *The Spirit of Modern Republicanism: The Moral Vision of the American Founders and the Philosophy of Locke* (Chicago: University of Chicago Press, 1988), 8.

[10] A recent summary of the languages of American politics during the country's founding years is given in Ronald J. Terchek, *Republican Paradoxes and Liberal Anxieties* (Lanham: Rowman and Littlefield, 1997), 305-16; see also Kramnick, 35-40.

[11] Quoted in A. J. Beitzinger, *A History of American Political Thought* (New York: Classworks, 1972), 3.

[12] Kramnick, 288.

[13] See R. H. Gabriel, *The Course of American Democratic Thought* (New York: Greenwood Press, 1986), 26-39.

[14] Ibid., 114.

[15] J. Nedelsky, *Private Property and the Limits of American Constitutionalism* (Chicago: University of Chicago Press, 1990), 1.

[16] J. W. Muller and W. Bennett, eds., *The Revival of Constitutionalism* (Lincoln: University of Nebraska Press, 1988), 87-103.

[17] Lane, 60.

Chapter 17

Bridging the Divide: Transatlantic Nuclear Diplomacy, NATO and the Dilemma of Extended Deterrence

Susanna Schrafstetter

> NATO's purpose is to keep the Americans in, the Germans down and the Russians out. (Lord Ismay)

At the end of World War II, American military forces based in Europe began to return home. US servicemen, who had recently fought the *Wehrmacht* from the Channel to the Elbe, re-entered civilian life. In less than 18 months, the size of the American armed forces declined dramatically. The Soviet Union did not demobilize. The Red Army was used to consolidate Soviet power in Eastern and Central Europe. The division of Europe had begun. In March 1948, to resist further Soviet expansion, the Western European powers signed the Brussels Treaty which provided common defense against attack. Initially, the Truman administration sought to distance America from events in Europe. The policy was soon reversed. In April 1949 the US administration signed the North Atlantic Treaty formally committing the US to the defense of Western Europe. The creation of NATO was the culmination of a diplomatic offensive initiated by members of the Brussels Treaty, particularly Britain, to tie the US to the security of Western Europe.[1]

The military alliance signified a new chapter in the transatlantic partnership: for the US, NATO represented a rejection of isolationism and an entangling alliance with European powers; for the Europeans, the creation of NATO was clear recognition that America was the only power able to prevent the continent being placed under Soviet domination. The new relationship brought to the fore sensitive political issues: what was America's role in Europe? How long would America be committed to the defense of Europe? Having entered both world wars reluctantly, could the US be trusted? On the one hand, the Europeans sought strong American leadership, but often complained about lack of consultation. On the other hand, although the US outwardly welcomed Europe as an equal partner, it was clearly recognized that a united Europe was potentially capable of challenging American military and economic power. In the early post-war period, however, Europe was far from speaking with one voice. Consequently, American policy and NATO policy were often perceived as synonymous. The charge that NATO was solely an extension of US foreign policy—an argument often used by the Soviets in an attempt to weaken the transatlantic relationship—proved difficult to counter.

This chapter provides an historical analysis of the nuclear dimension of the transatlantic relationship—the area in which tensions were particularly acute—from the beginning of NATO until the end of the Cold War. Initial analysis centers on Western nuclear diplomacy in the 1950s and 1960s. This period was mainly characterized by the question of which NATO members would be allowed to become nuclear powers, and by American efforts to create a NATO nuclear force under collective control. These questions were discussed both inside and outside the alliance, and decisions were often taken without consulting other NATO members. National interests and the question of control over Western nuclear forces dominated these discussions.

Only after the control question had been solved were European NATO members able to speak with one voice to the US. This was achieved by France's departure from NATO's integrated command structure in 1966 and West Germany's renunciation of nuclear weapons in the nuclear Non-Proliferation Treaty (NPT) of 1968. The late 1960s marked a turning point for the alliance: Britain, West Germany and, to some extent, Italy started cooperation on nuclear planning within NATO structures. At the same time, attention was shifting from which powers controlled Western nuclear weapons to how these weapons would be used. The control issue resolved, nuclear strategy became the main focus of alliance debate. The 1970s were characterized by the Europeans seeking reassurance from America as the Soviet Union achieved strategic nuclear parity with the US. These demands culminated in NATO's double-track decision of 1979 which provided for the deployment of US Intermediate Range Ballistic missiles (IRBMs) in Europe if the Soviet Union refused to remove its own IRBMs targeted at Western Europe. In the 1980s the divergence of opinion between the US and Europe widened. The increasingly strident tones of the Reagan administration worried many Europeans who feared the dawn of a Second Cold War.

North Atlantic nuclear policy has undergone change, but it has always been the litmus test for the seriousness of US commitment and alliance cohesion. With the collapse of the Soviet Union, many analysts believed nuclear weapons were marginalized and NATO's survival was strongly questioned. Is the Western world celebrating the victory over Communism and the "culture of contentment"?[2] Has NATO's role waned, changed or remained the same in the post-Cold War age of insecurity?

Nuclear Diplomacy and Intra-Alliance Politics 1945-1966

In accepting the need for NATO, the US entered a commitment to defend Western Europe against Soviet attack. The crux of the treaty was Article 5 which enshrined the principle of collective defense: an attack on one of the members would count as an attack against all.[3] The American nuclear guarantee was not made explicit. It was nevertheless clear that the ultimate defense of the alliance was based on the threat of instant nuclear retaliation carried out by US forces. The strategy raised a major dilemma: to deter the Soviets, the threat needed be credible. The credibility of the deterrent was not, however, based on the strength of Europe, but on those nuclear forces provided by the US. Another dilemma concerned intra-alliance control: the US, anxious to maintain undivided control of the Western nuclear deterrent, did not want more fingers on the nuclear trigger. For Europeans, equally determined to deter Soviet attack, such involvement was essential.

In its formative years NATO strategy relied on American nuclear capability (sword), with Europe reluctantly agreeing to enlarge conventional forces (shield). This division of resources did not suit the Europeans. The most important European NATO members had nuclear weapon programs under way (France, UK) or, in the case of West Germany, demanded some control over nuclear weapons. A number of factors explain this development. First, nuclear weapons were regarded as means to improve status and prestige—a belief reinforced by the fact that all members of the UN Security Council were nuclear powers. Second, they were considerably cheaper than conventional forces. Third, there was the question of control. NATO did not posses its own nuclear weapons: control remained firmly in the hands of the US government. Fourth, and most important was the problem of trust. In the case of limited attack on Western Europe, could the US be trusted to carry out a full-scale nuclear attack on the USSR? To address these concerns, the European powers pursued their own national interests.

The close cooperation between the UK and the US had been exemplified in the wartime program to build nuclear weapons: the Manhattan project. This cooperation was stopped abruptly in 1946 when the US Atomic Energy Act was passed, ending nuclear cooperation with other states. The McMahon Act, as it became known, demonstrated that the US was determined to preserve a nuclear monopoly. Undaunted, Britain initiated the development of its own nuclear bomb, which was seen as an essential element to resume nuclear cooperation with the US.[4] Only in 1958-59, in the afterglow of the British H-bomb test, did the Eisenhower administration accept that the UK was a nuclear power. The laws governing nuclear cooperation with other states were amended to include Britain—but only Britain.[5] This confirmed suspicions of NATO allies that the US and Britain shared a nuclear special relationship.

For Britain, nuclear power status promised not only a leading role in the Western alliance (albeit as junior partner of the US), but also a seat at the top table in international relations. In short, while the colonial empire was collapsing, nuclear weapons and exclusive cooperation with the US allowed Britain to relinquish its great power status on its own terms and, above all, influence in American nuclear policy.[6] British nuclear policy also reflected lessons from the Suez debacle: independent adventures were no longer advisable. Within the alliance Britain enjoyed a privileged position as the US junior partner—a position the British government jealously defended. France's rise as a nuclear power was reluctantly accepted, West German nuclear ambitions, however, were strongly opposed: the FRG was not allowed the same status as Britain.[7] In short, the US and Britain would provide the nuclear defense of the West and other NATO members were to accept this hierarchy.

While the US resumed nuclear collaboration with Britain, similar assistance to France was rejected, despite the fact that French scientists had worked on the Manhattan Project and France was preparing for its first atomic test. The Eisenhower government was willing to increase nuclear sharing within NATO but was not allowed to pass nuclear weapons directly into the hands of the allies—except to Britain. General de Gaulle, who returned to power in 1958, tried to secure parity with Britain, but he was only offered participation within a NATO framework. In Washington, this was seen as a means to accommodate European demands for some form of nuclear sharing. De Gaulle, however, felt blackmailed into nuclear dependence on the US. Ideally he sought global defense of the West led by a triumvirate of France, Britain and the US in which these three states would jointly decide over the use of nuclear weapons.[8]

The US rejected these demands, an outcome which led the French down a different path than the British: they stressed the independent role of their deterrent. French strategy became known as *la dissuasion du faible au fort*, implying that whilst France was not strong enough to inflict a fatal blow on the Soviet Union, the French arsenal could inflict sufficient damage to deter Moscow from aggression against France. France mistrusted the US guarantee and aimed at reducing American influence within Europe—the belief that the US was unreliable had been nourished by the Suez experience. Unlike Britain, France was not willing to sacrifice nuclear independence. However, de Gaulle agreed with the British: West Germany should not be allowed to gain any control over nuclear weapons. In short, the General wanted to build up a French nuclear force, the *force de frappe*, for the defense of Europe. France was to provide the nuclear umbrella and take the lead in the defense of Europe—or, in other words, play America's role in Europe.

For West Germany, nuclear abstention was the pre-condition for its admission into NATO in 1955. However, Bonn did not wish to preclude the nuclear option indefinitely and began to press for revision of its treaty obligations. Three main reasons are apparent. First, the threat of a nuclear option was seen as a powerful diplomatic lever in negotiations with the Soviets, especially in relation to German unification and augmented West German Chancellor Adenauer's "position of strength" approach towards Moscow. Second, the nuclear weapons programs of both Britain and France were seen as reinforcing West Germany's second-class status within the alliance. Finally, the lack of influence over NATO nuclear strategy worried the Germans as it was becoming clear to many in Bonn that in any future war, Germany (both East and West) would become a nuclear battlefield over which they would have no control. Exercise *Carte Blanche*, a NATO war game conducted in 1955, demonstrated that nuclear conflict with the Red Army would wipe Germany off the map.

Adenauer and Defense Minister Franz Josef Strauss put pressure on the US to provide Germany a greater say in the nuclear defense of Western Europe. Plans for joint nuclear weapons development with France and Italy within the framework of European integration had been halted by de Gaulle in 1958—much to German dismay.[9] In response, Bonn concentrated its efforts on extracting concessions from the US.

Wolfram Hanrieder argues that NATO had a dual function: to contain the Soviet Union via deterrence and West Germany via reassurance.[10] Reassurance in the form of "nuclear sharing" seemed necessary to contain nuclear aspirations of the Germans as the alliance was confronted with more or less veiled hints that West Germany might develop a national nuclear potential.

What explains the different paths pursued by Britain, France and Germany? Britain wanted transatlantic nuclear diplomacy to be an exclusive bilateral relationship. General de Gaulle denounced transatlantic nuclear diplomacy a means for America to dominate Europe and rejected cooperation with the Anglo-Saxons (without, however, rejecting the US nuclear umbrella). West Germany expected a revision of the 1954 agreements and some control over US weapons deployed in the FRG, but France and Britain did not welcome the German ambitions.

A NATO Nuclear Force?

The Eisenhower administration realized that lack of influence on nuclear decision making combined with Britain's special role were generating tensions within the alliance. In an attempt to solve these problems, Washington advanced plans for the creation of a NATO nuclear force, the MLF (multilateral force).[11] The initiative was ill-fated: it received lukewarm responses from Britain and France. Furthermore, no firm decision could be taken until after the 1960 presidential election. When the Kennedy administration came into office in 1961, Secretary of Defense McNamara's first priority was a review of defense policy. In 1957, *Sputnik*, the first Soviet satellite into orbit, had demonstrated that the Soviet Union could reach the US with Intercontinental Ballistic Missiles (ICBMs): American nuclear invulnerability was over. Under these conditions, massive retaliation was no longer in the US interest and consequently no longer credible. A new nuclear strategy, Flexible Response (as it became to be known later) was developed. It provided for limited conflict with the Warsaw Pact but avoided automatic escalation to an all-out nuclear war. To implement the strategy, tight control of the Western nuclear potential and increases in conventional forces were necessary. The US would control the nuclear sword; the Europeans the conventional shield.

Flexible Response raised European doubts about the America's nuclear guarantee. It implied that the US was no longer willing to retaliate automatically in response to a Soviet attack. In short, as America could be targeted by Russian nuclear weapons, Washington sought a graduated response prior to all-out nuclear war. The Europeans, however, demanded an early use of nuclear weapons: both to demonstrate resolve to escalate and to wed the US to Europe's defense. Early use of nuclear weapons, however, reaffirmed Bonn's worries of turning Germany into a battlefield. To reconcile this ambiguity, the Germans argued for an early use of nuclear weapons on Warsaw Pact rather than on NATO territory.

A NATO nuclear force did not fit easily with the new strategy. Centralized control and increases in conventional arms were the primary objectives. Nevertheless, the MLF was re-offered by Kennedy—albeit under different conditions. The US State Department saw political advantages in the MLF: implementation could promote European integration, foster the emergence of a single European voice in the alliance and assuage European fears about "annihilation without representation." Moreover, it could bring British and French nuclear arsenals under collective control and meet German demands for nuclear sharing. Against this, however, the force had no significant military value, was perceived in the Pentagon as assisting nuclear proliferation, and antagonized the USSR. Overall, the question of control was crucial: a veto-free force would undermine Flexible Response; a US veto would provide no incentive for the Europeans to join. The dilemma proved intractable. Consequently the MLF received low priority. Only in December 1962 when the British Prime Minister Macmillan secured the acquisition of *Polaris* missiles at Nassau did the MLF once again become the focus of interest. At Nassau Kennedy and McNamara agreed to supply the UK with *Polaris* missiles as replacement for the recently cancelled *Skybolt* missile. To downplay Britain's privileged position and maintain alliance cohesion, Kennedy insisted that Macmillan place the *Polaris* submarines within NATO's command structure. The Nassau Agreement strengthened French perception of special ties between the Anglo-Saxons and confirmed de Gaulle's decision to veto Britain's entry into the EEC in 1963.[12] The Macmillan government regarded nuclear collaboration as a bargaining chip for admission to the EEC, offering de Gaulle the prospect of Anglo-French cooperation. This, however, did not meet French objectives. The West Germans also felt snubbed by the Nassau Agreement: transatlantic nuclear sharing remained a solely British preserve.

Aware of the tensions Nassau had generated, the Kennedy Administration sought to promote the MLF as a means to placate the Germans and constrain French and British national nuclear arsenals. The French loudly rejected the scheme and sought to woo the Germans away from the MLF by renewing vague offers of Franco-German nuclear cooperation.[13] The Macmillan government also had no interest in sacrificing the special nuclear relationship for a NATO force in which Britain would stand on a par with Germany and Italy. The only NATO member pressing for the MLF was the Federal Republic. William Kaufmann has described the situation from the US perspective:

> Many Europeans were not happy with the existing arrangements. But they could not agree among themselves about objectives, they trusted one another less than they did the United States, and they had no particular inclination to incur the costs and risks of greater independence.[14]

Prime Minister Macmillan sought refuge in equivocation, issuing a flood of amendments and counter-proposals for the MLF. The 1964 Labour Government under Wilson continued this policy and stressed the importance of a global non-dissemination agreement to prevent proliferation of nuclear weapons. The agreement was seen as an opportunity to end German nuclear aspirations. This could only be achieved if the MLF was cancelled: Moscow had declared it would only sign a non-proliferation agreement if the MLF was abandoned. The Kremlin saw the MLF as a means of secretly transferring nuclear weapons to the FRG. Intended to strengthen the transatlantic relationship, the episode almost led to its collapse.

Crisis and Change 1965-1968

Divergent views over the MLF as well as criticism from Moscow led to strong intra-alliance tensions, culminating in the withdrawal of French forces from NATO's integrated military command in 1966, which led to a crisis of credibility for NATO in 1966-67.[15] French departure, however, was only symptomatic of a wider malaise that centered on the question of nuclear control. De Gaulle's move was primarily motivated by the desire to make France the only genuinely independent nuclear force in Europe. The West Germans insisted on the implementation of a nuclear sharing scheme, while the British urged the US to abandon the MLF in favor of a non-dissemination agreement. By the end of 1964, President Johnson was wary of the MLF. When some pro-MLF advisers from the State Department demanded he force Britain into the MLF, Johnson responded:

> Aren't you telling me to kick mother England out the door into the cold, while I bring the Kaiser into the sitting room? [...] What will be said by people in this country and in Congress, if the President kicks the English while welcoming the Germans?[16]

Johnson was ready to drop the MLF and his attention began to focus on a non-dissemination agreement.[17] The superpowers had a joint interest in preventing the spread of nuclear weapons. Firm control over nuclear weapons reduced the threat of nuclear blackmail. Furthermore, arms control was an area in which communication could be kept open during the Vietnam War. The French decision to leave NATO's integrated command structure coincided with a breakthrough in US-Soviet negotiations for the Non-Proliferation Treaty (NPT). Bonn was dismayed, describing the NPT as a "Morgenthau-Plan squared."[18] Bonn's unwillingness to sign the treaty was clear.

The crisis had cathartic effects: France's departure brought the other allies closer together, and the withdrawal freed the way for joint nuclear planning which the French had opposed. The MLF was now off the table. The new German government which came into power in 1969 signed the NPT, signaling a change in German foreign policy away from a hard-line approach to the Soviet Union towards "change through rapprochement." Détente was intended to bring the two Germanys closer together, but the Soviet demand of a non-nuclear FRG was identified as a precondition to a new *Ostpolitik*. Bonn's renunciation of nuclear weapons was equally welcome in London, Washington, Paris and Moscow; it not only marked the beginning of new relations with the East but also cooperation between the FRG and Britain in NATO.

The late 1960s and early 1970s also saw a shift of focus away from nuclear-sharing and towards strategy in transatlantic nuclear diplomacy— a process that had begun with the implementation of Flexible Response. Criticism of US nuclear policy and European unwillingness to fulfill their conventional commitments and their lack of support during Vietnam War led to renewed discussions over US disengagement and abandonment of the commitment in Europe. The NPT and Strategic Arms Limitation Talks [SALT] negotiations marked the dawn of superpower détente. However, détente raised fears that the US would put superpower dialogue before European security. Lack of proper consultation during the NPT and SALT negotiations (and later during the Yom-Kippur War) intensified these fears. Moreover as the Soviet Union had now reached strategic parity with the US (codified in the SALT I Treaty), the concept of extended deterrence became less credible. European NATO members therefore sought confirmation from Washington that the defense of Europe was a US priority.

Cooperation/Alienation: NATO and Nuclear Strategy 1969-1989

In 1966 Britain and Germany took the lead in creating the Nuclear Planning Group (NPG), an exclusive body of leading NATO members consisting of four permanent members (the US, Britain, the Federal Republic and Italy) and three members chosen in rotation. The origins of the NPG had been laid out by US Secretary of Defense McNamara, who in 1965 had proposed mechanisms to ensure greater transparency and consultation in US nuclear planning. The exclusive body allowed the Federal Republic and Italy to demonstrate their increasing importance as key members of the alliance without endangering British nuclear status or US ultimate control over nuclear weapons.[19]

One of the first examples of successful cooperation in the NPG was the working group on the use of tactical nuclear forces. The final paper, the Healey-Schröder report,[20] re-emphasized Western resolve to use nuclear weapons at a fairly early stage in a conflict. The Europeans were keen to underline this threat as they felt that the credibility of the deterrent had been reduced by Flexible Response, officially adopted by NATO in 1967. Denis Healey took a leading role in persuading the US to accept the goals of the Healey-Schröder report in November 1969.[21] For the first time, Europeans were speaking with one voice on nuclear matters both to defend European strategic interests and to establish consultation procedures on strategic planning within the alliance. Another new NATO body to emerge from British German cooperation was the Eurogroup, whose objective was to share defense spending more evenly among NATO members.[22] However, neither the Eurogroup nor the NPG was able to solve the central problem now facing NATO: the decline of the credibility of the extended deterrent.

For Britain the nuclear issue was closely linked with the European question. The Heath government considered close cooperation with Bonn a positive development. The British government also sought to improve relations with France—possible projects included Anglo-French cooperation to replace the *Polaris* system, and—in the long-term—the creation of a European deterrent. Heath was determined to avoid another Nassau. Lack of French interest, however, led to the replacement of *Polaris* by *Chevaline*, a British-designed warhead.[23] British governments offered nuclear cooperation in 1962 and 1967 to gain admission to the EEC. While this was never attractive enough to avert de Gaulle's *non*, it was largely irrelevant after de Gaulle's departure.[24]

In 1974 US Secretary of Defense James Schlesinger advanced a revised concept for the nuclear defense of the West that reflected the new geo-strategic balance in which the Soviet Union had achieved strategic parity. Starting from the assumption that extended deterrence was only credible if a nuclear war could be fought and won, the Schlesinger-Doctrine (as it was called) was the logical development of Flexible Response: it advocated flexible, limited options for the use of nuclear weapons in a wide range of contingencies. The strategy had two objectives: to raise the nuclear threshold by strengthening conventional forces to limit the danger of nuclear war in Europe; and to modernize tactical nuclear weapons to create thresholds against rapid escalation. Limited nuclear options were a way out of the fundamental problem posed by extended deterrence in the age of strategic parity—the strategy confirmed the US commitment to defend Europe. From a European perspective, however, it dramatically increased the possibility of limited nuclear war in Europe.

European worries were intensified by the modernization of Soviet IRBMs and deployment of *SS-20* missiles in Europe. The West German government responded by demanding deployment of NATO intermediate-range nuclear forces (INFs) to counter recent Soviet deployments, re-establishing the link between conventional forces and American strategic capabilities. Chancellor Schmidt argued that the Eurostrategic balance was strongly tipped in favor of the Warsaw Pact as the Soviets now possessed superiority in conventional and shorter-range nuclear missiles. The British government did not completely agree with Schmidt's analysis, but it supported the German demands.[25] The NATO double-track solution of 1979 sanctioned the deployment of US *Pershing* and *Cruise* missiles in Europe if arms control negotiations failed to persuade the Soviet Union to withdraw its IRBMs. The proposal was both military and political: it reflected American willingness to reassure the Europeans (especially the Germans) about US political intentions and their commitment to Europe.

The double-track decision reflected diverging German interests: on the one hand, the Germans insisted on a strategy in which deterrence was still the main element—rapid escalation demonstrating a willingness to use nuclear weapons. From this point of view deployment of new IRBMs was regarded as a necessary political signal to Moscow. On the other hand, nuclear policy could not be de-coupled from the policy of détente—demonstrating US commitment to deterrence was regarded as essential, but it should not threaten the fruits of *Ostpolitik* and the spirit of the Conference on Security and Cooperation in Europe (CSCE). Furthermore, the deployment of nuclear weapons was increasingly difficult to sell to the German (and European) public who strongly objected to the possibility of limited war being fought in Europe. For these reasons, the decision to re-arm was linked to arms control negotiations. Bonn's pressure was also an attempt to return America to a coherent transatlantic nuclear policy: President Carter's capricious decision to cancel the neutron bomb deployment in 1978 had strained German-American relations to the limit.

Tensions over nuclear strategy in the 1970s raise the question of whether the alliance was merely held together by the threat of the Soviet

Union. Indeed, had Moscow adopted a more constructive policy towards Europe, concepts of Europe as a third force between East and West (as discussed by the European left) may have been realized. France explored a path in this direction with the concept of a Europe "from the Atlantic to the Urals." With the end of superpower détente, however, the imaginative force underpinning such concepts evaporated.

Implementation of the double-track solution was left to the Reagan Administration which entered office in 1981. The intervention in Afghanistan demonstrated to the hawks in Washington that the "evil empire" (Ronald Reagan) could not be trusted and that power was the only language the Kremlin fully understood. The crusade was fought on political, military, economic and cultural levels. This hard line was reflected in US arms control policy: the American position in the negotiations was blunt and in the case of the zero solution (removal of all Intermediate Range Nuclear Forces from Europe) amounted to a take-it-or-leave-it ultimatum to the Soviets. This created immense difficulties for those European governments on whose territories the new missiles were to be deployed. The public demanded disarmament, with peace movements in Britain and West Germany organizing mass demonstrations. The angry climate made political support for the double-track solution problematic. This difficulty was compounded by Reagan's desire to create a defensive nuclear shield, the SDI or Star Wars program which further enflamed passions in Europe.

In contrast to the early1980s in which too little effort was made in arms control, in 1987 too much effort was made. The acceptance of the INF Treaty and a double zero solution (abolition of INFs and shorter-range intermediate nuclear forces) left the Europeans facing Soviet conventional superiority without a link to US strategic forces. European interests were again disregarded. Serious doubts were raised both in Bonn and London, but governments found it was difficult to object to the first-ever genuine disarmament agreement which received overwhelming public support. Washington clearly gave priority to arms control negotiations with the Soviets to the security interests of the allies. Paradoxically, German and British peace movements which attacked American "Imperialism" in the early 1980s were now more in line with US policy than European governments who were left with serious misgivings. With the collapse of the Soviet Union everything changed— or so it seemed.

Quo Vadis NATO?

When NATO was founded its major aim was to commit the US to the nuclear defense of Europe against a massive conventional attack by the

Soviet Union. Later, East and West were caught in a nuclear arms race. Nuclear weapons became the one area through which the Soviet Union gained superpower status.[26] Similarly, nuclear weapons represented status and political influence within NATO, and nuclear diplomacy always had political functions: as the MLF, the double-track decision and the NPT demonstrated. The NPT also showed that nuclear diplomacy East and West of the Iron Curtain was shaped by historical considerations. For Germany this meant a nuclear *Sonderweg*, a different path from that of Britain and France. Nuclear policy demonstrated the seriousness of the US commitment for the defense of Europe, and while it has been a major source of friction, it also proved a durable transatlantic link. However, the alliance was also held together by the failure of détente and the lack of alternative options.

With the end of the Cold War, nuclear confrontation which divided East and West began to thaw: Russia and the US successfully negotiated a reduction in strategic arms (START) while peace movements throughout Europe lost their momentum. France and the successor states of the Soviet Union readily agreed to join the NPT. In this new environment NATO's future seemed uncertain. At a stroke, NATO lost its two major roles: it was no longer required to contain either the Russians, who were withdrawing from Eastern Europe, or the Germans (at least not militarily). Should the peaceful dissolution of the Cold War be, as Ronald Steel has argued, NATO's last mission?[27] Is NATO's purpose now fulfilled?

Against expectations, the alliance has continued to survive. A number of reasons have been advanced to explain this tenacity. First, new tasks began to emerge, including peacekeeping and out-of-area operations. Second, the new age of uncertainty was regarded by some as equally dangerous as the bipolar world. Developments within the former Soviet Union raised concern, and the over-optimistic expectations about the Soviet Empire's graceful decline began to evaporate. German reunification raised new fears (and rekindled old ones) of the extension of German power over *Mitteleuropa*. Third, in comparison to NATO, neither the WEU (the defense organization of the Brussels Pact) nor the CSCE proved suitable candidates to maintain a credible European security system.[28] Genuine integration of European security policy, especially the pooling of the French and British nuclear forces, appears unlikely. In the words of former secretary general of WEU, Alfred Cahen:

> In the graveyard of aborted attempts to bring about a European Union, a graveyard where the tombs are many, the most numerous

ones contain the initiatives devoted to the creation of a European
security dimension.[29]

Britain and other European NATO members (Denmark, the Netherlands)
eager to maintain strong transatlantic links, oppose French initiatives for
a European security and defense identity (ESDI). Realizing the lack of
support, France has abandoned efforts for a genuine European security
system, in favor of gradual partial reintegration into NATO.[30] Once
again, the creation of a second, European pillar within the Transatlantic
Alliance is back on the agenda.

David Yost has recently argued that "there is a strong case for the US
to maintain nuclear forces and commitments in Europe and to continue
working closely with NATO allies in developing and implementing
nuclear policy."[31] He contends that the main factors against a US
withdrawal from Europe are Russia's increased emphasis on nuclear
weapons in her military doctrine; political uncertainties in the FSU; the
lack of an European alternative to US nuclear forces; and US acceptance
of new extended-deterrence responsibilities through NATO
enlargement.[32] Deterrence, non-proliferation—this was made painfully
obvious by the Indian and Pakistani tests in 1998—and alliance cohesion
remain, despite some new roles for NATO, the key tasks of the alliance.
Plus ça change, plus c'est la même chose.

---

[1] John Baylis, *The Diplomacy of Pragmatism: Britain and the Formation of
NATO, 1942-49* (Basingstoke: Macmillan, 1993), 116.
[2] Ken Booth, "Liberal Democracy, Global Order and the Future of
Transatlantic Relations," in *Brassey's Defence Yearbook 1993* (London:
Brassey's, 1993), 353-66.
[3] Baylis, 161.
[4] Margaret Gowing, *Independence and Deterrence: Britain and Atomic
Energy* (London: Macmillan, 1974), 184.
[5] See Jan Melissen, *The Struggle for Nuclear Partnership: Britain, the United
States and the Making of an Ambiguous Alliance, 1952-1959* (Groningen:
Styx, 1993).
[6] Stephen Twigge and Len Scott, *Planning Armageddon: Britain, the United
States and the Command of Western Nuclear Forces, 1945-1964*
(Amsterdam: Harwood, 2000), 100ff.
[7] Susanna Schrafstetter, *Die dritte Atommacht, Britische Nichtver-
breitungspolitik im Dienst von Statussicherung und Deutschlandpolitik*
(Munich: Oldenbourg, 1999), 42-43.
[8] Ibid., 38-39.
[9] For the Franco-German-Italian nuclear cooperation, see Colette Barbier,
"Les négotiations franco-germano-italiennes en vue de l'établissement d'une

coopération militaire nucléaire au cours des années 1956-1958," *Revue d'Histoire Diplomatique* 104 (1990): 81-114; Eckart Conze, "La coopération franco-germano-italienne dans le domaine nucléaire dans les années 1957-1958: Un point de vue allemand," *Revue d'Histoire Diplomatique* 104 (1990): 115-32; Leopoldo Nuti, "Le rôle de l'Italie dans les négotiations trilatérales 1957-1958," *Revue d'Histoire Diplomatique* 104 (1990): 133-56.

[10] Wolfram Hanrieder, "The FRG and NATO: Between Security Dependence and Security Partnership," in *The Federal Republic of Germany and NATO*, ed. Emil Kirchner (London: Macmillan, 1992), 195.

[11] For the MLF, see Pascaline Winand, *Eisenhower, Kennedy and the United States of Europe* (New York: St. Martin's Press, 1993); Christoph Bluth, *Britain, Germany and Western Nuclear Strategy* (Oxford: Oxford University Press, 1995); Christoph Hoppe, *Zwischen Teilhabe und Mitsprache* (Baden Baden: Nomos 1993); John Steinbrunner, *The Cybernetic Theory of Decision* (Princeton: Princeton University Press, 1974).

[12] Maurice Vaisse, "General de Gaulle et la Première Candidature Britannique au Marché Commun," *Revue d'Histoire Diplomatique* 108 (1994): 147.

[13] Beatrice Heuser, *NATO, Britain, France and the FRG: Nuclear Strategies and Forces for Europe, 1949-2000* (London: Macmillan, 1998), 154-57.

[14] William Kaufmann, *The McNamara Strategy* (New York: Harper and Row, 1964), 104.

[15] Helga Haftendorn, *NATO and the Nuclear Revolution: A Crisis in Credibility, 1966-1967* (Oxford: Clarendon, 1996).

[16] LBJL, NSF, Country File: UK, box 214, Record of Conversation, 6 December 1964.

[17] See Glenn Seaborg, *Stemming the Tide: Arms Control in the Johnson Years* (Lexington: Lexington Books, 1987).

[18] Matthias Küntzel, *Bonn und die Bombe* (Frankfurt: Campe, 1993), 157.

[19] The example of Italy shows how much the nuclear question was an issue of status and prestige. Once the Italians were admitted to the NPG, they were happy to be a member of the body, but they did not participate actively. Leopoldo Nuti, "Me Too Please: Italy and the Politics of Nuclear Weapons, 1945-1975," *Diplomacy and Statecraft* 4 (1993): 132.

[20] The paper was named after the British and German Defense Ministers.

[21] Heuser, 54.

[22] Bluth, 197-98.

[23] Heuser, 159-160.

[24] The French, it seems, found a more attractive partner. Richard Ullman has argued that the Nixon administration, which entered office in 1969, sought to improve relations with France. This aim was primarily achieved by covertly aiding the French nuclear program. The aid consisted in the solution of French technical problems, not in the delivery of hardware, which was still forbidden under the Atomic Energy Act. If this account is true, the independent development of the *force de frappe* is a myth rather than reality. Richard Ullman, "The Covert French Connection," *Foreign Policy* 75 (1989): 3-33.

[25] Bluth, 221-22.

[26] West German Chancellor Schmidt called the Soviet Union "Upper Volta with nuclear weapons." Hannes Adomeit, *Imperial Overstretch: Germany in Soviet Policy from Stalin to Gorbachev* (Baden-Baden: Nomos, 1998), 41.

[27] Ronald Steel, "NATO's Last Mission," *Foreign Policy* 79 (1989): 83-95.

[28] See Tom Lansford, "The Triumph of Transatlanticism: NATO and the Evolution of European Security after the Cold War," *Journal of Strategic Studies* 22 (1999): 1-28.

[29] Alfred Cahen quoted in David Haglund, "NATO's Expansion and European Security after the Washington Summit—What Next?" *European Security* 8 (1999): 10.

[30] Lansford, 12-14.

[31] David Yost, *The United States and Nuclear Deterrence in Europe,* Adelphi Paper 326 (Oxford: Oxford University Press, 1999), 70. For an assessment of NATO's future, see also Susan Eisenhower, *NATO at Fifty: Perspectives on the Future of the Transatlantic Alliance* (Washington: Centre for Political and Strategic Studies, 1999).

[32] Ibid., 72.

Selected Bibliography

Abraham, H. J. et al, eds. *Essays on the Constitution of the United States.* London: National University Press, 1978.

Alexander, Grant S. *Commodity and Property: Competing Visions of Property in American Legal Thought.* Chicago: University of Chicago Press, 1997.

Alheit, P., and E. Kammler. *Lifelong Learning and Its Impact on Social and Regional Development.* Bremen: Donat Verlag, 1998.

Archer, M. S., ed. *The Sociology of Educational Expansion: Take-off, Growth and Inflation in Educational Systems.* London: Sage, 1992.

Arciniegas, Germán. *America in Europe: A History of the New World in Reverse.* Translated by Gabriela Arciniegas and R. Victoria Arana. San Diego: Harcourt Brace Jovanovich, 1986.

Bailyn, B. *The Peopling of British North America.* New York: Knopf, 1986.

Bakhtin, Mikhail. *The Dialogic Imagination.* Austin: University of Texas Press, 1990.

Barthes, Roland. *Mythologies.* Translated by Annette Lavers. London: Jonathan Cape, 1972.

Baylis, John. *The Diplomacy of Pragmatism: Britain and the Formation of NATO, 1942-49.* Basingstoke: Macmillan, 1993.

Bellamy, R., and D. Castiglione, eds. *Constitutionalism in Transformation: European and Theoretical Perspectives.* Blackwell: Oxford, 1996.

Bellamy, Richard, ed. *Constitutionalism, Democracy and Sovereignty. American and European Perspectives.* Avebury: Aldershot, 1996.

Bernstein, R. *Dictatorship of Virtue.* New York: Alfred A. Knopf, 1994.

Betten, L., ed. *The Human Rights Act: What It Means.* London: Martinus Nijhoff Publishers, 1999.

Bhabha, Homi. *The Location of Culture.* London: Routledge, 1994.

Blethen, H. T., and C. W. Wood, eds. *Ulster and North America: Transatlantic Perspectives on the Scotch-Irish.* Tuscaloosa: University of Alabama Press, 1997.

Bluth, Christoph. *Britain, Germany and Western Nuclear Strategy.* Oxford: Oxford University Press, 1995.

Bogdanor, V., ed. *Constitutions in Democratic Politics.* Aldershot: Gower Publishing, 1988.

Borjas, George J. *Friends or Strangers: The Impact of Immigrants on the U.S. Economy.* New York: Basic Books, 1990.

Bradbury, Malcolm. *Dangerous Pilgrimages: Trans-Atlantic Mythologies and the Novel.* London: Secker and Warburg, 1995.

Braudel, Fernand. *After Thoughts on Material Civilization and Capitalism.* Baltimore: Johns Hopkins University Press, 1977.

Breakwell, G., ed. *Threatened Identities.* Chichester, England: Wiley, 1983.

Breakwell, G., and E. Lyons, eds. *Changing European Identities.* Oxford: Butterworth Heinemann, 1996.

Brimelow, Peter. *Alien Nation: Common Sense About America's Immigration Disaster.* New York: Random House, 1995.

Bryan, William Jennings et al. *Republic or Empire? The Philippine Question.* Chicago: Independence Co., 1899.

Burroughs, William, and Brion Gysin. *The Third Mind.* London: John Calder, 1979.

Butterworth, G., and P. Bryant, eds. *Causes of Development: Interdisciplinary Perspectives.* Chichester, England: Wiley, 1987.

Cell, John. *The Highest Stage of White Supremacy: The Origins of Segregation in South Africa and the American South.* Cambridge: Cambridge University Press, 1982.

Chambers, Iain. *Migrancy, Culture, Identity.* London: Routledge, 1994.

Clifford, James. *Routes: Travel and Translation in the Late Twentieth Century.* Cambridge: Harvard University Press, 1997.

Conway, A. *The Welsh in America: Letters from the Immigrants.* Cardiff: University of Wales Press, 1961.

Cronon, E. David. *Marcus Garvey and the Universal Negro Improvement Association.* Madison: University of Wisconsin Press, 1969.

Dahl, Robert A. *A Preface to Democratic Theory.* Chicago: University of Chicago Press, 1956.

Devine, T. M., ed. *Scottish Emigration and Scottish Society.* Edinburgh: John Donald, 1992.

Domville-Fife, Charles. *The Real South America.* London: George Routledge, 1922.

Eisenhower, Susan. *NATO at Fifty: Perspectives on the Future of the Transatlantic Alliance.* Washington, D.C.: Centre for Political and Strategic Studies, 1999.

Elliott, J. H. *The Old World and the New, 1492-1650.* Cambridge: Cambridge University Press, 1970.

Elster, J., and R. Slagstad, eds. *Constitutionalism and Democracy.* Cambridge: Cambridge University Press, 1993.

Fifer, J. Valerie. *American Progress: The Growth of the Transport, Tourist and Information Industries in the Nineteenth-Century West.* Chester, Conn.: The Globe Patriot Press, 1988.

Fisher, S. *Recreation and the Sea.* Exeter, England: Exeter University Press, 1997.

Flores, William V., and Rina Benmayore. *Latino Cultural Citizenship: Claiming Identity, Space, and Rights.* Boston: Beacon Press, 1997.

Flynn, M., ed. *Scottish Population History from the Seventeenth Century to the 1930s* Cambridge: Cambridge University Press, 1977.

Franklin, D. P., and M. J. Baun, eds. *Political Culture and Constitutionalism: A Comparative Approach.* Armonk, N.Y.: M. E. Sharpe, 1995.

Franklin, John Hope, and Alfred A. Mosse. *From Slavery to Freedom: A History of African-Americans.* New York: McGraw Hill, 1947.

Frederick, Howard. *Global Communication and International Relations.* Belmont, Cal.: Wadsworth Publishing Co., 1993.

Fryer, Peter. *Staying Power: The History of Black People in Britain.* London: Pluto Press, 1984.

Fukuyama, Francis. *The End of History and the Last Man.* London: Penguin, 1992.

Furlough, E., and S. Baranowski, eds. *Tourism and Consumption in Modern Europe.* Ann Arbor: University of Michigan Press, forthcoming.

Furnham, A., and S. Bochner. *Culture Shock: Psychological Reactions to Unfamiliar Environments.* London: Routledge, 1986.

Fussell, Paul. *Abroad: British Literary Traveling Between the Wars.* Oxford: Oxford University Press, 1982.

Gabriel, R. H. *The Course of American Democratic Thought.* Westbury, Conn.: Greenwood Press, 1986.

Giddens, Anthony. *The Consequences of Modernity: Self and Society in the Late Modern Age.* Cambridge: Polity Press, 1990.

Giere, U. *Adult Learning in a World at Risk: Emerging Policies and Strategies.* Hamburg: Unesco Institute of Education, 1996.

Gierke, O.T., *Natural Law and the Theory of Society, 1500 to 1800* Cambridge: Cambridge University Press, 1950.

Gilroy, Paul. *The Black Atlantic: Modernity and Double Consciousness.* London: Verso, 1996.

Goffman, Erving. *Stigma: Notes on the Management of Spoiled Identity.* Harmondsworth, England: Penguin, 1976.

Gowing, Margaret. *Independence and Deterrence: Britain and Atomic Energy.* London: Macmillan, 1974.

Greenslade, D. *Welsh Fever: Welsh Activities in the United States and Canada Today.* Cowbridge, Wales: D. Brown, 1986.

Habermas, Jurgen. *The Structural Transformation of the Public Sphere: An Inquiry into a Category of Bourgeois Society.* Translated by Thomas Burger with the assistance of Frederick Lawrence. Cambridge: Polity Press, 1989.

Haftendorn, Helga. *NATO and the Nuclear Revolution: A Crisis in Credibility, 1966-1967.* Oxford: Clarendon Press, 1996.

Hall, Stuart, et al, eds. *Modernity and Its Futures.* Cambridge: Polity Press, 1992.

Hammar, Thomas. *European Immigration Policy: A Comparative Study.* Cambridge: Cambridge University Press, 1985.

Hargreaves, D. *Interpersonal Relations and Education.* London: Routledge and Kegan Paul, 1975.

Held, D., and C. Pollitt. *New Forms of Democracy.* London: Sage, 1986.

Heuser, Beatrice. *NATO, Britain, France and the FRG: Nuclear Strategies and Forces for Europe, 1949-2000.* London: Macmillan, 1998.

Hirschman, Albert O. *The Passions and the Interests: Political Arguments for Capitalism Before Its Triumph.* Princeton: Princeton University Press, 1977.

Hirst, P., and G. Thompson. *Globalization in Question: The International Economy and the Possibilities of Governance.* Cambridge: Polity Press, 1996.

Hobbes, Thomas. *Leviathan.* Indianapolis: The Library of Liberal Arts Press, 1958.

Hobbes, Thomas. *Man and Citizen.* Indianapolis: Hackett Publishing Co.,1991.

James, C. L. R. *Black Jacobins.* London: Vintage, 1963.

Jarvis, P. *Adult and Continuing Education: Theory and Practice.* New York: Routledge, 1995.

Jones, W. D. *Wales in America.* Cardiff: University of Wales Press, 1993.

Kanter, R. *World Class: Thriving Locally in the Global Economy.* New York: Simon and Schuster, 1995.

Kaplan, Caren. *Questions of Travel: Postmodern Discourses of Displacement.* Durham: Duke University Press, 1996.

Kiernan, V. G. *The Lords of Human Kind: European Attitudes to the Outside World in the Imperial Age.* Harmondsworth, England: Penguin, 1972.

King, Russell, et al, eds. *Writing Across Worlds: Literature and Migration.* London: Routledge, 1995.

Kirchner, Emil, ed. *The Federal Republic of Germany and NATO.* London: Macmillan, 1992.

Kirk, N., ed. *Northern Identities.* Aldershot, England: Ashgate, 2000.

Klapper, Joseph T. *The Effects of Mass Communication.* New York: Free Press, 1960.

Kowaleski, Michael, ed. *Temperamental Journeys: Essays on the Modern Literature of Travel.* (Athens: University of Georgia Press, 1992.

Kramnick, I.. *Republicanism and Bourgeois Radicalism: Political Ideology in Late Eighteenth-Century England and America.* Ithica: Cornell University Press, 1990.

Kujawinska-Courtney, K., and R. M. Machnikowski, eds. *The Role of Great Britain in the Modern World.* Lódz, Poland: Lódz University Press, 1999.

Kymlicka, Will. *Multicultural Citizenship.* New York: Oxford University Press, 1995.

Lane, J-E. *Constitutions and Political Theory.* Manchester: Manchester University Press, 1996.

Lawrence, Karen R. *Penelope Voyages: Women and Travel in the British Literary Tradition.* Ithica: Cornell University Press, 1994.

Lencek, L., and G. Bosker. *The Beach: The History of Paradise on Earth.* Harmondsworth: Penguin, 1999.

Lind, E. A. and T. Tyler. *The Social Psychology of Procedural Justice.* New York: Plenum, 1988.

Locke, John. *Two Treatises of Government.* New York: Hafner Publishing, 1947.

Lorimer, Douglas. *Colour, Class and the Victorians.* New York: Holmes and Meier, 1978.

Lowery, Shearon A., and Melvin L. DeFleur. *Milestones in Mass Communication Research.* White Plains, N.Y.: Longman, 1995.

Macpherson, C. B. *The Political Theory of Possessive Individualism Hobbes to Locke.* Oxford: Oxford University Press, 1964.

Mannheim, Karl. *Ideology and Utopia.* New York: Harcourt, Brace, Jovanovich, 1991.

Marshall, T. H. *Class, Citizenship, and Social Development.* New York: Doubleday, 1964.

Massey, D., and P. Jess, eds. *A Place in the World?* Oxford: Oxford University Press, 1995.

Mayo, M. *Imaging Tomorrow: Adult Education for Transformation.* Leicester, England: National Institute of Adult Continuing Education, 1997.

McKay, D. *American Politics and Society.* Oxford: Blackwell, 1993.

McMillan, C. J. *Early History of the Township of Erin.* Cheltenham: Boston Mills, 1974.

Mead, G. *Mind, Self and Society.* Chicago: Chicago University Press, 1934.

Melissen, Jan. *The Struggle for Nuclear Partnership: Britain, the United States and the Making of an Ambiguous Alliance, 1952-1959.* Groningen: Styx, 1993.

Mischel, T., ed. *The Self: Psychological and Philosophical Issues.* Oxford: Blackwell, 1977.

Mowlana, Hamid. *Global Information and World Communication.* New York: Longman, 1986.

Muller, J. W., ed. *The Revival of Constitutionalism.* Lincoln: University of Nebraska Press, 1988.

Nedelsky, J. *Private Property and the Limits of American Constitutionalism: The Madisonian Framework and Its Legacy.* Chicago: University of Chicago Press, 1990.

Newby, Eric, ed. *Travellers' Tales.* London: Picador, 1986.

Newman, F., and D. Weissbrodt. *International Human Rights: Law, Policy, and Process.* Cincinnati: Anderson Publishing, 1996.

Nye, Joseph Jr. *Bound to Lead: The Changing Nature of American Power.* New York: Basic Books, 1990.

Onuf, N. G. *The Republican Legacy in International Thought.* Cambridge: Cambridge University Press, 1998.

Pangle, T. L. *The Spirit of Modern Republicanism: The Moral Vision of the American Founders and the Philosophy of Locke.* Chicago: University of Chicago Press, 1988.

Parenti, Michael. *Against Empire.* San Francisco: City Light Books, 1995.

Perea, Juan F., ed. *Immigrants Out! The New Nativism and the Anti-Immigrant Impulse in the United States.* New York: New York University Press, 1997.

Perry, L. *Intellectual Life in America: A History.* Chicago: University of Chicago Press, 1989.

Pettinger, Alasdair, ed. *Always Elsewhere: Travels of the Black Atlantic.* London and New York: Cassell, 1998.

Pettit, P. *Republicanism: A Theory of Freedom and Government.* Oxford: Oxford University Press, 1997.

Pratt, Mary Louise. *Imperial Eyes: Travel Writing and Transculturation.* London: Routledge, 1995.

Priestley, J. B. *English Journey.* London: Heinemann, 1934.

Pritchard, Annette, and Nigel J. Morgan. *Power and Politics at the Seaside.* Exeter: Exeter University Press, 1999.

Reischmann, J., et al. *Comparative Adult Education.* Ljubljana: Slovenian Institute for Adult Education, 1999.

Rich, Paul B. *Race and Empire in British Politics.* Cambridge: Cambridge University Press 1990.

Robertson, George, et al, eds. *Travellers' Tales: Narratives of Home and Displacement.* London: Routledge, 1994.

Robertson, N. *The History of the County of Bruce.* Toronto: William Biggs, 1906.

Rushdie, Salman. *Imaginary Homelands.* London: Granta, 1991.

Rutherford, J., ed. *Identity, Community, Culture, Difference.* London: Lawrence and Wishart, 1990.

San Juan, E. Jr. *Beyond Postcolonial Theory.* London: Macmillan, 1998.

Schlesinger, Arthur Jr. *The Disuniting of America.* New York: Norton, 1992.

Schramm, Wilbur. *Mass Media and National Development.* Palo Alto, Cal.: Stanford University Press, 1964.

Seaborg, Glenn. *Stemming the Tide: Arms Control in the Johnson Years.* Lexington: Lexington Books, 1987.

Shields, R. *Places on the Margin.* London: Routledge, 1991.

Shumpeter, Joseph. *Capitalism, Socialism and Democracy.* New York: Harper and Brothers, 1950.

Skevington, S., and D. Baker, eds. *The Social Identity of Women.* London: Sage, 1989.

Skinner, Q. *The Foundations of Modern Political Thought.* Cambridge: Cambridge University Press, 1978.

Smagula, Howard J. *Currents: Contemporary Directions in the Visual Arts.* Englewood Cliffs, N.J.: Prentice-Hall, 1989.

Smith, D. *Wales: A Question for History.* Bridgend, Wales: Seren, 1999.

Spybey, T. *Globalization and World Society.* Cambridge: Polity Press, 1996.

Stein, Judith. *The World of Marcus Garvey: Race and Class in Modern Society.* Baton Rouge: Louisiana State University Press, 1986.

Steinbrunner, John. *The Cybernetic Theory of Decision.* Princeton: Princeton University Press, 1974.

Tajfel, H., ed. *Differentiation Between Social Groups.* London: Academic Press, 1978.

Tajfel, H., ed. *Social Identity and Intergroup Relations.* Cambridge: Cambridge University Press, 1982.

Terchek, R. J. *Republican Paradoxes and Liberal Anxieties: Retrieving Neglected Fragments of Political Theory.* Lanham: Rowman and Littlefield, 1997.

Thibaut, J., and L. Walker. *Procedural Justice: A Psychological Analysis.* Hillsdale, N.J.: Erlbaum, 1975.

Towner, J. *An Historical Geography of Recreation and Tourism in the Western World, 1540-1940.* Chichester: Wiley, 1996.

Twigge, Stephen, and Len Scott. *Planning Armageddon: Britain, the United States and the Command of Western Nuclear Forces, 1945-1964.* Amsterdam: Harwood, 2000.

Van Vyver, J. D., and J. Witte, eds. *Religious Human Rights in Global Perspectives: Legal Perspectives.* Amsterdam: Kluwer, 1996.

Waters, M. *Globalization.* London: Routledge, 1995.

Watson, G. *Passing for White.* London: Tavistock, 1970.

Winand, Pascaline. *Eisenhower, Kennedy and the United States of Europe.* New York: St. Martin's Press, 1993.

Woodward, S. L. *Balkan Tragedy: Chaos and Dissolution After the Cold War.* Washington: The Brookings Institution, 1995.

Yack, Bernard, ed. *Liberalism Without Illusions: Essays on Liberal Theory and the Political Vision of Judith N. Shklar.* Chicago: University of Chicago Press, 1996.

Yardley, K., and T. Honess, eds. *Self and Identity: Psychosocial Perspectives.* Chichester: Wiley, 1987.

Yoshino, Kosaku. *Cultural Nationalism in Contemporary Japan.* London: Routledge, 1992.

Yost, David. *The United States and Nuclear Deterrence in Europe* (Adelphi Paper 326). Oxford: Oxford University Press, 1999.

Zuckert, M. P. *Natural Rights and the New Republicanism.* Princeton: Princeton University Press, 1994.

INDEX

Ideology, 87-89, 92, 95
Immigrant policy, 50, 51, 52, 53, 54, 55, 57, 58, 59, 61, 62, 64
Immigrants, 34, 35, 33, 38
Immigration policy, 50, 51, 55, 56, 64
Immigration, 2, 5, 19, 27, 28, 49, 50, 51, 52, 53, 54, 55, 56, 57, 59, 60, 61, 62, 64, 65
Imperialism, 3, 7
Information Revolution, 111, 112
International Criminal Tribunal for the Former Yugoslavia, (ICTFY), 213, 218, 219, 220, 221, 222, 223, 224, 225
International law, 4, 11
International Monetary Fund, 99
Isolationism, 59, 60

Jefferson, Thomas, 99, 102, 103, 106

Kymlicka, Will, 7, 10, 12, 14, 15, 53

Latin America, 2, 3, 4, 5, 6, 7, 10, 14, 145, 146, 154, 239
Law, 229, 230, 232, 233, 239
Locke, John, 98, 105, 106, 232, 234

Mannheim, Karl, 87, 88, 89, 95
Marcos, Subcommandante, 8, 9, 10, 14
Media, 90, 91, 94, 95, 112-16, 118, 119, 120, 121
Migrants, 33, 34, 35, 36, 33, 37, 38, 39, 40, 49, 61.
Migration, xix, xx, xvii, 1, 35, 36, 40, 41, 49, 54, 59, 62, 65
Multiculturalism, 2, 4, 5, 6, 53, 55, 57, 59, 62
Multilateral Force (MLF), 248, 249, 250, 251, 255

Museums, 187, 188, 191, 195, 196, 197, 198

NAFTA, 5, 6
Nativism, 57, 58, 61, 63, 64
NATO, 214, 216, 243, 244, 245, 246, 247, 248, 249, 250, 251, 252, 253, 254, 255, 256
Neo-liberalism, 2, 6, 97, 98, 99, 104, 107, 108
News flow, 113, 115, 118
Non-Proliferation Treaty, 244, 251
North Atlantic bloc, 111, 112, 114, 121, 124
North Atlantic, 111, 112, 114, 115, 116, 117, 118, 119, 120, 121, 122, 123, 124
Nuclear diplomacy, 243, 245

Pan-Africanism, 18, 23, 24, 26
Pettinger, Alisdair, 161, 165, 169
Pratt, Mary Louise, 173, 177, 183
Property, 98, 99, 102, 103, 104, 105, 106, 107, 108

Race, 17, 18, 19, 20, 21, 22, 23, 24, 25, 26, 27, 28, 29
Religion, 202, 203, 204, 205, 206, 207, 208, 209, 210
Republicanism, 9, 229, 230, 231, 232, 234, 236, 237, 239, 240

Seaside resorts, 143, 144, 146, 152
Soft power, 112, 114, 117, 118, 119, 120, 121, 124
Supreme Court, The US, 202, 203, 204, 205

Tourism, 143, 159, 160, 162, 163, 164, 165, 167, 174
Tourists, 159, 160, 162, 163, 164, 165, 166, 167

268

About of Contributors

Robert Barford is Professor Emeritus at Eastern Illinois University. He is the co-founder and editor of *The Acorn, A Ghandian Journal* (1983-1990) and is presently at work on developing a political ethic.

Neil Campbell is the Subject Leader in American Studies at the University of Derby, UK. He is the co-author of *American Cultural Studies* (Routledge, 1997) and has just completed a second book, *The Cultures of the American New West* (Edinburgh, 2000).

Kathleen Kadon Desmond is a Professor of Art at Central Missouri State University. She has published over 20 articles on contemporary art and education. She was the Faculty Director of the Maastricht Center for Transatlantic Studies in 1999.

Peter W. Edge is a Reader in Law and Religion at Oxford Brookes University, UK. He has published in the *International and Comparative Law Quarterly*, the *Anglo-American Law Review*, and the *Journal of Civil Liberties*.

Lesley Hodgson is a Ph.D. research student at the University of Glamorgan, Wales. Lesley attended the Maastricht Center for Transatlantic Studies as an undergraduate and attributes much of her success to date to that visit.

Will Kaufman is a Senior Lecturer in English and American Studies at the University of Central Lancashire, UK. His wide-ranging research interests include comedy, the Civil War, and Transatlantic Studies. He is the author of *The Comedian as Confidence Man*, (Wayne State University Press, 1997). He is a founder and co-director of the Maastricht Center for Transatlantic Studies.

Tamás Kozma is the Director of the Hungarian Institute for Educational Research in Budapest and Professor of Sociology of Education at the University of Debrecen, Hungary. He is the author of several books, including *Ethnicity and Education* (Peter Lang, 1992).

Ryszard M. Machnikowski is employed by the Institute of International Studies, University of Lódz, Poland. He was the Soros Scholar at Hertford College, Oxford University, in 1992-93, after

271

which he became a Fulbright Scholar at Columbia University. He has published 20 articles and one book.

Javier Maestro is a Professor in the Department of History of Social Communication at Complutense University, and lectures on American government and politics for the University of Alcalá. His recent publications include *History of Trade and Shipping between Spain and Sweden-Norway in the 19th Century* (University of Cádiz, 1999).

Heidi Slettedahl Macpherson is a Senior Lecturer in English and American Literature at the University of Central Lancashire, UK and a co-director of the Maastricht Center for Transatlantic Studies. She is the author of *Women's Movement: Escape as Transgression in North American Feminist Fiction* (Rodopi Press, 2000).

Camilo Pérez-Bustillo is a Research Professor of Media Studies and Law at the State of Mexico campus of the Instituto Tecnologico y de Estudios Superiores de Monterrey. He is the author and editor of several books and articles on issues of human rights, indigenous rights, and multiculturalism, published in both English and Spanish.

Jane Prince is a Principal Lecturer in Psychology at the University of Glamorgan, Wales. Her research interests are primarily in transitional identities. She is working on a confidential area of government policy looking at the discourses within decision-making groups.

Kuldip R. Rampal is a Professor of Mass Communication at Central Missouri State University. His research on political communication, press regulation, media ethics, and international broadcasting has appeared in a variety of books and journals. The Republic of China awarded him the 1993 International Communication Award.

Susanna Schrafstetter is a Lecturer in European History at the University of Glamorgan, Wales. She is the author of *Die dritte Atommacht. Britische Nichtverbreitungspolitik im Dienst von Statussicherung und Deutschlandpolitik1952-1968* (Oldenbourg, 1999).

John W. Sheets is a Professor of Anthropology at Central Missouri State University. His publications appear in *Annals of Human Biology, Current Anthropology, Journal of Biosocial Science, Man, Northern Scotland, Scottish Studies*, and *Social Biology*.

Andrew Thompson is a Lecturer in Sociology at the University of Glamorgan, Wales. His recent publications include, as co-editor, *Nation, Identity, and Social Theory* (University of Wales Press, 1999) and *Wales Today* (University of Wales Press, 1999).

Don H. Wallace is a Professor of Criminal Justice at Central Missouri State University. He has presented papers on international human rights and has had articles published on the death penalty and the history of prisoners' rights.

John K. Walton is a Professor of Social History at the University of Central Lancashire, UK. His books include *The English Seaside Resort: A Social History, 1750-1914* (Leicester University Press, 1983), *Blackpool* (Edinburgh University Press, 1998), and *The British Seaside: Holidays and Resorts in the Twentieth Century* (Manchester University Press, 2000).

Miles W. Williams is a Professor of Political Science at Central Missouri State University. His publications include *Illegal Aliens in the Western Hemisphere* (Praeger), co-authored with Kenneth Johnson.

Neil A. Wynn is a Reader in History and American Studies at the University of Glamorgan, Wales. His books include *The Afro-American and the Second World War* (1976) and *From Progressivism to Prosperity* (1986), both published by Holmes and Meier. He is a co-director of the Maastricht Center for Transatlantic Studies.